Digital Research Methods in Fashion and Textile Studies

Digital Research Methods in Fashion and Textile Studies

Amanda Sikarskie

BLOOMSBURY VISUAL ARTS
LONDON • NEW YORK • OXFORD • NEW DELHI • SYDNEY

BLOOMSBURY VISUAL ARTS
Bloomsbury Publishing Plc
50 Bedford Square, London, WC1B 3DP, UK
1385 Broadway, New York, NY 10018, USA

BLOOMSBURY, BLOOMSBURY VISUAL ARTS and the Diana logo are
trademarks of Bloomsbury Publishing Plc

First published in Great Britain 2020

Cover design: Dani Leigh
Cover image © saskia fairfull on Unsplash

A catalogue record for this book is available from the British Library.

A catalog record for this book is available from the Library of Congress.

ISBN: HB: 978-1-3500-4250-6
PB: 978-1-3501-3447-8
ePDF: 978-1-3500-4251-3
eBook: 978-1-3500-4252-0

Typeset by Integra Software Services Pvt. Ltd.
Printed and bound in India

To find out more about our authors and books visit www.bloomsbury.com
and sign up for our newsletters.

To the Black Queen.

Contents

List of Illustrations xi
Acknowledgments xiv
About the Author xvi

1 Introduction: A New Maximalism 1

About this Book 2
Postmodernism and Positivism in Mixed-Methods Research 4
Mixed-Methods Research as Maximalism 6
Roadmap to the Book 8
Part 1: Searching: Chapter 1: Text-based Searching Strategies 9
Part 1: Searching: Case Study: In Search of Kate Moss 10
Part 1: Searching: Chapter 2: Visual Searching 10
Part 2: Connecting: Chapter 3: Blogging, Instagram, and Research 11
Part 2: Connecting: Chapter 4: Critical Reading of Social Media Texts 12
Part 2: Connecting: Case Study: Reading Moschino's "Capsule Collection" 13
Part 3: Visualizing: Chapter 5: Data Visualization 13
Part 3: Visualizing: Chapter 6: Mapping 14
Part 3: Visualizing: Case Study: Coding *Fashion Is Kale* 14
Responding to the Critique of Minimalism: Why Use Mixed Methods? 14
Futurism, Maximalism, and the Black Queen 15

Part 1 **Searching** 19

2 Text-based Searching Strategies 21

Keyword Generation for Boolean Queries 21
SEO and Searching the Web 25
What is Metadata? 27
National, Local, and Regional Databases 28
Australian Dress Register 29
Europeana 30
Commercial Pattern Archive 33
Encyclopedic Databases 34
Fashion History Timeline 35
Fashion Photography Archive 36

Case Study: In Search of Kate Moss 38
Kate as Mermaid 39
In Search of the Fashion Model 41
When Text-based Searches Fail 45

3 Visual Searching 47

Why Images? 47
Images and Memory 51
Five Types of Queries 53
Sourcing Images Responsibly 54
Computer Vision in Museum Work 56
Searching for Patterns: Harlequin and Ichimatsu 58
Searching for Colors: Millennial Pink, Tiffany Blue, and Historical Colors 60
Reverse Image Searches 61
John Lennon's T-Shirts 62
Limitations of Reverse Image Searches 62

Part 2 **Connecting** 65

4 Blogging, Instagram, and Research 67

Conducting Research on Social Media 67
The Wisdom of the Crowd 70
Who is the Crowd? 70
#georgianjanuary 72
Citing Social Posts 73
Disseminating Research on Instagram 76
Conferences: If You Hashtag It, They Will Tweet 76
The Importance of Hashtags 77
Emojis in Academic Communication 78
The Semiotic Power of Emojis 81
Bricolage and Polyvore 82
Instant Gratification in Fashion Scholarship 83
Style Blogging 84
Street Style 85
Blogging as Research Method 87
Academic #ootds and the Simmelian Dandy 88
Fashion Blogger Poses and Normative Chic 90
Academic Style Blogging as Academic Work 92
Fashion Blogger Ethics and the Role of the Independent Blogger 93

5 **Critical Reading of Social Media Texts** 95

Applied Theory 95
Hermeneutics 96
Hermeneutics ... and Cleavage 97
Scholarly Communication, Professionalism, and Social Media
Controversy 99
Social Media Outrages: Women in Politics Wear Clothes on the Internet 99
Case Study: Reading the Moschino "Capsule Collection" 103
Opiates: An Historical Background 106
Heroin Chic 106
Popular Criticism of "Fashionable" Drug Use 107
Simmel and Psychoanalytic Readings 108
Simmel and Marxist Readings: Modesty, Class, and Imitation 109

Part 3 **Visualizing** 111

6 **Data Visualization** 113

The History of Visualization and its Practitioners 115
The Visualization Wheel 117
Density and Transparency 118
The Importance of Color 119
Data Visualization Ethics 119
Types of Visualizations 120
The Visualization Process 122
Single Number Visualizations 123
Icon Arrays 127
The Cleveland-McGill Scale 127
Gestalt Theory 129
Pie Charts 130
Bad Pie Charts and Donut Charts 130
Word Clouds 131
A Word about 3D Modeling 136

7 **Mapping** 139

Reading Maps 140
Types of Maps 141
Projections 142
Remote Sensing and GIS 143
Density, Scale, and Color 144

The Participatory Turn in Mapping 146
The OpenStreetMap and Crowdsourced Mapping 147
Qualitative and Quantitative Mapping 149
Trade Routes of Viking Silk 150
Overlaying Data Sets and Mapping Transport History 151
Mapping the Discovery of the Hope Diamond 153
Visualizing Qualitative Data 156
Case Study: Coding *Fashion Is Spinach* 157
Coding and Code ... with Highlighters 158
Document Annotation Methods and Annotation as Method 159
Why Spinach?: The Binary of Style and Fashion 160
Shopping as Research Method 161

Conclusions: Responding to the Critique of Minimalism 165

Post-script: Maximalist Muse: A Conversation with Kristen Bateman 171

Glossary 174
Notes 178
Bibliography 193
Join the Conversation on Instagram! 208
Index 209

List of Illustrations

Chapter 1: Introduction: A New Maximalism:

1.1 Maximalist runway show fashion photograph, Pexels.com 2

1.2 Film Still: Anita Pallenberg as the Black Queen in *Barbarella*, Paramount Pictures (1968) 16

Part 1: Searching

Chapter 2: Text-based Searching Strategies:

2.1 Screenshot: Dawn Waterhouse ballgown on the Australian Dress Register, Image courtesy of the Canberra Museum and Art Gallery 31

2.2 Screenshot: Maison Martin Margiela bodysuit on Europeana Fashion, CC BY-SA 32

2.3 Screenshot: Panniers on the Fashion History Timeline, Image taken by Justine de Young and courtesy of the Fashion Institute of Technology, State University of New York 36

2.4 Screenshot: Bloomsbury Fashion Photography Archive: Search page with explore tab, featuring a runway look by YSL 37

2.5 Screenshot: Bloomsbury Fashion Photography Archive: Kate Moss in Martine Sitbon (1994) 42

2.6 Screenshot: Bloomsbury Fashion Photography Archive: Mermaid silhouette by Nina Ricci (1984) 43

2.7 Virginia Oldoini, Countess of Castiglione, photograph by Pierre-Louise Pierson, *c.* 1863–6 45

Chapter 3: Visual Searching:

3.1 Boy's kimono with dogs, horses, and pigeons, Japan, 1940s, Metropolitan Museum of Art, Purchase, Friends of Asian Art, 2014 49

3.2 Rin in *Inuyasha*, Yomiuri Telecasting Corporation (YTV) (2001) 50

3.3 Film still: Jerry Hall, second from left, in *Princess Caraboo*, TriStar Pictures (1994) 54

3.4 Betty Ford supporting the Equal Rights Amendment, Gerald R. Ford Presidential Library & Museum 56

3.5 Fragment of a *kosode* (kimono) featuring the *shippo* pattern of interlocking circles, Japan, Edo period (mid-19th century), Los Angeles County Museum of Art, Gift of Miss Bella Mabury 57

3.6 Film still: Anna Magnani in *The Golden Coach*, Cinecittà Studios (1952) 59

3.7 Film still: John Lennon's UFO Sighting in New York City (1974) 63

Part 2: Connecting

Chapter 4: Blogging, Instagram, and Research:

4.1 Fall 1991 James Galanos sequined gown, detail shot as seen in an FHCC Instagram post from December 1, 2017, Image courtesy of the Robert and Penny Fox Historic Costume Collection at Drexel University 69

4.2 Robe de Style, as seen in a Facebook post to the group Fashion Historians Unite! by Andrea Melvin, Grand Rapids Public Museum, Grand Rapids, Michigan 71

4.3 Open source unicode emojis from the Emojidex 79

Chapter 5: Critical Reading of Social Media Texts:

5.1 The hermeneutic circle, visualized with ice skating, from *Skating with Bron Meyer* (1921) 97

5.2 #JustSayMoschiNO, #JustSayNoToMoschino, and #JustSayMoschiNoThanks hashtags as seen on Twitter, Image created by Amada Sikarskie 105

Part 3: Visualizing

Chapter 6: Data Visualization:

6.1 Data Visualization: Packing list for Florida created using emojis, Amanda Sikarskie 114

6.2 Color wheel, *Art in Dress* (1916) 117
6.3 UFO Sightings Chart, National Archives UK (1969) 120
6.4 London Underground Map, *Electric Railway Journal* (1908) 122
6.5 Single number visualization of the ten most common quilt patterns on the Quilt Index, Amanda Sikarskie 128
6.6 Data visualization: The cost of a wedding, Amanda Sikarskie 128
6.7 Pie chart: Quilt Index, Amanda Sikarskie 131
6.8 Pie chart: Prince death reaction, Amanda Sikarskie 132
6.9 Word cloud data visualization: Macarons, Amanda Sikarskie 133
6.10 Number cloud data visualization: Angel numbers, Amanda Sikarskie 134
6.11 Tag cloud: Common patterns on the Quilt Index, Amanda Sikarskie 136

Chapter 7: Mapping:

7.1 Open Street Map: Spitalfields, London 141
7.2 Open Street Map: Boutiques of Milan, Italy 148
7.3 Nineteenth-century map of India, from *Reports of the Missionary and Benevolent Boards and Committees to the General Assembly of the Presbyterian Church in the United States of America* (1891) 155
7.4 Open Street Map: Kollur, with added text by Amanda Sikarskie 156
7.5 Data visualization: *Fashion Is Kale*, Amanda Sikarskie 159

Conclusions: Responding to the Critique of Minimalism:

8.1 A look from LA swim week 2018 in which maximalism meets retro futurism. 2aSJKCX 169

Acknowledgments

Thanks to Matthew for over ten years of marriage, for hearing about the minutiae of this book for the past three years, and for reading it and making suggestions when it was in a much rougher state. Thanks to Prada (the cat) for purring sweetly on my pillow every morning and to Tanly (another cat) for meowing less sweetly and getting me up to write every morning. (That's certainly why he wakes me up, I tell myself.) Thanks also to my Mom, Rick and Mary Jo, Jayne, and the whole family for supporting me always.

A big thank you to Adriane Little for all of her generous correspondence about the *Mapping Mrs. Dalloway* project. And thank you to Christina Mitchell for the help with Japanese kimono pattern names. *Ichimatsu* for the win! I also need to thank, in no particular order, Holly Kent for the suggestion about research bursts (aka research nuggets), Colleen Hill, Sarah Scaturro, Amy Milne, Kristen Bateman, Sarah Hegge, Clare Sauro, and also Andrea Melvin, Deirdre Clemente, Eleanor Houghton, Caroline Millbank, Justine de Young, Michael Shepherd, and the Fox Historic Costume Collection at Drexel University, Eleanor Kenny and Adrian Murphy of Europeana, Sarah Pointon of the Australian Dress Register, and Michael Bailey and Ruth Oliphant of the Canberra Museum and Art Gallery for permission to use the images that appear in this book. Thank you also to my department chairs: Michael Mamp in Fashion, Merchandising, and Design at Central Michigan University, and Chris Waters in Art & Art History at the University of Michigan—Flint, for fostering such supportive working environments for Lecturers

Finally, I wish to offer my heartfelt thanks to the wonderful team at Bloomsbury: Hannah Crump, the Acquisitions Editor who first spotted potential in this project and convinced me to go for it, Publisher Frances Arnold, and Assistant Editors Pari Thomson and Yvonne Thouroude, who answered my many questions promptly and cheerfully, put up with various cover image changes and permissions questions, and generally kept things running smoothly. Many thanks also to the permissions team at Bloomsbury for allowing me to use some beautiful images from the Fashion Photography Archive in this book. And thanks to Carly Bull, Senior Marketing Manager at Bloomsbury, for astutely advising me to abbreviate the book's hashtag for social media to #digifashresearchbook—my initial idea of "#digitalresearchmethods4fashiontextilestudies" would have been much too long!

And a huge thank you to the design team at Bloomsbury who beautifully incorporated my aesthetic preferences into the cover design of this book. (I asked for pastel, and they delivered!) The attention to detail that went into this cover was truly top notch, as with how the dove gray of the model's manicure is picked up in the dove gray font of "Bloomsbury" just below. I really wanted to be happy with the cover, and the designers have achieved that! Job well done! Thank you, everyone!

About the Author

Amanda Sikarskie is a fashion historian whose current work investigates the methods and best practices for doing the history of dress and textiles in a digital age. Since receiving her Ph.D. in 2011, she has published two other books—*The Duprees of Spitalfields* (Amazon CreateSpace, 2015) and *Textile Collections* (Rowman & Littlefield, 2016)—and taught undergraduate and graduate-level courses in art and design history and museum studies. She currently teaches history of dress and culture in the Department of Fashion Merchandising and Design at Central Michigan University, as well as various art history courses in the University of Michigan system. She is also working on a new book project on digital heritage storytelling for luxury brands. In her spare time, she loves music—rock and roll, blues, and country—thrifting, cats, squirrels, and flowers. Follow her on Instagram @sikarska.

1 Introduction: A New Maximalism

maximalism *noun*: an aesthetic or philosophy that prizes multiplicity

Maximalism in fashion refers to the new turn in fashion toward the mixing of numerous, seemingly incongruous prints in the same ensemble, but the sheer variety of new methods ushered in by our use of digital technologies has led to what I call a new maximalism in research practices. Mixed-methods approaches using multiple digital sites and strategies have been the norm for some time in the social sciences, but fashion history is catching up. The year that I began writing this book, 2016, was a year of maximalism in the word of fashion.[1] Whereas just a few years ago, brands like Céline were being touted for their clean, restrained touch, in 2016, it was suddenly acceptable and even desirable to mix prints beyond the point of clashing. Coco Chanel's old adage that a person should take off one accessory before going out went straight out the window; now, it is put two extra rings on before going out. Alessandro Michelle's reinvigoration of luxury fashion house Gucci typifies this new maximalism, mixing colors and textures, fabrics and prints. Dolce & Gabbana have also adopted the maximalist aesthetic, even creating odd wearable technology meets glamor juxtapositions by adding headphones to tiaras. Enormous and elaborate handbag charms that do not coordinate with the rest of the bag seem to be the newest iteration of maximalism.

Maximalism is certainly fun, but is it also merely frivolous, or is there some deeper philosophy undergirding all the prints and tiaras and handbag charms? Legendary Bauhaus turned American architect and Illinois Institute of Technology professor Ludwig Mies van der Rohe famously uttered the maxim: "Less is more." While that may have been true for International Style architecture in the 1950s and '60s—those steel and glass boxes totally devoid of ornament, today in architecture as in the fashion world, more is more. Or, as one of the postmodern starchitects,[2] Robert Venturi put it, "Less is a bore." In fashion, the new "more is more" aesthetic has taken on the moniker of "maximalism" (Figure 1.1).

Figure 1.1 *Maximalist runway show fashion photograph, Pexels.com.*

About this Book

In English, we use "fashion," "dress," and "costume" to describe the clothing that people wear, fashion in particular referring to the endless succession and repetition of the popular styles of the moment. But as Heike Jenss, editor of *Fashion Studies* (2016) notes, "In the Romance languages as well as in many Germanic languages, through interestingly not in English, the word for fashion is *mode* or *moda* derived from the Latin word *modus* for shape or manner, which is also a root of the word 'modernity,' associated with the fast-paced urban life in European capitals for which fashion (or *la mode*) became a symbol or metaphor" (see Baudelaire 2004).[3] I would love to have titled this book *Research à la Mode* or something similar, as *mode* is linguistically more suggestive of a method or way of doing things than any of the English terms listed above. Many readers of this book undoubtedly not having a background in the Romance or Germanic languages, however, *Research à la Mode* sounds a bit too much like research with a side of ice cream, which would not necessarily be a bad thing in practice but is certainly not in keeping with the spirit of the book.

Thus, this volume is titled *Digital Research Methods for Fashion and Textile Studies*, and I have chosen to use the term "fashion" primarily in this book, rather than its sister terms "dress" and "costume." I decided not to use costume, even though it is the preferred term for the field among academic historians in the United States, as evidenced by the name of their professional association, the Costume Society of America. But I find that whenever I mention "costume" to someone outside academia, they invariably think I am talking about theatrical costumes. So, for the sake of minimizing confusion, "costume" was not a good option or this project. "Dress" is the more frequently used term among academics in the UK, and as Jonathan Faiers noted in his essay "Dress Thinking: Disciplines and Interdisciplinarity," dress is a more universal term, while "fashion" has implied in the past a more Western, elite mode of dress.[4] Both the field of costume/dress/fashion studies and its terminology are changing, however. Globalism in the apparel and textile complex, the closing of university home economics departments, and the recognition of designing clothing as an art and not just a craft have all contributed to the increase in the preference for the term "fashion," even among academic historians of the subject, as seen in recent titles such as Harriet Walker's *Less Is More: Minimalism in Fashion* (2011). And of course, as a practical matter, many readers of this book are undoubtedly graduates of or students in fashion (rather than "costume" or "dress") courses of study.

Costume. Dress. Craft. Art. Home economics. History. Fashion studies in the early twenty-first century, like an Alessandro Michelle ensemble, is an idiosyncratic object, made of many components some of which—like art and craft—seem diametrically opposed to each other, and yet which function as a harmonious, albeit complex, and at times cacophonous, whole. This book takes maximalism as a metaphor for mixed-methods research, as well as for multi-theory hermeneutic critical reading (see Chapter 4), but maximalism also serves as a metaphor for fashion as an academic discipline. To extend the metaphor further, our field is not the clean, pared down minimalism of the university art department, nor the practical street wear of the school of home economics or human ecology, but rather a combination of the two in the same outfit—the paint-splattered khaki all-in-one with a floral print day dress worn over it.

Just as the discipline of fashion studies combines ideas and practices from a variety of related fields, so too does fashion studies rely on a mixed bag of research methodologies. This is increasingly true in the digital age. *Digital Research Methods in Fashion and Textile Studies* presents the reader with a variety of digital methodologies to aid in better searching for, analyzing, and discussing vintage design, photography, and writing on fashion, as well as historic and ethnographic dress and textile objects themselves. This book will help you to:

- Gain a familiarity with various digital research methods and explore through practical case studies how they can interface with work in fashion and textile studies.

- Learn how to incorporate digital methods to enliven and enrich a research project in progress.
- Benefit from simple changes that you can make to integrate digital activities into your day-to-day working life as a fashion researcher, such as joining new channels for scholarly communication and feedback from peers.

Each chapter focuses upon different methods, problems, or research sites, including:

- Searching large databases effectively
- Family history
- Pattern recognition and visual searching
- Mobile methods for communicating with other scholars digitally
- Maximalism and mixed-methods approaches to research
- Data visualization
- Mapping
- Critical reading of social media texts

Much like fashion itself, research methods are constantly evolving. In today's rapidly changing climate, we are all beginners in some respects. Younger readers will likely be more familiar with many of the resources, but perhaps not with the methods. Established scholars will surely be more familiar with many of the methods, but possibly not with the new contexts engendered by the digital. From advanced undergraduate and postgraduate students working on research projects to veteran professionals in fashion and textile history and beyond, everyone can benefit from a diverse set of fresh approaches to conducting and disseminating research. In the current age of instant gratification, with users snapping and posting images from runway shows long before the clothes will ever appear in stores, the world of fashion is increasingly digital and fast-paced. Research on fashion is, too. *Digital Research Methods* will help you keep up.

Postmodernism and Positivism in Mixed-Methods Research

Dick Hebdige, in particular, has been a pioneering force in the mixing of qualitative methods and theories in fashion studies research. His 1979 book, *Subculture: The*

Meaning of Style, uses semiotics, structuralism and post-structuralism, as well as draws upon Claude Lévi-Strauss's concept of bricolage. With the digital turn in fashion and textile studies, however, scholars can now add quantitative methods into this mix as well. Further, as Heike Jenss notes:

> The field of fashion studies in the United States (and beyond) now encompasses a substantial number of scholars who are located in academic programs that bring together social science approaches, economics, and the physical or natural sciences. These include for example, textile and apparel programs, which are located in university departments for human development, family and nutrition sciences, or in the departments for design, technology and management, marketing and merchandising, or consumer studies—fields in which quantitative studies are used frequently.[5]

On the escalation of interdisciplinarity and the need for mixed-methods research, Jenss writes:

> Fashion and fashion studies' wide reach and also its 'in-between-ness' (Granata 2012) makes for an exciting field of research, yet the 'escalation of interdisciplinary research' (Taylor 2013, 23) can also feel overwhelming, not least for students and emerging scholars, who are trying to find their footing in the field … the field's dense disciplinary entanglements, which bring a wide range of methods to the field—and the essential need for the use, combination, and adaptation of multiple methods in the exploration of fashion.[6]

Kaiser and Green note that the International Textile and Apparel Association's journal, the *Clothing and Textiles Research Journal*, has recently published several articles focused on causality in marketing using structural equation modeling (SEM) as a methodology.

> Yet in the 2005 edition of their handbook, they [Denzin and Lincoln] described the "re-emergence" of "scientism" in the United States in the early years of the twenty-first century, promoted by the National Research Council's call for objective, rigorously controlled studies that employed causal models (Denzin and Lincoln 2005, 8). Advanced statistical techniques such as structural equation modelling (SEM) have become fashionable in the context of consumer studies.[7]

But while the sub-discipline's of fashion retailing and marketing are largely positivist in their research at present, the larger discipline (and indeed the case studies in this book), even while adopting and adapting some quantitative techniques, is still largely qualitative and a product of the postmodern turn of the 1980s.

Mixed-Methods Research as Maximalism

Sometimes called "messy methods," mixed-methods research is fundamentally a form of assemblage, much like the maximalist impulse in fashion. In their introduction to *Deleuze and Research Methodologies*, Rebecca Coleman and Jessica Ringrose define assemblage as "a key concept that seeks to account for multiplicity and change (or becoming)."[8] Coleman and Ringrose also construct method as a form of crafting, writing, "method is the crafting of the boundaries between what is present, what is manifestly absent, and what is Othered."[9] Assemblage and craft are apt metaphors for this type of research, and indeed in their book, *Foundations of Multimethod Research: Synthesizing Styles*, John Brewer and Albert Hunter note that metaphor is one technique for generating research problems that lends itself to mixed-methods work. They give examples such as "night as frontier," "neighbourhood as fashion," and "cities as organism."[10] In fact, the idea for this book is based on the metaphor of maximalism in fashion for mixed-methods research. No one set of methods—qualitative or quantitative—should be seen as inherently better than the other; nor are they philosophically irreconcilable. For example, in a research project, one could use both qualitative analysis of texts such as a film and fashion and textile objects themselves, along with raw objective spatial data taken from a mapping program (quantitative). This is the mixed-methods approach in a nutshell—using a variety of qualitative and quantitative techniques to answer your research question and tell a designer, wearer, or dress or textile object's story. The following is a brief overview of the qualitative and the quantitative.[11]

	Qualitative	**Quantitative**
data	based on texts	based on numbers
focus	meanings	facts
relationship between researcher and subject	close/more interaction	distant/less interaction

Types of research methods include archival (historical, statistical), field work (ethnographic), and surveys and experiments. These basic methodologies can be mixed in one study in various ways, either concurrently or sequentially, for example: two forms of the research question, two types of data analysis (numerical vs. text-based or visual), or two types of conclusions (objective vs. subjective).

Carolyn S. Ridenour and Isador Newman call qualitative and quantitative a false dichotomy. "The research question initiates any research study. [I always ask my students: 'What's your thesis?' 'What are you trying to prove about the designer/garment/etc.?'] The research question is fundamental, much more fundamental than the paradigm (qualitative or quantitative) to which a researcher feels allegiance."[12] According to David E. Gray, one of the major benefits of mixing methods is "initiation," which "uses mixed methods to uncover paradoxes, new perspectives, and contradictions. The focus of initiation, then, is the generation of new insights which may lead to the reframing of research questions, in the words of Rossman and Wilson: 'a feeling of a creative leap.'"[13] One of the ways to make that creative leap is to use narrative to tell your story. Narratives have ethical, political implications, causality, a sense of identity (of the narrator and of the characters). In *Using Narrative in Social Research: Qualitative and Quantitative Approaches*, Jane Elliott unpacks an "existing debate about whether it is possible to integrate approaches that emphasize individuals' subjective beliefs and experiences with approaches that provide a numerical description of the social world."[14] Add to this the additional layer of digital tools, and quantitative data can tell stories.

The following example is a story from my own research practice: I used qualitative methods to test my hypothesis of a connection—a single pattern or original, unique image source—for various Depression-era appliqué peacock medallion quilts. Many of the appliquéd peacocks looked to my eye quite similar, and many of the quilt-makers chose turquoise and the background color for these peacock quilt tops. During archival research at the International Quilt Study Center and Museum in Lincoln, Nebraska, I found my hypothesis to be invalid, however, that there were, in fact, many disparate sources for the peacocks in question. One quilt studies was created after a painting of a peacock in the family's collection, and no definitive published pattern or kit could be found. Similarities of style and color were to do with the Art Deco influence in American quilt-making, and trends in dyes in cotton calicoes during the 1930s, and not the fact that the patterns had a common origin. Research narratives ultimately prove (or seek to prove) theories. What is the role of research? Theory generation or theory confirmation? Both! We usually think of qualitative research as exploratory, whereas quantitative is used to test a hypothesis, but this is not always the case. Sometimes, your research disproves your hypothesis, and if this is the case, you should keep an open mind to results, not seek to prove a theory in the absence of data to back it up or hope for a particular outcome that is not borne out in the evidence.

Rossman and Wilson (1985) suggest three types of researchers: purists, situationalists, and pragmatists. Purists use either qualitative or quantitative methodologies exclusively, no matter what the situation. Situationalists, by contrast, use either qualitative or quantitative methods, depending on needs, demands, and ultimately, the best fit for the nature of the research question. Pragmatists mix methodologies in a single study as a matter of course. But as Brewer and Hunter note, "If individuals are to be their own theoreticians, however, then each must also accept some responsibility for synthesis, otherwise, we risk inundation by idiosyncratic theories that may be firmly grounded in their authors' research but are of problematic significance in the larger scheme of things."[15] In this instance, maximalism equals pragmatism.

In addition to its inherent pragmatism, maximalism of research methods can help to combat androcentrism in scholarship. Even women, as researchers, can be unintentionally sexist. "Androcentricity is essentially a view of the world from a male perspective. It manifests itself when ego is constructed as male, rather than female, such as when 'intergroup warfare' is defined as 'a means of gaining women and slaves.'"[16] Is gynocentrism the answer? "Familism is a particular instance of gender insensitivity. It consists of treating the family as the smallest unit of analysis in instances in which it is, in fact, individuals within families (or households) who engage in certain actions, have certain experiences, and so on."[17] Chapter 5 of Liz Jones and Ian Barron's *Research and Gender* deals with undertaking research in a field that is feminized. With its origins in home economics, perhaps no discipline has been constructed as feminine more than apparel and textile studies. Jones and Barron urge a move beyond binaries and essentialism (such as we see in much of the feminist art of the 1970s—Miriam Schapiro, Judy Chicago, etc.). Indeed, I initially considered Schapiro's concept of *femmage*—a portmanteau of feminist and collage—as the guiding metaphor for this book on mixed-methods research. I opted instead for the new maximalism because it lacks the historical and cultural baggage associated with essentialism, while preserving the basic idea of assemblage and craft inherent to mixed methods.

Roadmap to the Book

Gerunds are those words that end in "ing" and signify the activity understood in a verb, but also function as nouns—ideas, things, concrete. The titles of each chapter in this book begin with a gerund—searching, connecting, and making. This reflects that this book is fundamentally about both ideas and actions—and ideas put into action, about the practice and praxis of digital research methods in fashion and textile studies, and not just the theory. Joanne Entwistle (2000) argues that fashion is a situated practice, its performance inseparable from its context. For Heike Jenss, research, too, is a situated practice, and therefore notes that research methods books often disappoint because they divorce the methodologies from their research contexts.[18] Jenss writes, "'Methods books' can also have a tendency to be (like the word 'method' itself) rather abstract when they isolate or decontextualise the discussion of methods from the broader trajectories or bodies of research."[19] With this book, I am keen to correct—or at least to begin to correct—this problem by continuously situating the discussion of various research methods and tools within the contexts of concrete research problems, specifically within the case studies at the conclusion of each chapter, but also with various examples and mini case studies throughout the main body of each chapter as well. It is my sincere hope that this will be one methods book that, rather than dealing in abstractions, will provide researchers both expert and novice with ideas that they can actually use while offering general advice that will remain relevant for years to come.

The following paragraphs lay out a roadmap to the various methods to be covered in this book. The book is divided into three parts—*Searching, Connecting,* and *Visualizing*—each with two chapters and an extended case study. Part 1: Searching begins with methods and strategies for novice researchers before moving on to more advanced methods. Part 2: Connecting explores the connections that one can make with other fashion studies scholars through social media, how various social media can further one's research, and methods for doing research using social media, both in terms of using critical theory and quite practically in terms of properly citing social posts. Part 3: Visualizing profiles digital tools that fashion studies scholars can use to make visual aids both as research method and to disseminate research, chiefly data visualization and mapping, though 3D modeling is discussed as well. Case studies in each unit—centered on topics ranging from Kate Moss to Moschino's "Capsule Collection" to Elizabeth Hawes's *Fashion Is Spinach*—connect theory to practice, demonstrating how to put these digital research methods into action through specific, concrete examples using current digital resources.

Part 1: Searching: Chapter 1: Text-based Searching Strategies

This chapter is all about the theory and practice of searching databases. While this chapter is aimed at beginners, it will also be of use to researchers at any age or stage who wish to be introduced to new digital resources or new tricks for conducting searches. Scholars may be unaware of how to effectively parse metadata, and many research projects in the history of dress and textiles will necessitate that scholars go outside their comfort zone and conduct object-based research in databases with which they may be totally unfamiliar. Indeed, much of research fashion and textiles today is navigating and mining the ever-expanding multitude of online archives of thematic collections such as the Australian Dress Register, Berg Fashion Library, the Bloomsbury Fashion Photography Archive, Commercial Pattern Archive, Dress Discover, Europeana, the Fashion History Timeline, the FIDM (Fashion Institute of Design and Merchandising) Museum and Galleries Online Collections, Minnesota Dressmakers, Modemuze, Pockets of History, the Quilt Index, Tapestry, Texas Fashion Collection, and the Vintage Patterns Wiki. The sheer breadth and variety of search possibilities on these sites can intimidate students and some scholars, causing them to fall back on doing research in what are sometimes perceived as less desirable places, such as Instagram and Pinterest, where the factuality of posts and tags cannot be reasonably guaranteed. This introductory chapter to the world of digital research methods gives examples of some of the major databases for fashion and textile history and tips for searching digital collections like a pro.

Part 1: Searching: Case Study: In Search of Kate Moss

Sometimes, the most ubiquitous subjects are the most difficult to search for in databases, not because the searches return too few results, but because they return *too many*. In this first case study, inspired by the real-world problem of trying to wade through a mass of search results on a very popular topic in fashion studies, iconic supermodel Kate Moss, we will undertake various Boolean searches of the Fashion Photography Archive online to model searching techniques outlined earlier in the chapter. Ultimately, the reader can discover the fastest and most efficient way arrive at our quarry—just the query language to yield just the right images of Moss for several different research projects.

Part 1: Searching: Chapter 2: Visual Searching

This chapter peers into the emerging future of visual (as opposed to text-based) searching, profiling a variety of tools. Content-based image retrieval technologies can help researchers find like garments or textiles from a particular period or culture. As an example, Seminole patchwork dress and quilts, with their many, regular, and vaguely similar patterns, each with a different name that is not well known outside the Seminole culture, make excellent subjects for visual, rather than text-based searching. In the second half of this chapter, the author demonstrates how to use TinEye and Google Reverse Image Search to search for specific patchwork designs, even without using the name of the pattern. Also covered in the second half of this chapter is visual stylometry, an artificial intelligence-based method to identifying the authenticity of visual and material culture.

So you're ready to publish your research? For young academics, securing image rights is one of the biggest barriers to publishing one's scholarly research. This chapter also explores ways in which scholars can leverage the public domain, including sourcing free public domain images on Flickr Commons, as well as strategies for giving back, such as applying Creative Commons licensing to one's work.

Part 2: Connecting: Chapter 3: Blogging, Instagram, and Research

This chapter concerns itself with the theory and practice of connecting with other scholars on social media for the production and dissemination of fashion research. Of utmost importance given the current degree of confusion, even among scholars, on how to cite such posts correctly are the ethics of using social media texts in one's research and how to cite texts like tweets and Instagram posts effectively. Listservs are increasingly unpopular with postgraduate students and young faculty. How does one communicate with other scholars in one's field in the late age of the listserv? This chapter gives ideas for scholarly communication, including Facebook groups such as Fashion Historians Unite!, the increasing internationalization of academic communication, the use of hashtags as a means of academic communication, and style blogging as research method. This chapter also offers advice for citing social media posts—including tweets, direct messages, and Facebook and Instagram posts in the Chicago, MLA, and APA styles.

Chapter 1 makes the case that digital repositories such as the FIDM Museum and Galleries Online Collections are vitally important resources for students and give advice on using them effectively, noting that these scholarly databases are superior research tools when compared to repositories of images on social media sites such as Pinterest and Instagram. That is not to say, however, one should avoid using such sites for research purposes entirely. Instagram has a couple key advantages as a research site: it is optimized for mobile (whereas online archives such as Europeana, sadly, are not) and is used frequently and proficiently by many fashion students. This chapter proves that one really can do research on Instagram, provided that one is smart about the hashtags for which they search. In the mobile world, hashtags are the new metadata.

In recognition of the highly international, post-anglophone, and increasingly post-alphabet fashion communities on these sites, this chapter also explores how those in fashion studies use emojis as part of their academic communication. Articles of clothing, including, shirt, pants, sun hat, top hat, boots, and high-heeled shoes, hearts of various colors, a variety of fruits and vegetables, as well as flowers and other flowers, such as cactus and palm tree, animals, including the unicorn, meteorological phenomena such as snowflake and rainbow, and various symbols, such as the red "100."

Part 2: Connecting: Chapter 4: Critical Reading of Social Media Texts

Reading and research habits are changing rapidly in the late age of print. Whereas ten years ago, professors found themselves in a losing battle to dissuade their students from doing research on Wikipedia, today an increasing number of faculty point their students (and themselves) toward user-generated media for research purposes. Social media accounts of designers, journalists, models, museum curators, and others in the fashion world can be wonderful primary sources for scholars of dress and textiles. Social networks can be fruitful research sites for interrogating questions relating to fashion and the popular imagination. As a recent example: How did women respond online to a 2016 *Vogue* (UK) article that asked whether or not cleavage is "over"?[20] But how do we critically read these posts, recognizing the author's purpose and bias in order to make value judgments about the validity and suitability of the posts for research purposes? This chapter discusses how to find—and more importantly to critically analyze—style blogs and social posts on sites like Facebook, Twitter, and Instagram, using critical theory, especially Marxist and psychoanalytic hermeneutics.

This chapter also considers the decidedly uncritical side of social media in the fashion studies community. *The Daily Mail* and other media outlets reported in November 2015 that Sir Mark and Carol Thatcher had offered to donate many items from the late Prime Minister Margaret Thatcher's wardrobe to the Victoria & Albert Museum, only to be spurned because her wardrobe was not of "outstanding aesthetic or technical quality."[21] The online brouhaha that followed, in which museum professionals, fashion academics, those that loved Thatcher, and those that hated her, weighed in on the value (or lack thereof) of Thatcher's clothing makes for an excellent test case for the critical analysis of a variety of social media posts from blogs to tweets to Facebook statuses. Academics' social communication about the role of dress in the perception of women in power will also be considered, including future First Lady Melania Trump's wearing of a Gucci "pussy bow" blouse to a presidential debate and Prime Minister Theresa May's leather trousers and leopard print heels.

Part 2: Connecting: Case Study: Reading Moschino's "Capsule Collection"

Using Georg Simmel's dialectical thought on fashion and the concept of the hermeneutic spiral, this case study demonstrates how to apply sociological theory to the analysis and interpretation of social posts about Moschino's "Capsule Collection." Moschino's Capsule Collection featured apparel and accessories covered in prints and embellishments representing various psychoactive prescription drugs. Unsurprisingly, many people took to social media to express their views on the collection. This case is also a particularly apt example of how a quite ephemeral moment can still provide timeless lessons that have already outlasted this controversy, not only in critical reading skills and digital ethics, but also in the nature of morality and shame in relation to the ongoing opiate crisis.

Part 3: Visualizing: Chapter 5: Data Visualization

This chapter explores the theory and practice of making data visualizations and 3D models both as research method and to communicate one's ideas. Data visualization goes beyond visual communication of research results and is a research method onto itself, helping the researcher discover new patterns and connections in their work. Particularly helpful when dealing with "big data," massive amounts of quantitative data that can be difficult to conceptualize, data visualizations run the gamut from simple tag clouds (groups of words arranged visually to highlight the words that appear most often in a given text) to more complex visualizations, such as maps populated by location-based data. Visualization programs profiled in this chapter will be student-friendly, with low or no costs, a WYSIWYG (what you see is what you get) user interface, and a shallow learning curve. 3D modeling will also be discussed.

Part 3: Visualizing: Chapter 6: Mapping

Trade, migration, colonialism, and globalization are important topics in dress and textile studies, and digital mapping programs allow researcher and audience alike to visualize the journeys of makers and objects and spot new patterns in location-based data. Although this chapter discusses GIS (Geographic Information Systems), the focus will be on platforms such as OpenStreetMap and Google Map Maker—open access tools with a shallow learning curve and low or no cost that students and technophobic researchers can start using right away. A real-world research problems in textile history—the nature of trade routes for Viking-era silk—make the discussion of the various software programs concrete.

Part 3: Visualizing: Case Study: Coding *Fashion Is Kale*

Love it or hate it, online shopping is an unavoidable reality for many. Historians of the fashion business likely already visit retail sites as a part of their research. But shopping, as American designer Elizabeth Hawes noted in her foundational book, *Fashion Is Spinach* (1938), can be highly problematic. Hawes called fashion a "deformed thief," stealing the value of the goods we buy. This case study demonstrates how to present writing on fashion, such as *Fashion Is Spinach*, in a new, visual way as a data visualization of coded themes within the text. Both coding and code are discussed as research methods.

Responding to the Critique of Minimalism: Why Use Mixed Methods?

The conclusion to this book considers, and responds to, the critique of minimalism, both in fashion and in research. Why use mixed methods? After all, some researchers dislike the sense of disorder that may come with mixing research methods. As Coleman and Ringrose note, however, "reality is messy and methodologies that seek to convert this mess into something smooth, coherent, and precise" miss the point entirely.[22] Mixed-methods approaches are applicable to the various stages of the research process, from formulating the research problem, including interpreting and synthesizing theories from multiple disciplines, finding the objects to study, collecting data with multiple methods, explaining social phenomena causally, and making research public. The multi-method researcher is especially able to navigate inter- and multi-disciplinarity. Brewer and Hunter make a case for mixed methods as follows:

> In this arena of competing perspectives [apparel and textiles, history of art, studio art, sociology, etc.], multimethod researchers have a vested interest in bridging differences and bringing about common understanding. They may play an almost ambassadorial role ... they serve to mitigate conflict within the system as a whole ... Multimethod research offers a possible solution to this dilemma. In research that must reach both a professional and a more general audience [which is more or less all research in fashion studies], some methods might be employed for their appeal to the methodologically sophisticated, while others (equally rigorous, but less esoteric) might be used for their accessibility to a wider group.[23]

Many journals already publish mixed-methods research, not only those specializing in that pursuit. "It has become increasingly clear that research methods cannot be assumed a priori to be neutral or atheoretical tools."[24] Research methods have historical, cultural, and political implications, so choose wisely for your audience and project. This book will help you to navigate these complex choices.

Futurism, Maximalism, and the Black Queen

Anita Pallenberg, the Black Queen in the cult classic film *Barbarella*, was an actress, Italian fashion icon, and rock and roll muse. The woman was known for her bangs, her pointy, carnivorous teeth, for slinging a chunky belt over absolutely anything, and for mixing patterns and textures like a mad woman. When I heard of her passing in June 2017, it was like my fairy godmother had died. I spent a day in bed eating gelato and watching *Barbarella*. The simultaneously futuristic and maximalist aesthetic of director Roger Vadim's 1968 sci-fi fantasy *Barbarella: Queen of the Galaxy*, starring Jane Fonda as the title character and Anita Pallenberg as the evil Black Queen, became highly influential for me as I was thinking through what it means for this book, and indeed for fashion writing generally at present, to be both futuristic—situated in a nascent and rapidly evolving digital age—and maximalistic (Figure 1.2).

Figure 1.2 *Film Still: Anita Pallenberg as the Black Queen in* Barbarella, *Paramount Pictures (1968).*

In fashion at least, futurism is often associated with minimalism, while maximalism can read as kitsch, or what architect Robert Venturi liked to call, "good, old-fashioned Victorian clutter." A popular perception of futuristic clothing based on space suits worn by astronauts comprises cold, sleek, shiny white or silver metallic fabrics, simply cut and practical, with no embellishments or accessories. Such a vision of futurism is minimalist indeed. In her book, *Space Oddities*, Marie Lathers proposes a different kind of minimalist dress for women in space—nudity.[25] The 1960s space flicks such as *Nude on the Moon* (1961) and *Barbarella* were populated by female astronaut characters who often found themselves in a state of undress.

While Lathers is primarily interested in the "cosmic striptease" of Jane Fonda's "five-star double-rated astronavigatrix earth girl" character, she does note the importance of the varied clothing worn by Barbarella when she does not appear in the nude:

> Barbarella is not defined so much by her specific clothing as by her multiple changes of attire. She wears a tight black and white outfit only to trade it for an emerald green, only to choose another black one, again and again. Each outfit has matching boots, some reaching up to her thighs. Barbarella's very being, and along with it her stance as an astronaut, is defined by the removal and then changing of clothes: her adventure in space is an adventure in sex and wardrobe.[26]

The costuming in the film was done by Jacques Fonteray and Paco Rabanne (who also appears in the film), and is at once rooted in the speculative, space-age look of the 1960s and totally over-the-top maximalism (this is especially the case for Pallenberg's costumes), with feathers and horns and sequins disrupting the clean, sleek aesthetic one often associates with futurism in fashion. Thanks to the Black Queen, I had reconciled in my own mind the dichotomy, and (I think) a false one, between the digital age and maximalism in dress. And I was determined that this methods book would take a new direction toward maximalism.

The fashion photograph on the cover of this book is similarly simultaneously futuristic, which hints at the "digital age" aspect of the book, and maximalistic, with all its disparate pieces that should not necessarily go together. The silk roses on the headpiece are *perfect* in that they should in no way complement the cool, sleek, silver, and clear, iridescent fabrics and general futuristic spirit of the outfit, and yet somehow they just work. Much like this book itself, which espouses methods that one would not necessarily associate with academia and academic communication, like emojis and Instagram research bursts, and methods that traditionally have not been seen as going together, such as qualitative and quantitative approaches to the same research question, and yet somehow, it all just works. I hope that you enjoy this book, and as you embark on your own digital fashion research in a time in which Instagram research bursts and data visualizations are no longer the future but the present, I hope that you take a cue from the Black Queen and incorporate some sequins and feathers along the way.

PART 1

Searching

This introductory part starts at the beginning: the commencement of the research process. In my younger days, like many students, I liked to leave research papers until the night (or more responsibly, the weekend) before they were due and then, in heroic hours of mania, churn out what I thought was a brilliant paper. Eventually, though, the wisdom of experience, combined with the ever-lengthening page counts of my writing projects led me to adopt a different and ultimately much more effective strategy: developing (and using) a research plan.[1] A good research plan begins with a schedule, determining when the work of research and writing will be done and establishing internal deadlines to follow. Next comes narrowing down the research topic. In choosing a research topic, a good place to start is to look for gaps in the existing literature. What kinds of objects, such as menswear and children's wear, have been under-studied? What subjects have been studied a great deal, but always ignoring a particular method, theory, or context?

Writing assignments, especially at the advanced undergraduate and graduate levels, are often quite open ended. Doing some preliminary research almost always helps to narrow a broad topic that could be fully addressed as a book down to a more manageable topic best addressed as an essay. For example, the very broad topic "punk fashion" might be best addressed as a book (which, in fact, it has been in Monica Sklar's *Punk Style*), but a narrower topic, such as "punk fashion in Munich," would work well as a long essay. (And be sure to keep track of all of the sources consulted along the way. There is nothing worse than the time-consuming process of creating a long bibliography from scratch after the fact.)

2 Text-based Searching Strategies

There are some basics to searching any database, from library catalogs to these fashion and textile-specific databases. Searching these databases effectively often means employing search strategies beyond simple keyword searches. Truly productive searches start out with an understanding of Boolean language. Christy Gavins opens Chapter Three of her book, *Teaching Information Literacy*, with the pithy line: "Most people have learned about [online] searching the way they learned about sex—from their friends."[1] Boolean queries are a must for attaining best results in searching library catalogs and many other databases. Boolean logic is used in many disciplines, including mathematics (especially algebra), logic, and computer science. In the field of library science, "Boolean" refers to the logical use of keywords in a search, combined with operators, such as AND and OR, and truncations, such as *. Gavins lays out a five-step system for constructing Boolean search queries: stating the topic, determining the most important concepts of the topic, expressing each concept as a keyword, truncating, and finally, rewriting the keywords as parenthetical statements.[2]

Keyword Generation for Boolean Queries

Keyword generation is arguably the most important step in constructing a search. Helpfully, in their book, *Successful Keyword Searching*, MacDonald and MacDonald supply lists of commonly used keywords for many academic disciplines, including fashion studies.[3] Keywords included in their fashion list are:

A
apparel
attire

B
belt
bodice

C
cape
casual
chemise
cloak
clothing
costume
costume design
cotton

D
design
dress
dress design

F
fabric
fad
fashion
fashion designer
fashion industry
fashion photography
formal

G
garment
garment industry
garter
girdle
gown

H
hat

K
kilt

L
loincloth

M
minimalism

N
natural fibers
needle trades
New Look
nylon

O
ornamentation

P
pattern making

R
rayon
retail
robe

S
seamstress
sewing
shirt
shoes
skirt
sleeves
stockings
stole
storage
style
suit
synthetic

T
tailor
tailoring
textiles

toga
traditional dress
trousers
tunic

U
uniform

V
vesture

W
weave
Western dress
wrap

While lists such as this one are very useful, don't rely solely on such resources as you conduct your searches. Even the most comprehensive keyword list will be missing many useful terms. This list, for example, is missing "knit" or "knitwear," both very important terms for apparel design students. It is also missing "models," the crucial keyword from our previous example. And while MacDonald and MacDonald's list includes "minimalism," they have omitted "maximalism," the fashion concept on which this book is based.

Another important point to keep in mind is that keywords change with place and time. An American database might use "costume," as the preferred term for clothing, while a British database might use "dress," for example. Research projects on the history of dress often require extra forethought in the form of period-specific language in creating search queries. For instance, researchers beginning projects on eighteenth-century dress should consider eighteenth-century language. In her essay on humanities databases in *Women Online: Research in Women's Studies Using Online Databases*, Joyce Duncan Falk discusses searching the *Eighteenth Century Short Title Catalogue*, a database of British library holdings of works published in the eighteenth century. Ideal for historic dress research, the database contains period writing on "woman's character, conduct (vices, virtues, follies), dress, education, and rights are typical entries, as are works of fiction about the loves and adventures of women."[4] If Falk's description of the database sounds like something out of a Jane Austen novel, that's because she's sensitive to the particular qualities of the English language as it was spoken and written in the eighteenth century. This doesn't mean that a person needs to read *Pride and Prejudice* or *Sense and Sensibility* before beginning their research project on historic dress, however. Being mindful of period language should suffice in most cases. Falk suggests searching for the keywords "woman" and "women" in this way: "(wom#n OR lady OR ladies)."[5] Meanwhile, placed in the middle of the word, the # symbol does not denote a hashtag; rather, it acts as a wild card, returning search results for any character. In this case, both "woman" and "women." She uses "lady" and "ladies" as keywords because they were frequently used terms for women in the 1700s. ("Lady" is not truncated here, presumably because such a search would also return results for "laddie," which is quite the opposite!) Above all, be thorough and creative in your keyword generation. Keywords such as these may be used when searching a search engine, such as Google, or in searches of databases.

SEO and Searching the Web

Embarking on the research project in earnest, once the topic has been narrowed down to a set of concepts expressible as keywords, means asking research questions. Many novice researchers are overwhelmed by the sheer number of possibilities when it comes to where to begin searching for sources, and many unfortunately (but understandably) turn to Google. Search engine optimization, or SEO, has largely changed our expectations about how to search for information on the Web. One simply has to type "1910s Lanvin" or "that jumpsuit that Mick Jagger wore" or whatever into the search bar in Google and the search engine's algorithm will return useful results in the order of relevance. Right? Ordinarily, this is sadly not the case.

While SEO does make it easier and faster to search for content on the Web, it is also changing the character and quality of the content, especially as regards fashion. For her book, *Remake, Remodel: Women's Magazines in the Digital Age*, Brooke Erin Duffy interviewed an editorial assistant at magazine giant *Condé Nast* about a recent presentation the staff there had been given on writing material for the Web with SEO in mind. According to the interviewee:

> [The title of an article] should have a number in it, and it should be as basic as possible, something like "Ten Cute Hair Ideas" ... Because when people are Googling, it's all SEO ... what happens is someone out there Googles "cute haircuts" because they want a cute haircut. And we come up first, we give you "Fifteen Cute Haircuts for Fall," "Fifteen Cute Haircuts for Spring."[6]

The widespread practice of writing more for SEO than for readers creates a standardization of Web content—both in writing style and in the nature of the material itself. For anyone who authors Web content on a regular basis, this represents a conundrum—to sacrifice SEO, and thus the article's place in a users' search results, or style and content. In his article for *Art Journal Open*, "Citation Bombing: Tactical and Symbolic Subversion of Academic Metrification," creator of the Citation Bomb app Zachary Kaiser asks, "What numerical value applies to achieving the arc of a compelling paragraph? What algorithm measures the importance of the time spent sitting in front of a painting with a colleague, developing ideas and discussing the artist's engagement with complex visual problems?"[7] SEO, Kaiser argues, can only lead to the "fetishization of data and concomitant information gathering" and the degradation of academic prose.[8]

Imagine scholarly prose written with SEO in mind; the results seem amusingly absurd. If, for example, I had titled a blog post about the *Duprees of Spitalfields*, a family of Huguenot silk weavers living and working in the East End of London (see Chapter 6), as "Twelve Amazing Historic Silks You Need to Know about Right Now," I would almost certainly have received more traffic. SEO can also produce frustrations for students and researchers. Barring someone publishing "Ten Cute Lanvin Frocks from the 1910s" and "Ten Times Mick Jagger Wore That Ossie Clarke Jumpsuit," library, museum, and archival databases remain the best places to begin a search project that requires study of period object and primary sources in fashion and textile studies. While Google is a convenient place to begin, searching databases is ultimately a better strategy for a research project in fashion or textile studies, perhaps especially one rooted in a family story. Jane Devine and Francine Egger-Sider explain why in their book, *Going beyond Google … Again*. They note:

> The largest contributor to the Invisible Web [the part of the Web that cannot be easily accessed by search engines] consists of resources locked away in *databases*. Databases are collections of materials with their own organization and their own search and retrieval functions. Databases often offer valuable resources that have been vetted by a review or editorial process. Search engine spiders can find the databases but they cannot necessarily enter into them for content. The spider programs used to gather and index sites simply cannot fill out the necessary query forms that databases rely on.[9]

Besides library catalogs and databases of peer-reviewed articles, researchers in the field of fashion and textiles studies are also served by several excellent databases, each with their own collection strengths, containing fashion photographs and images of dress and textile objects, along with their metadata.

What is Metadata?

You may have heard the phrase, "that's so meta!," or perhaps read the prefix in other contexts, such as "meta-analysis" or "metacognition." "Meta" refers to that which is an abstraction of itself or a concept which is an order higher than itself. It may sound complicated in theory, but in practice it is actually pretty simple. Metadata, very simply defined, is data about data. Let us take the example of an object in a museum collection that appears in a database: a cologne bottle shaped like a moose from the FIDM collection. The bottle itself is the data, while all of the information about it—that it is brown, made of glass, moose-shaped, dates to the 1970s—, was produced by Avon, is called "Alaskan Moose Deep Woods," etc—are its associated metadata. When searching for an object in a database, one searches using metadata. One might be looking for an object made by Avon, for cologne bottles from the 1970s, or for moose-themed material culture, and would search accordingly using either a keyword search box on the database's website, or if the databases' metadata scheme and frontend website design allow for it, one could search by specific metadata fields, such as "date," "title," "color," or "maker." In the example, searching the database by metadata field for date (1970s) and maker (Avon) is quite straightforward, but what about searching for "moose"? While only the most complicated custom metadata schemes are likely to have a field for animal-shaped objects, "moose" can still be queried in the title field in this case. To search like a pro, it is helpful to understand how databases work.

Databases are created using content management systems, computer software programs such as Omeka and KORA that store object files (such as TIFF and .JPG) and connect them with their metadata, organized by metadata schemes. A variety of types of objects may be associated with metadata in such schemes—objects, such as clothing and accessories, images, such as fashion photographs, and even sound and video. Organizations may create a custom metadata scheme to suit the needs of their user base and the particular types of objects in the collection.

The Quilt Index, for example, uses a highly detailed custom metadata scheme with over 150 individual metadata fields, created in-house specifically for describing quilt objects. Alternately, an institution might use a standard metadata scheme, such as Dublin Core or VRA Core. These standard metadata schemes are lighter and less detailed than custom schemes, with fewer metadata fields, because they are meant to work for a wide variety of types of objects and collections. The original Dublin Core Metadata Element Set, for example, which is the result of an international conference on metadata held in Dublin, Ohio in 1995, features only fifteen fields: title, creator, subject, description, publisher, contributor, date, type, format, identifier, source, language, relation, coverage, and rights. These core or standard metadata schemes specify only basic metadata about an object, but have the advantage of interoperability with other databases, facilitating collaboration and connectivity between institutions and collections. Now that we have a better understanding of how databases are built and organized around metadata, let us explore several key databases in the field of fashion and textile studies.

National, Local, and Regional Databases

Even a few years ago, it was much more difficult to find information and images about fashion—especially recent fashion—than it is today. Writing of her own work on Martin Margiela (published in 2016, but conducted beginning *c.* 2000), Francesca Granata writes, "When setting out to study experimental fashion at the turn of the millennium, I thought that it would be quite simple to reconstruct and access such a recent past. However, I found the opposite to be the case."[10] This difficulty stemmed from the fact that early image databases, such as firstVIEW.com, catwalking.com, and the Contemporary Fashion Archive (contemporaryfashion.net), were challenging to search and hardly encyclopedic in nature. Happily, these databases have now largely been replaced by richer and easier-to-use resources.

In fashion and textile history, discipline-specific databases usually yield more relevant and trustworthy results than simply searching within a web browser's search engine. Below is a current list of key databases, a few of which are described in the sections that follow:

- Australian Dress Register, australiandressregister.org
- Berg Fashion Library, bloomsburyfashioncentral.com
- Commercial Pattern Archive, copa.apps.uri.edu
- Costume Institute Fashion Plates, https://www.metmuseum.org/art/libraries-and-research-centers/watson-digital-collections/costume-institute-collections/costume-institute-fashion-plates
- Dress Discover, https://dressdiscover.org/
- Europeana, europeana.eu
- Fashion History Timeline, fashionhistory.fitnyc.edu
- Fashion Photography Archive, bloomsburyfashioncentral.com
- the FIDM (Fashion Institute of Design and Merchandising) Museum and Galleries Online Collections, fidmmuseum.org
- Minnesota Dressmakers, collections.mnhs.org

- Modemuze, modemuze.nl
- Pockets of History, vads.ac.uk
- the Quilt Index, quiltindex.org
- Tapestry, tapestry.philau.edu
- Texas Fashion Collection, digital.library.unt.edu
- We Wear Culture, https://artsandculture.google.com/

Along with these databases, we will also note the value of genealogical databases in fashion and textile research and the role of family history as fashion and textile history. In discussing these databases in the pages that follow, I have given much greater time to some than to others. I have chosen a few representative sites that show the breadth of material that can be found in historic costume databases, as well as projects that provide a sense of the increasingly global state of the field.

Australian Dress Register

The Australian Dress Register, a database of both historical and contemporary Australian fashion, features a bit of everything fashion from the land down under. According to the Australian Dress Register's about page:

> The Australian Dress Register is a collaborative, online project about dress with Australian provenance. This includes men's, women's and children's clothing ranging from the special occasion to the everyday. Museums and private collectors are encouraged to research their garments and share the stories and photographs while the information is still available and within living memory. The Register encourages people to consider their collections very broadly and share what they know about members of their community, what they wore and life in the past. This provides access to a world wide audience while keeping their garments in their relevant location.[11]

The scope of the Australian Dress Register spans from humble woolen clothing and cotton day dresses to high fashion and the work of Beril Jents (known as Australia's first couturier) to contemporary Australian brands and designers. More recently, the Bicentennial Wool Fashion Parade of 1988 included woolen designs by international designers (Missoni, Sonia Rykiel, and Versace to name a few) and by seven Australian designers. In her essay, "Interlaced: Textiles for Fashion," Liz Williamson observes that "the well-known saying 'wool: the fabric of a nation' illustrates the Australian perception of wool as a material embedded in the history of European settlement."[12] Beyond wool, the Australian Dress Register also features staple Australian brands such as Brown Sugar, and of course, what Australia is best known for in the world of fashion: swimwear.

In "Against the Grain: Australia and the Swimsuit," Christine Schmidt argues that Australian fashion, and in particular its swimwear, is especially grounded in a sense of place, writing:

> Fashion commentator Norma Martyn described the Australian look as 'fashioned by geography' (Martyn 1976, 11) and influenced by sea, sand and sun. Reflecting on an Australian fashion landscape, when Kimberly Busteed, Miss Universe Australia 2007, appeared wearing a swimsuit and lifesaving cap for the national costume segment of the pageant, Martyn said to the world that Australia had undoubtedly taken the crown for its swimwear—and it would seem that, in Australia, less is definitely more.[13]

To search for swimwear, browse by theme and select "sportswear." Owner's names are connected with the objects whenever possible, such as Mina Wylie's swimming costume, *c.* 1910–12, and Violet Armstrong's lifesaving club swimsuit, *c.* 1930–45.

Australian-made couture can be found on the site by selecting "Australia" as the country of origin and then also selecting a theme such as "ball," "debutante," "evening dress," "fancy dress," "special occasion," and "wedding." In an Instagram post, dress historian Kate Strasdin showcased gowns by Australian designers, calling for more exposure for this rich, though under-utilized resource.[14] Collection highlights include an evening dress designed by Lisa Ho and worn by Delta Goodrem and a red satin and tulle ballgown worn by Dawn Waterhouse to the state ball given in honor of Queen Elizabeth II in 1954 (Figure 2.1).

Europeana

Europeana is a free database sponsored by the European Union and aims to be "an online collection of millions of digitized items from European museums, libraries, archives, and audiovisual collections."[15] The ModeMuseum in Antwerp and the Victoria and Albert in London are two museums with strong fashion collections included in Europeana. This trend toward not only digitization of museum collections and metadata, but also their free and open access online as evidenced by not only the database itself but also by LODLAM Europeana, which shares open linked data about the objects, has been echoed in the United States

Figure 2.1 *Screenshot: Dawn Waterhouse ballgown on the Australian Dress Register, Image courtesy of the Canberra Museum and Art Gallery.*

through recent projects at the Metropolitan Museum of Art in New York and by the Los Angeles County Museum of Art, which makes images from its costume collection available to the public under a public domain Creative Commons license on Flickr Commons. As Agiatis Bernardou and Alastair Dunning (2018) note, however, since Europe is so pan-lingual, translation software built into the website would further facilitate not only use by individual users but also sharing of data between institutions.[16]

Europeana features over five million objects. Those wishing to use images from the site in their research or elsewhere online should browse by "openly licensed images." If one is not searching for anything in particular and simply wishes to peruse the site, a good strategy is to choose "explore" and then "people." Profiles and linked objects exist for designers and artists such as Judith Leyster, Maria Sybilla Merian, William Morris, Yves Saint Laurent (YSL), and Madeleine Vionnet. Or, search for a specific person in the search box on the main page. Be sure to delete each previously used keyword search by clicking the "X" to the right of the search term, as keywords stack in Europeana's search design. Unless, of course, the goal is to search multiple terms at the same time. In this case, consider each term to be separated by "AND" rather than "OR." Boolean queries will be discussed later in this chapter.

Also be specific in phrasing searches when using this database, though. Europeana's search algorithm casts a very wide net. Let us take the example of the fashion house of Martin Margiela. Margiela is known for meta-fashion, that is, fashion about fashion. Databases use metadata—data about data—to return relevant search results. But if the metadata queried is too broad or vague and the search algorithm favors breadth, many unusable search results may be returned. A search for "Margiela," for example, returns over 1,600 results, many of which are irrelevant, returning results for *Margiela I Margielka* (1953), among others. A better keyword search strategy is to use "Margiela, Martin" or "Maison Martin Margiela" (Figure 2.2).

Costume Institute Fashion Plates and the Fashion Institute of Design and Merchandising (FIDM) Museum and Galleries Online Collections are two more key

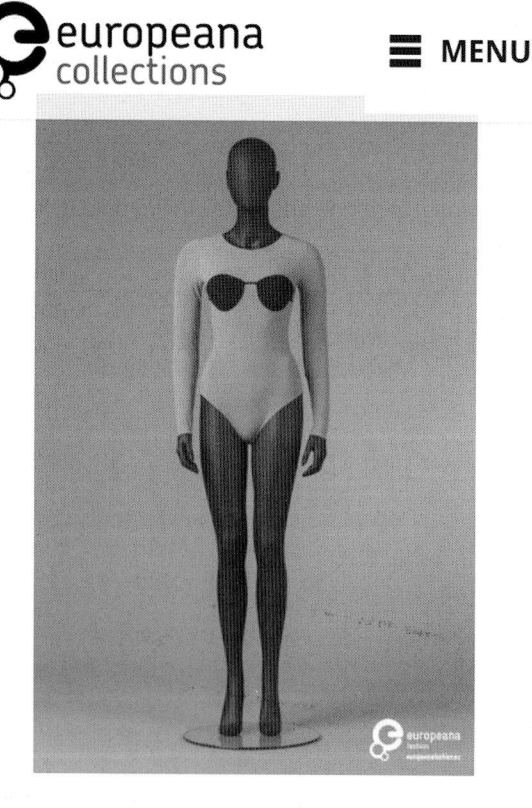

Figure 2.2 *Screenshot: Maison Martin Margiela bodysuit on Europeana Fashion, CC BY-SA.*

museum-based databases. FIDM is particularly important for researchers working on fragrance. To browse the fragrance collection, choose "collections" and then scroll down to "fragrance." Users may then search within only the fragrance collection among a variety of other Dublin Core-based metadata fields, including title, date, creator, material, credit line, object ID number, and early and late date ranges. To find a bottle of Alaskan Moose Deep Woods, an aftershave about which I happen to have fond childhood memories, I put "Avon" in the creator field. Other notable collections on the FIDM site include the Hollywood costume collection, the FIDM jewelry and costume collections, and the Versace Menswear Archive. The FIDM site was created using the ubiquitous PastPerfect museum cataloging software and is quite intuitive and user-friendly. It also has a fast and functional mobile site. Indeed the screenshots of the Australian Dress Register, Europeana, and FIDM databases illustrated in this chapter are all taken from these databases' mobile websites.

Modemuze, Minnesota Dressmakers, and the Texas Fashion Collection are three other major place-based databases for fashion studies. Modemuze is mostly in Dutch, but is well-organized, user-friendly, and has an active blog with occasional English articles. Among the textile and accessory-specific databases are Pockets of History, the Quilt Index, and Tapestry. The Pockets of History project takes users back to the time when pockets were independent and tied on, rather than part of a larger garment's construction. Hundreds of eighteenth- and nineteenth-century pockets are browsable by various materials and decoration types (embroidery, patchwork, etc.). The site also contains information about how pockets were made and used, and the all-too-common problem with detached pockets: what one did in case of the loss of one's pocket. (A common sight in eighteenth-century newspapers were advertisements that began "lost in my pocket … " and proceeded with a litany of lost valuables.)

Commercial Pattern Archive

Of particular import for working on sewing patterns is the Commercial Pattern Archive (COPA). The COPA at the University of Rhode Island Libraries is an archive built around the paper pattern collection of Betty Williams, historical costumer and vintage pattern expert. In contrast to some of the other databases described in this chapter, such as Europeana, which are largely populated by museum pieces (and thus by high-end fashion), sewing patterns by nature are a more populist, democratic object, and they can provide researchers with a valuable visual record of the sorts of lowbrow or everyday fashions—especially of menswear and children's wear—that rarely made it into museum collections. Besides giving researchers a picture of popular fashion of decades past, Joy Spanabel Emery notes two other important reasons for the study of paper patterns: (1) Taken together, a pattern archive is essentially a visual dictionary of garment technology, an important resource for students studying garment construction. (2) Although many patterns were not dated, the date of a pattern can usually be determined by other metadata that describe the pattern. This offers a means to accurately date trends in popular clothing from about the 1840s to the present.[17]

Sewing patterns may be dated by the style of the garment, style of the pattern company logo, pattern number, and price.[18] Unlike many other media, such as vinyl records, that have unique numbers (e.g., the Beatles's *Abbey Road* is PCS 7088 and no other record may share this number),[19] the same pattern number may be used by more than one paper sewing pattern. As Joy Spanabel Emery notes: "In general, the numbers, usually four digits between 1000 and 9999, are recycled. Recycling is not influenced by calendar year; consequently, the lower numbers can overlap higher numbers in the same year."[20] This fact alone can make sewing patterns particularly tricky for which to search. Thus, when searching the COPA or Vintage Pattern Wiki for a particular pattern, never search for the number alone as one might be a library call number or museum accession number. Instead, search for the style of the pattern, the company, if known (e.g., Butterick, Qwik Sew, McCall's, Simplicity, or Vogue) *and* the pattern number. Of course, when browsing an archive (rather than searching for one specific example), one need to search only for the style (e.g., apron, bodysuit, cowl neck, petticoat), or the company, depending on the nature of the research question.

The COPA website unveiled a new redesign in January 2018, featuring more objects—over 55,000 images of garments and pattern schematics—as well as more metadata fields by which to search. Unfortunately, access to the site is not currently immediate. To use the site, users must first download, complete, and send back an access form to receive login credentials.

Encyclopedic Databases

Some of these databases are created and maintained by scholars in conjunction with academic publishing houses, such as Bloomsbury. While these databases are behind a pay wall for the general public, students and university faculty can usually access them for free through their college or university library. Others are free to the public, collaborations with tech companies, such as Google, or coming out of universities, such as the Fashion Institute of Technology. One exception to this general rule that Google is not the best place to conduct a research project is the Google Arts & Culture site, We Wear Culture,[21] a collaboration between Google and several major museums and cultural institutions that features stories about designers, as well as the muses who inspired and wore the clothes, and is a great place to start looking for a topic. The site features a timeline of dress from 6,000 BCE to the 1930s.

Fashion History Timeline

The Fashion History Timeline is a project of the Art History program at the Fashion Institute of Technology. It is a hybrid scholarly crowdsourced resource featuring essays and dictionary entries browsable alphabetically, by time period and by designer. The whole database is built using Zotero. The site has the look and feel of a blog. Clicking on "designers," for example, brings up the most recent additions to the designers category, rather than a traditional browse or advanced search interface. A search for "Margiela, Martin," the same search from the Europeana example, brings up only one result, a book review of Radical Fashion (2001). Undoubtedly, as additional scholarly contributions grow the database, more information will become available. It does seem in its early days (I am writing this on the day on which the site went live: February 13, 2018) that the Fashion History Timeline is more geared toward fashion history before about 1970, rather than contemporary history. This may change as the site grows.

In the meantime, the real beauty of the site is its dictionary and timeline. In the dictionary, fashion students can find reliable definitions for terms such as "leg-of-mutton sleeves" and "robe a l'anglaise," many of which have been submitted by students at FIT. Each definition is accompanied by an illustration from the history of art or fashion. The entry for "Panniers," for example, posted by Kimberlei McNamara (March 24, 2017) reads: "An under-structure used in eighteenth century fashion that created a shape wide at the sides and flat at the front and back" (Figure 2.3). In addition to the dictionary, an encyclopedia-style timeline is browsable by the ancient world, early middle ages, and 14th, 15th, 16th, 17th, 18th, 19th, 20th, and 21st centuries. Clicking on a century breaks the period down by decade, with illustrated introductions to the fashion of each ten-year period. Many of these timeline entries were written by FIT students as well. Elsewhere on the site, a blog post by Justine de Young entitled "How to Research Fashion" encourages students to: (1) look carefully, (2) identify the date, (3) compare to other objects from the same decade, (4) dig deeper into primary and secondary sources for the decade (or century), and (5) assess how the garment fits within its time period.[22]

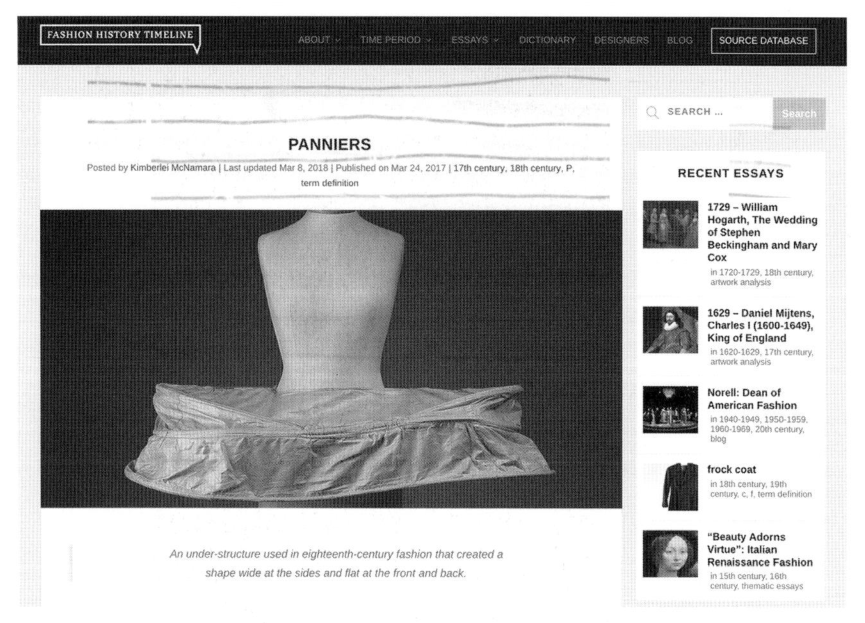

Figure 2.3 *Screenshot: Panniers on the Fashion History Timeline, Image taken by Justine de Young and courtesy of the Fashion Institute of Technology, State University of New York.*

Fashion Photography Archive

The Berg Fashion Library and the Fashion Photography Archive are both subscription-based services available in the same place: bloomsburyfashioncentral.com. Many colleges and university libraries already provide free access to their students and faculty. The Berg Fashion Library contains 13,000 images, as well as the Berg Encyclopedia of World Dress and Fashion, and is a good place to start at the beginning of a research project, before the topic is well-refined, or to learn about the history of dress more broadly.

The Fashion Photography Archive, by contrast, features over 750,000[23] catwalk, backstage, and street style photographs and fashion by over 400 designers from the 1970s to the present searchable across a wide array of metadata fields. This is the place to look for very specific images to foster research in progress on the fashion of the last few decades. It is particularly useful for projects on models and muses. Basic metadata given for each object include maker, date, and reference number. Searches can be refined by selecting additional metadata options on the left-hand side of the screen under "explore," such as accessories, colors, dress type, garments, organizations such as design houses, people, and seasons. This example record for a runway photograph of YSL Spring/Summer 1988 illustrates some of the many possibilities (Figure 2.4).

Figure 2.4 *Screenshot: Bloomsbury Fashion Photography Archive: search page with explore tab, featuring a runway look by YSL.*

Susan Sontag writing for *Vogue* in 1978 famously observed, "Great fashion photography is more than the photography of fashion."[24] Fashion photography tells us a great deal about the aesthetic and moral values of a particular time and place. Writing twenty years later on the importance of the fashion photograph in the 1990s, Elliott Smedley noted, "It therefore seems that realist fashion photography in the 1990s has that function that photojournalism has lost, perhaps through sheer volume. Furthermore, realist fashion photography can reach a wider audience than social documentary or art photography could ever hope to achieve."[25] Ultimately, fashion photography documents a culture's vision of who and what is beautiful, and who and what fascinates a society, often with an ugly or dangerous tinge to the initial beauty of the model and the clothes she or he wears. Thus, a database of fashion photography can be one of the most important weapons in the fashion scholar's arsenal. Now that we have an idea of the strengths and specific uses of many fashion and textile databases, we can explore searching for a particular topic: Kate Moss.

Case Study: In Search of Kate Moss

At the end of the *Absolutely Fabulous* movie (2016), when the viewer discovers that Kate Moss has not drowned in the Thames, but rather has been washed up on the coast of the European continent like some glamorous castaway, but looking more like a mermaid, I thought "how perfect a use of Kate, because she really is a mermaid." That is not to say that she is half fish, but rather something like a nymph. "The essence of these nymphs [mermaids], whether lively or languorous, is their sexuality. At a time when it was taboo to display genitalia in art, a mermaid could be shown 'entirely naked,' yet 'decent.' She is the nineteenth century equivalent of a Page 3 girl, exposed above but unavailable below."[26] According to Sophia Kingshill, author of *Mermaids*, "Much of the mermaid's legend centers on her ambivalence. She's presented as a seducer, yet obviously, given that she is woman only down to her waist and fish below, she cannot achieve intercourse. Arousing but never satisfying desire, she is a tease, an unobtainable flirt."[27] This modern image of the beautiful model as nymph or mermaid has roots in the Sirens in Homer's *Odyssey*. "One one level, what they offer is a reflection of fame, a hymn to a hero's own greatness that would sound sweet in that hero's ears: holding up a flattering mirror, you could say."[28] Inspiration for a research project can truly strike at any time, even when one is supposedly taking a break from research to watch a zany film.

Each case study in this book sets out to demonstrate the relevance of the theory and more abstract information presented in the main body of the chapter to dress and textile studies research through practical application. In demonstrating potential searches of the Bloomsbury Fashion Photography Archive using Kate Moss as subject, we return to the research plan from Chapter 1. I have opted here not to focus on Moss's most infamous role, as the poster child (and scapegoat) of the heroin chic, size zero look of the 1990s, nor on her more recent and perhaps less famous roles: her recent magazine work, collaborations with other designers such as Alexander McQueen, her work in the business of fashion, and her growing inscrutability in the face of her status as one of the most legendary fashion icons of all time, but to concentrate instead on demonstrating searches for her in the context of a single research question modeling, a hypothetical research project inspired by the *Ab Fab* movie: to what extent can Kate Moss be read as an allegorical mermaid?

Kate as Mermaid

To return search results for images of mermaid silhouette dresses on the Bloomsbury Fashion Photography Archive, one can either search for "mermaid" by typing it into the keyword search box or check "mermaid" under "garments" within the "explore" tab on the left. The records for the photographs on this site have been so richly laden with metadata that browsing and searching often return similar results and it is easier to just browse. (In many databases, this is not the case!) "Mermaid" is quite a specialized term in the context of fashion metadata, and is usually too specific to appear in a database's metadata scheme. While the very large number of objects on this site makes it worthwhile for advanced researchers looking for a very particular sort of image—such as Kate Moss doing runway in a mermaid silhouette gown. The richness of the explore feature also makes the Fashion Photography Archive quite helpful for beginning researchers who may not always be familiar with the vocabulary of fashion (and thus not yet have the instincts for which terms to search).

The Fashion Photography Archive contains dozens of images of Moss on the runway, as well as numerous articles about her, along with articles that reference the mermaid silhouette or mermaids in popular culture, but checking the "mermaid" box under "garments" does not return with results of Kate Moss. So, to test our theoretical hypothesis that Moss is an allegorical mermaid, a change in search strategy was called for. Instead of using the explore tab, I did a keyword search querying the keywords "Moss, Kate AND mermaid." "AND" in this example is a Boolean operator. To demonstrate a simplified version of Gavins's system for articulating Boolean search queries discussed in Chapter 1, let's suppose that a student wants to write a research paper on the embodiment of the mermaid archetype among fashion models.[29]

Step one: State the topic

Example: "fashion model as mermaid."

Example question: "To what extent can runway fashion models of the 1970s, '80s and '90s, such as Kate Moss, be read as allegorical mermaids?"

A research question such as this, while vital for the researcher's own understanding of what they hope to accomplish and what sources they hope to find, is difficult, if not impossible, to search for in many museum and other databases. This is why the research question must first be distilled down to a few key concepts.

Step two: Determine the most important concepts of the topic

Example: "fashion models," "mermaids," "1970s," "1980s," "1990s."

The key concepts for this topic are temporal—the time period, the 1970s, '80s, and '90s—and relational, how fashion models embodied the mermaid archetype at the time.

Step three: Express each concept as a keyword

Example: "fashion," "models," "mermaids," "siren," "splash."

Here is where the search query really begins to take shape. The phrase "fashion and models" became the keywords "fashion" and "models." This is quite straightforward. Less straightforward was the extrapolation of "mermaids" to the additional keywords "siren" and "splash." In both cases, works in the field of popular culture—Roxy Music's 1975 album *Siren* (on the cover of which model Jerry Hall appears in the guise of a mermaid) and the 1984 film *Splash* starring Daryl Hannah as a mermaid—gave rise to mermaid crazes in the popular imagination, which filtered into the world of fashion. Finally, the decades "1970s," "1980s," and "1990s" were omitted completely, not only because many unrelated things happened in those decades, but also because most databases have a separate search parameter for time period, apart from the keyword entry.

Step four: Truncation

Example: model* returns results not just for "model," but also "models," "modeling," etc.

Don't go overboard with truncations, however. According to Gavins, "Students misapply truncation when they fail to consider the meaning of words. For example, they will truncate *sexism* as 'sex*,' not realizing that this will bring a great deal of irrelevant hits that have nothing to do with sexist behaviour."[30] Thus, truncation should only be used as necessary or if appropriate.

Step five: Rewrite the keywords as a parenthetical statement

Example: (fashion OR models) AND (mermaid OR siren).

The parenthetical statement "(fashion OR models) AND (mermaid OR siren)" is the best way to articulate this Boolean query. This is because the most important Boolean operator is the one between the parenthetical statements. The statement "(fashion AND models) OR (mermaid OR siren)," for example, would return results about either fashion and models or cocaine or heroin, which would not be particularly useful. The statement "(fashion OR models) AND (mermaid AND siren)" is better, but again, the operators, this time within the parentheses, are used incorrectly. The best statement would be "(fashion OR models) AND (mermaid OR siren)."

I chose not to truncate "models" in this query. The search term "model*," in this case, returned too many results about statistical models, rather than fashion models, which was of course unhelpful. Finally, note that while this example did not use proper names, when searching for a particular person as a key term, always give their name as "last name, first name" in a Boolean query, for example: "Hall, Jerry" or "Moss, Kate."

Frustratingly, there are many records for runway photographs of mermaid silhouette dresses, such as this example of Nina Ricci from Fall/Winter 1984, but none worn by Moss (Figure 2.5). In this case, the "AND" operator returns too few results, while the "OR" operator returns too many only tangentially related results (Kate Moss or mermaid silhouette, but not both). Even if a Boolean search does not produce enough quality results, a researcher can still find what they are looking for, or at least a very close approximation. The third and final search strategy used was to revisit the "explore" tab, that set of metadata options on the left side of the screen. By searching for Kate Moss and selecting for mermaid-looking colors in the "colour" section—blue and turquoise (the Fashion Photography Archive allows users to get fairly specific with colors), I was able to find an image close to that for which I was looking—Kate Moss in cerulean blue, quite mermaid style eye makeup walking for Martine Sitbon Spring/Summer 1994 (Figure 2.6).

In Search of the Fashion Model

Sometimes the most ubiquitous person is the most difficult to search for, because so many irrelevant results are returned for each query. Kate Moss is certainly one

Figure 2.5 *Screenshot: Bloomsbury Fashion Photography Archive: Kate Moss in Martine Sitbon (1994).*

Figure 2.6 *Screenshot: Bloomsbury Fashion Photography Archive: Mermaid silhouette by Nina Ricci (1984).*

of the most ubiquitous people in fashion. Key to a successful research project on the study of fashion models is the understanding that models are not just dress-up dolls or muses. Models are creative professionals, artists, and laborers, just as the fashion designers are. I know a few former models, all of whom are very intelligent. They consider their bodies to be works of art. They're muses, but they're also artists themselves. In their essay, "Models as Brands: Critical Thinking about Bodies and Images," Joanne Entwistle and Don Slater take labor-centric approach to the study of models and modeling: "Here it is the working models themselves and not their representational bodies that are analysed, with the focus on the model's labouring body, working economically, emotionally, aesthetically, under determinate and fluctuating conditions of employment and contract."[31] Moss is multi-faceted, known for her early work with Corinne Day "Under Exposure," magazine covers such as *Hello* and *Another Man*, collaborations with designers such as Alexander McQueen, and her work in the business of fashion with the Kate Moss Agency.

Many writers have attempted to describe, not only her style but her image. Kira Jolliffe and Bay Garnett, of *Cheap Date* Magazine, wrote in the *Cheap Date Guide to Style*:

> She must have drunk in images of Riviera, punk, Anita Pallenberg; she can identify brilliant creativity and interpret it in her own way. Her look doesn't come from nowhere—she pulls in her own knowledge and humour. Clothes are used as a language and she has a keen, intelligent use of the semiotics ... Kate Moss is endlessly fascinating precisely because she is stylish. She seemed to land effortlessly as style queen of the universe, single-handedly propping up fashion as we know it ... People want a bit of her looseness, a bit of her style, which is why they copy her.[32]

In a 2017 cover story interview with *W Magazine*, Moss promises the reader that she will "reveal all of her secrets."[33] The interview itself is unremarkable. She does not tell the reader anything that someone who follows fashion would not already know. She still gets nervous. She still arrives to shoots on time, or even early. She got her start at sixteen as a makeup free, freckle-faced youth in 1990 on the cover of *Hello* Magazine. Her shoot was rather more revealing, in a literal sense; Moss was nude. But revealing her body in such a way again reveals nothing that the fashion faithful did not already know about her. She has appeared topless in photographs frequently, even recently. She reveals all, except for her secrets. Moss is very much the Mick Jagger of fashion in so much as her interviews are notoriously repetitive, uninformative, and short. It is up to the researcher to attempt, through her body of work, to plumb the depths and reveal some of her secrets.

Figure 2.7 *Virginia Oldoini, Countess of Castiglione, photograph by Pierre-Louise Pierson, c. 1863–6.*

When Text-based Searches Fail

Searching for fashion photography images provides its own set of challenges for student researchers. Inevitably, some students will encounter an aspect of a costume for which they cannot find the term and thus not generate keywords effectively. Especially for students, not knowing the sometimes arcane word for a particular dress object or fabric pattern is a common occurrence. This makes discussion of the piece difficult. A student searching for the iconic image of the

Countess of Castiglione by Louis Pierson (previously attributed to Adolphe Braun), for example, might not know the sitter's name (the best keyword for the search) and might instead search for something like "the lady looking through the circle" (Figure 2.7). (In the photograph, she looks through an oval picture frame as a lorgnette.) Text-based searching is likely going to fail this researcher because he or she is searching from visual memory, and unless the student has already found a digital copy of the image, he or she would not be able to use a reverse image search to identify the name of the sitter. The second chapter of this book, on visual, rather than text-based searching, explains how researchers are beginning to be a case study.

3 Visual Searching

So far, we have focused upon language-based search strategies, methods for searching databases using key terms and Boolean queries. This works quite well provided that one knows the word for the thing for which they're searching. But what happens when that's not the case, when the word that should be the key term is unknown? Previously, this would be a major stumbling block to research that would need to be overcome before proceeding further. New technologies facilitating visual rather than text-based searching of the Web and databases, however, are beginning to change this.

Why Images?

From the mid-nineteenth century on, the history of fashion is very much the history of images. Heliographic experiments in Europe in the 1820s by Joseph Nicéphore Niépce paved the way for the invention of true photographic processes by Louis Daguerre and William Henry Fox Talbot in the 1830s and 1840s. Much early fashion photography appeared in the form of the cartes-de-visite churned out by Victorian portrait studios such as André Adolphe Eugène Disdéri's portraits of a woman in a Greek key motif dress from the early 1860s. Pioneers of commercial fashion photography in Paris in the early 1900s included Bissonais et Taponnier, Reutlinger Studio, and Seeberger Frères.[1] Later, in the 1920s, Baron Adolf de Meyer created pictorialist images for *Vogue* such as that of the wedding dress modeled by Helen Lee Worthing, and Edward Steichen "in his role as chief photographer for Condé Nast Publications in the United States, was the catalyst behind the 'new look' in fashion photography during the 1920s."[2] Fashion photography in the 1930s drew from many influences, including the history of art and the then-contemporary Surrealist movement. Historian of photography Naomi Rosenblum calls Cecil Beaton's 1932 portrait of Marlene Dietrich, for example, "lush baroque fantasy with a modern touch."[3] In contrast, American fashion photographers of the 1930s often made use of the unique geological features, flora, and fauna of the United States, such as in Toni Frissell's photograph of a woman in a fur coat and a jaunty hat walking a Dalmatian on a precarious rocky outcropping, "Boom for Brown Beavers," reproduced in the August 1939 issue of *Vogue*. If fashion photography can be said to have an heroic period, as painting, music, and various other arts do, it is likely the period from the 1940s to the 1960s, when photographers such as Richard Avedon, David Bailey, Erwin Blumenfeld, Louise Dahl-Wolfe, Irving Penn, and John Rawlings created images for *Harper's Bazaar, Vogue*, and the like.

Beyond the ubiquity of photography in fashion and fashion in photography, images fulfill many roles for the researcher. Photographic images stand in for objects when one cannot be in the object's presence. How immensely impractical and inconvenient it would be to have to see every fashion or textile object one reads about in person! Photographs also document ephemeral events, such as runway fashion shows. In the absence of the object or event, images offer a satisfying kind of proof of the veracity of a thing or events' existence, even though photographs, of course, can be manipulated, cropped, filtered, and otherwise made to mislead. Most often, images serve as illustrations of concepts, people, places, objects, and patterns. In fashion and textile scholarship, where the look of the object is such an important part of its reason for being, and where small visual details may be the only thing to distinguish one object from another, images are crucial to both the reader and the researcher. Specific kinds of images—called data visualizations—can be produced by scholars to more effectively communicate research findings (data visualization will be discussed in Chapter 5).

Images can also inspire curiosity and provoke new research questions. For example, upon seeing a photograph of a boy's kimono in the collection of the Metropolitan Museum of Art, I was immediately struck with a question. The rayon kimono is decorated with images of horses, dogs, and spy pigeons (equipped with tiny cameras!), *katakana* lettering that reads "*aikoku*" (patriotism) and "*hinomaru*" (rising sun), and a checkerboard pattern of orange and pale yellow (Figure 3.1). I had seen this pattern in the same colors before—on a child's kimono worn by Rin, a young human girl character in the manga and anime series *Inuyasha*, which is set during Japan's Warring States period (Figure 3.2). Is the orange and pale yellow checkerboard pattern—known as *ichimatsu*—common on traditional children's kimonos in particular, or is this merely a coincidence? Rumiko Takahashi, the creator of *Inuyasha*, certainly seems to have been interested in traditional Japanese textile patterns. Two other characters in the series are named after such patterns: kagome (which is also the name for the wickerwork pattern) and shippo (which is also the name for the seven treasures or interlocking circles pattern).

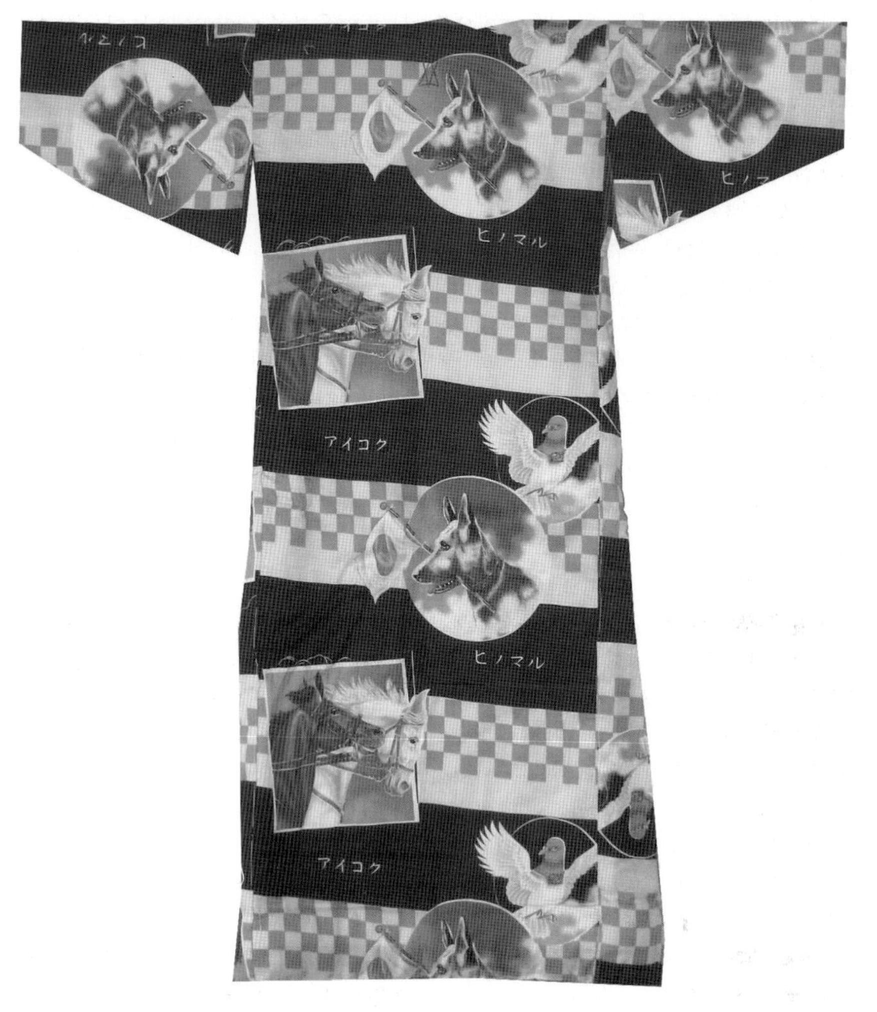

Figure 3.1 *Boy's kimono with dogs, horses, and pigeons, Japan, 1940s, Metropolitan Museum of Art, Purchase, Friends of Asian Art, 2014.*

While this is a research project for another day, it demonstrates the power of images to spur new directions in one's research.

Finally, photographic images also play a profound role in human memory. Images may be quite documentary and impersonal, or quite personal. Emotionally laden photographs help us to remember people, places, and things that we have known on a personal level. In *Mrs. McGinty's Dead* (1951), detective novelist Agatha Christie describes three functions that images can perform in relation to human memory—commemorating vanity, sentiment, and hate:

Figure 3.2 *Rin in* Inuyasha, *Yomiuri Telecasting Corporation (YTV) (2001).*

Why do people keep photographs?
Why? Goodness knows! Why do people keep things—junk—trash, bits and pieces. They do—that's all there is to it!
Up to a point I agree with you. Some people keep things. Some people throw everything away as soon as they have done with it. That, yes, it is a matter of temperament. But I speak now especially of photographs. Why do people keep, in particular, *photographs*?
As I say, because they just don't throw things away. Or else because it reminds them—.
Poirot pounced on the words.
Exactly. *It reminds them*. Now again we ask—*why*? Why does a woman keep a photograph of herself when young? And I say that the first reason is, essentially, vanity. She has been a pretty girl and she keeps a photograph of herself to remind her of what a pretty girl she was. It encourages her when the mirror tells her unpalatable things. She says, perhaps, to a friend, 'That was me when I was eighteen … ' and she sighs … You agree?
Yes—yes, I should say that's true enough.
Then that is reason No. 1. Vanity. Now reason No. 2. Sentiment.
That's the same thing?

No, no not quite. Because this leads you to preserve, not only your own photograph, but that of someone else ... A picture of your married daughter—when she was a child sitting on a hearthrug with tulle around her ... Very embarrassing to the subject sometimes, but mothers like to do it. And sons and daughters often keep pictures of their mothers, especially, say, if their mother died young. 'This was my mother as a girl.'

I'm beginning to see what you're driving at, Poirot.

And there is, possibly, a *third* category. Not vanity, not sentiment, not love—perhaps *hate*—what do you say?

Hate?

Yes. To keep a desire for revenge alive. Someone who has injured you—you might keep a photograph to remind you, might you not?

--from Agatha Christie's *Mrs. McGinty's Dead* (1951)[4]

While all of these examples are orientated to a murder mystery, the basic premise—that photographs help people to remember—is a universal one. Undergirding the many roles that photographs, including fashion photographs, play is memory.

Images and Memory

Computer scientist Simone Santini likens visual database queries to calling forth images in the human memory.[5] Think back to a pivotal fashion moment in your own personal development, a moment in which you saw something so beautiful, or somehow strangely compelling, that you knew you wanted to pursue dress and textiles in the future. You probably remember the name of the model or the magazine or the shop associated with the memory quite well, probably the year (and possibly even the month or season) as well. But how well do you actually remember the garment, textile, or look? Can you accurately describe it? My fashion moment came *c.* 1989. I was staying with my grandparents, and my Grandma magnanimously decided that I could ransack her closet to play dress up. I fell in love with a sleeveless mint green sheath dress. I remember she said that she had worn it to a family graduation in 1976 or 1977, and the terrific thing about this (what must have been rather unremarkable) dress to me, a child in the 80s, was that this totally radical mint color seemed so fresh and timely, not like the drab oranges, maroons, and browns that my younger self associated with the 70s. When we see something that reminds us—for whatever reason—of our visual memory, Santini states that we feel an "eerie sense of deja vu."[6] But my memory of the actual dress is elusive and, undoubtedly, colored by my later experiences studying fashion. The material was certainly synthetic, maybe polyester or a poly-rayon blend. Was there a border at the hem? The dress had a narrow belt—was that mint green as well? Did it have darts? I can picture this dress so well in my mind's eye, and yet, I can't. This is the fleeting nature of human visual memory.

Santini argues that there are two basic types of visual memory: holistic and detail-oriented, yet fragmented.

> On the one hand, there is the somehow 'holistic' way of remembering visual scenes: one can have a very vivid and emotionally rich memory [as with my mint sheath dress example] but remember practically no detail—the whole can stand by itself without being supported by its parts. On the other hand, one finds a clear but fragmented memory of disconnected details which stand without being connected to a whole.[7]

This discussion of memory may seem like a *non sequitur*, but memory is actually foundational to querying databases, especially visual queries. According to Santini, this is

> because users look for images based on some imagined referent. The modalities with which these referents are built in the mind of the user are similar to those with which images are remembered: The holistic aspects of the referent are invariant to considerable change in details. A search in traditional databases, on the other hand, is a business of details—we ask for certain values in well-defined fields and certain relations between fields. The 'overall' or holistic aspect of a record never enters a query specification.[8]

There are several different ways to organize and allow for querying of image databases: by similarity, by generality, by interaction or comparison, or by data complexity.[9] The most successful model for visual queries—in terms of prevalence, popularity, and ease of use—is called "query by example."[10] This model, quite simply, returns results most *visually* similar to the original query image selected by the user, along the parameters set by an algorithm such as shape/form, color, and more advanced parameters such as whether the image appears to contain a human face.

Complicating searching for images is that they have both semiotic—that a user can interpret as a sign—and technical qualities.[11] In the early days of visual searching, computer vision was so focused on the outlines of forms that the results returned would often have what is termed a "similarity mismatch." Santini gives the example of a photograph of a rounded arch door and a photograph of a brunette with her wet hair plastered to her head.[12] In this case, the images, though visually similar (in a rudimentary way) in form, were not semiotically similar, and thus those search results were unhelpful. Fortunately, computer vision has come a long way in the last twenty years, and such glaring similarity mismatches rarely occur these days.

Five Types of Queries

- In the days before the internet, (fashion) journalists wishing to populate their stories with images had to contact an image archive by phone or fax and ask a real human being (an archivist) for images suitable for their story. Ornager (1997) and Markkula and Sormounen (1998) identified five specific types of archival image querying journalists: the specific enquirer, general enquirer, story teller enquirer, story giver enquirer, and space-filler enquirer.[13] Importantly, these five modes of image-seeking still apply today for queries made by researchers using search engines and databases.
- A specific image query would be: "I need that one photo of Jerry Hall wearing that one look at that one show."
- A more general inquiry, by contrast, would be: "Just give me ten or twenty images of Jerry Hall from 1987–89. I'll choose the one that works best."

The specific and general enquirers maintained a fairly limited collaborative relationship with the archival staff, unlike story tellers and story givers, who worked directly with the archivist to find the image(s) they needed.

- A story teller might call the archivist, explain the story that he was trying to tell about Jerry Hall, and then get the archivist to select the most appropriate images, while the story giver would simply send the archivist the copy of his still-unpublished article, and have the archivist read the piece and then choose appropriate images.
- Finally, the space filler simply wants any image tangentially related to his topic to fill space in his article: "Just give me an image of Jerry Hall—I don't care which one," such as Ms. Hall in period dress for *Princess Caraboo* (1994) (Figure 3.3).

In the example of the mermaids from the previous case study, an image of Jerry Hall from the cover shoot of Roxy Music's *Siren* album would have been most appropriate. In research projects, it is generally best to be a specific enquirer,

Figure 3.3 *Film still: Jerry Hall, second from left, in* Princess Caraboo, *TriStar Pictures (1994).*

though in the publishing world, the realities of budgetary and other constraints can sometimes turn specific enquirers and story tellers into space fillers. Significantly, these five types of image seekers—specific, general, story teller, story giver, and space filler—still represent the various ways in which we try to find archival images in today's mobile, digital world.

Before selecting an example image to query from, or even selecting the search tool or image database to use, it is important to know the purpose of the search. Is it a specific inquiry—a search for one particular image, or a more general inquiry on the topic? Santini cautions that "there are as many modalities of interaction with a repository of image data as there are users. One of the most limiting and unfounded assumptions in content-based retrieval is that for each query there is *a* target image."[14] Serious researchers will not often be looking for space-filler images, but they may, like the story teller, need help in choosing an image. Even in the digital, impersonal world of today, it is still common practice to contact a library or archive when trying to locate an image for a project. Don't be afraid to be the story teller, if that will best serve your research.

Sourcing Images Responsibly

Any discussion of using found images in one's research, either in print or simply posting them online, should include the responsible sourcing of images. Getty

Images, while ubiquitous, is a poor starting point for most academics. To purchase a license of an image of a Gucci Press event featuring maximalist fashion at Bergdorf Goodman, for example, would cost $575. The Metropolitan Museum of Art, on the other hand, is a good place for academics to begin searching for images to use in research online, in conference presentations, or in print. Supported by Bloomberg Philanthropies, their quite liberal open access policy reads as follows:

> Open Access Policy
>
> The Metropolitan Museum of Art creates, organizes, and disseminates a broad range of digital images and data that document the rich history of the Museum, its collection, exhibitions, events, people, and activities.Images of artworks in the Museum's collection fall into two categories:
>
> 1. images of works the Museum believes to be in the **public domain**, or those to which the Museum waives any copyright it might have
> 2. images of works the Museum knows to be **under copyright or other restrictions.**
>
> On February 7, 2017, The Metropolitan Museum of Art implemented a new policy known as Open Access, which makes images of artworks it believes to be in the public domain widely and freely available for unrestricted use, and at no cost, in accordance with the Creative Commons Zero (CC0) designation and the Terms of Conditions of this website.
>
> It also makes available data from the entire online collection—both works it believes to be in the public domain and those under copyright or other restrictions—including basic information such as title, artist, date, medium, and dimensions. This data is available to all in accordance with the Creative Commons Zero (CC0) designation.[15]

The Los Angeles County Museum of Art (LACMA) has also donated many images of objects in their collection to the public domain. Other great places to find free fashion images to post online and/or use in scholarship include: New York Public Library, Europeana, LOC American Memory, Flickr Commons; archival projects conducted by individual US states, such as Florida Memory; US Government images including photographs taken by those working in government departments such as State and Defense while in the course of fulfilling their duties; and the Presidential Museums of the United States. Presidential museums are a great reserve of images and information on dress, and because they are government entities, most of this material is in the public domain. This image of Betty Ford supporting the Equal Rights Amendment appears here gratis from the Gerald R Ford Presidential Museum and Library (Figure 3.4).

Figure 3.4 *Betty Ford supporting the Equal Rights Amendment, Gerald R. Ford Presidential Library & Museum.*

Computer Vision in Museum Work

Returning to the example of my grandmothers mint green sheath dress, since I do not know the pattern name (if any) or the designer or the company that produced it, I would likely need to become a story teller enquirer to find an image of that particular dress. Now, if I only wanted to find an image of a quite similar sort of dress, I would not use a visual search engine at all, but instead would use a text-based search of a traditional database as discussed in the previous chapter. This is because (1) I don't have a photograph of the dress in question to query from (which was my problem in the first place) and (2) I already know much of the metadata related to the dress, even though I cannot remember what it looked like in detail. Date: 1970s, Color: mint, Style: sheath, and so on. General query-by-example visual searches make sense (as opposed to text-based searches) when the user has an idea of what the thing should look like, but does not know any of the metadata. The most common reason for this is not knowing the technical jargon for a type of object: "I saw this really cool dress/shoe/detail/pattern/textile, and I want to learn more about it, but I don't know what it's called." Searching for "leg-of-mutton" sleeves in a traditional, text-driven database is next to impossible, for example, unless the user knows the term "leg-of-mutton sleeve." Visual

Figure 3.5 *Fragment of a* kosode *(kimono) featuring the* shippo *pattern of interlocking circles, Japan, Edo period (mid-nineteenth century), Los Angeles County Museum of Art, Gift of Miss Bella Mabury.*

searching is also helpful for students when dealing with non-Western terms, such as the Japanese ichimatsu, kagome, and shippo patterns. Queries like these demonstrate the power and utility of computer vision (Figure 3.5).

In psychology, visual searching is the ability of people to scan a complex visual landscape to find a specific image—a person, object, symbol, or pattern—hidden in plain sight among many visual distractions. The popular children's book series *Where's Wally?* (or its American counterpart *Where's Waldo?*) is an example of visual searching. From childhood, people are quite good at visual searching, provided that the amount of images to be searched is on a human scale and that everything to be searched is within their field of vision at the same time. People are significantly poorer at visual searching on the internet, where a seemingly array of images exist on a seemingly endless litany of webpages and on object records in databases. And, until recently, computers themselves have struggled with visual searching across vast sets of images as well. This is beginning to change.

Searching for Patterns: Harlequin and Ichimatsu

Properly trained, computer algorithms can become very good at visual searching over large amounts of images across multiple plains. This has tremendous implications for fashion and textile research and museum work. For example, anthropologist Hilda Davis documents twelve patterns, all of them unnamed, in her foundational 1955 essay, "The History of Seminole Clothing and Its Multi-Colored Designs."[16] Davis wrote, "There are no recorded designs, no written patterns to follow; all the designs are developed entirely from memory."[17] Geometric patterns with names such as fire, rain, storm, arrow, turtle, bird, and diamondback [rattlesnake] make Seminole patchwork patterns even more difficult for most laypeople to identify than traditional Euro American quilt patterns such as log cabin. Content-based image retrieval (CBIR) technology could be used to help researchers identify discrete patterns and plot the occurrence of patterns over time. Returning to the example of the two children's kimonos from the beginning of the chapter, CBIR could also help to search for other kimonos with the ichimatsu pattern, or more specifically for only ichimatsu patterns of orange and yellow, helping a researcher to build database of images featuring the pattern.

So often we want to search for objects that look similar to an object we have already found—maybe for other objects with that orange and yellow checkerboard pattern, or perhaps with polka dots or with beadwork in a spiral shape or with green feathers. The problem is compounded if the novice researcher does not know the technical term for the object, material, or embellishment technique for which they are searching. Imagine, for example, the frustration of searching a collections database for "harlequin" or "ichimatsu" without knowing the term. Entering "checkerboard pattern" instead of "ichimatsu" or "that circus pattern" instead of "harlequin" into a museum's database is not likely to be very effective!

The example of Anna Magnani explores how these tools will allow for a new approach to evaluate the authenticity of theatrical period pieces, as well as give novice researchers (who might not even know the term "harlequin") an entirely visual-based strategy for searching similar pieces (Figure 3.6). A favorite written research assignment for fashion design and interior design students is the analysis of costumes or sets in a period film. For this assignment, I ask students to carefully watch the film and then write a three- to four-page analysis briefly describing the film's location, the decade/time period and style(s) represented, and the basic plot, and then, write an analysis of the historical accuracy of the film's costume design. In their analyses, they consider issues such as: the accuracy of the style(s) represented, in which instances (and why) the period or style actually depicted does not match the intended period or style of the piece, and the degree to which (and how) the film is a reflection of the time that the film was made, rather than the time it is trying to represent. I ask students to be careful to focus only on the

Figure 3.6 *Film still: Anna Magnani in* The Golden Coach, *Cinecittà Studios (1952).*

costumes, rather than on the architecture, interior architecture and furnishings, and to use vocabulary terms from our key terms lists when possible throughout the essay.

La carrozza d'oro (The Gold Coach, 1952), an eighteenth-century period piece known for its iconic costumes worn by Anna Magnani, Italian neorealist film star and fashion icon of the 1940s, 1950s, and 1960s, is one of the films on my list for design students.[18] Magnani was known for her style both on-screen and off, and one of her most distinctive costumes was a harlequin print dress that she wore for the *The Gold Coach*. Magnani was made for channeling the eighteenth century, and in *The Gold Coach*, she plays the leading lady of an itinerant *commedia dell'arte* troupe in eighteenth-century Spanish colonial Peru, and she wears this incredible harlequin-patterned dress that is part of an eighteenth-century period piece and at the same time like something straight out of Picasso's Rose Period (which has been called his circus period). Say, for example, a student was conducting research on Magnani's harlequin costume. Without knowing the term "harlequin," how could they search for the pattern? By querying an image of Magnani wearing the costume in a visual image search, the student would return results of the image across many websites. Such a search would still require a little digging on the part of the student, clicking on each image result to learn more about the object and (crucially when doing research online) evaluating the credibility and authority of each source, but it is likely that one or more of the results would describe the pattern as "harlequin."

Searching for Colors: Millennial Pink, Tiffany Blue, and Historical Colors

Computer vision is not only for searching for patterns. Colors, as well, can be seen and differentiated more accurately by an algorithmic eye than by the human eye. Millennial pink is hard to define. It is the new neutral of the mid-2010s, to be sure, but exactly what shade of pink it is, is a matter of debate. The Pass Notes column in *The Guardian* opined: "It's sort of a grapefruit shade of apricotty salmon."[19] Actually, though, by using a hex code, one can quantifiably define millennial pink or any other color. The hex code for millennial pink is #FBD287, for example. The quantification of colors through hex codes, the six-digit three-byte hexadecimal numbers used in the digital rendering of color, makes searching for elusive hues like millennial pink much more straightforward. Just as not everyone agrees on exactly what color constitutes millennial pink, different individuals may even perceive proprietary and brand-associated colors such as Tiffany Blue, #0ABAB5, differently. Such colors are also easier to search for by their hex codes as the hex codes remove the variables of human eyesight and perception from the naming of color.

Historical colors and dyestuffs also benefit from being queried by hex code. In her analysis of medieval silks found in Scandinavia (see Chapter 6 for more on this topic), Marianne Vedeler notes that three types of dyestuffs were found, all in the red and purple family: lichen purple, madder root (which quiltmakers will know is used in the production of Turkey red dye), and *kermes* or *kirmiz*, an insect that inhabits oak trees and which can be dried and crushed into a fine red powder.[20] Lichen "Byzantine" purple can be written as #702963, Turkey red as #A91101, and kirmiz (or cochineal red or carmine) as #960018. Although these three colors have multiple colloquial names, they each represent only one discrete hex code.

Reverse Image Searches

Much lower-tech than content-based image retrieval and available for researchers and museums to use today, reverse image searches are quite useful both for finding the source of an image (if the researcher was not careful to note the source at the time of download) and for finding higher resolution versions of the image one already has for publication purposes. Reverse image searches are also beneficial to researchers who have a digital copy of an image that contains text, but the text is illegible because of poor image resolution. A reverse image search using a free website called Tin Eye[21] for this nineteenth-century French fashion plate with difficult-to-read text returned a link to a higher-resolution (and much easier to read) copy of the same image. While reverse image search engines may look much like traditional, text-based query search engines, they search for images rather than strings of text. To conduct a reverse image search, rather than typing your query, simply drag and drop or upload the image for which you wish to search into the search bar of a reverse image search engine such as Google Reverse Image Search[22] or Tin Eye.

One of the most obvious uses for reverse image searches in fashion history, especially museum work, is wearer provenance—that is, identifying if a garment was actually worn by the famous person purported to have worn it, such as was a particular t-shirt worn by John Lennon? When the provenance metadata accompanying the object indicate that an object may have been worn or owned by a notable personage, visual search technology might be able to prove (or disprove) the validity of such a provenance.

John Lennon's T-Shirts

John Lennon, sometime in 1980, created a list of clothing items he believed to have been stolen from the two storage cupboards that he and Yoko Ono rented in the Dakota Building, their home in New York City. In the list, he included many jackets and fur coats, as well as Beatles costuming from the Magical Mystery Tour and Sergeant Pepper eras. It turned out that several of the articles were not, in fact, stolen; they reappeared, had been taken down to Florida, or gifted away. This inventory of "stolen" goods documents that Lennon, like many artists of his day, had some difficulty in looking after his personal belongings, and that many of his clothes were likely given away.[23]

There is ample photographic evidence for Lennon's enthusiasm for clothing in general and T-shirts in particular. For a short time in the swinging sixties between 1967 and 1968, the Beatles owned their own clothing shop in Marylebone, London, Apple Boutique, a competitor to Chelsea's Granny Takes a Trip. John Lennon was photographed wearing his famous cut-off "New York" T-shirt worn in New York in 1974.[24] In that same year, he wore a Mickey Mouse T-shirt when he took his son Julian to Disneyland.[25] And in 1978, he was photographed wearing a Rolling Stones' *Some Girls* album tee.[26] "Lennon loved New York. For him, it was the hottest, and the fastest, city on earth."[27] "It's almost the difference between Liverpool and London, and London and New York. I like New Yorkers because they have no time for the niceties of life. They're like me in this."[28] It was also in New York where Lennon wore a black T-shirt in a television interview regarding his and May Pang's recent UFO sighting. "Flying low, barely above the height of the apartment rooftops, the UFO hovered, coasting quietly like a tourist, Lennon later recalled."[29] In the future, image searches will likely be so good that they would be able to match the T-shirt Lennon wore in that interview from even a complicated image such as this film still (Figure 3.7).

Limitations of Reverse Image Searches

For the immediate future, these searches do have their limitations, however. If you are the original poster of the original image (not a derivative of an image that is already online), reverse image search will likely be unable to help you find similar, but not quite the same, images. Also, reverse image searches may fail if like images have different watermarks, or differences in resolution, or if one image is cropped in any way. These free online tools simply are not that good, yet. Thus, in the case of the New York T-shirt from the 1974 photograph, neither Google Reverse Image

Figure 3.7 *Film still: John Lennon's UFO Sighting in New York City (1974).*

Search nor Tin Eye was able to make a match to any images in museum collections (or elsewhere) because they can only match the original photograph of Lennon wearing the shirt, without alteration in variables like resolution or lighting (and museum photographs are known for utilizing studio lighting and an archivally high resolution, often 600 dpi). For images originating with the researcher, the best way (for now) to search for like images online—like a vintage photograph of Lennon actually wearing the shirt—is to use traditional text-based search techniques in browsers and databases. Unfortunately, as we saw with images of Kate Moss in Chapter 1, often the most famous people are the most difficult to search for because so many irrelevant results are returned. Traditional text-based searching is incredibly frustrating in this particular example because Lennon was famously photographed wearing a different T-shirt that read "New York"—a white cut-off with a black ringer. Because of images of him wearing that shirt clogging the results, old-fashioned, low-tech interviews with people who knew him in the 1970s are probably the only way to solve this provenance mystery at the present time. In a few years, though, online content-based image retrieval will likely have progressed far enough that a reverse image search will be able to answer the question once and for all. Until then, perhaps, researchers just need to be patient. In the meantime, crowdsourcing research queries by connecting with other scholars on social media can help beginner and advanced researchers alike to find the terms and images they seek.[30]

PART 2

Connecting

Many of the examples in the previous chapter—images and objects related to Kate Moss and John Lennon—are held in collections in London and New York. As we have seen, online databases make it immeasurably easier to do work in fashion scholarship from outside the world's fashion capitals. So, too, does social media, the subject of this chapter.

On Being a Fashion Historian in a Fly-over State

Being a historian of costume in a "fly-over" state is not easy. I really do not know how historians of dress living west of the Ohio and east of the Rockies managed before the days of social media. That is not to say that Middle America lacks fashion sense, nor that there is a lack of collections to research between the coasts. There are the historic costume collection at Kent State University being a shining example. Most of the Big Ten and Big Twelve universities also have very fine costume collections including not only regional and everyday examples of dress, but works by high-style designers as well, as do many of the civic museums, including the Cincinnati Art Museum. There are also engaged, motivated students in apparel and textiles, home economics and human ecology, art and art history, and history departments at these schools. No, speaking as a historian of dress and textiles who has only ever worked in Michigan as of the writing of this, the problem for fashion historians in the center of the United States is not a lack of students or collections—it is a lack of access to peers. In these places being the only person on the faculty who studies the history of dress is a common enough occurrence, and before social media, I can only imagine that fashion historians must have truly felt alone at times.

Digital marketing expert Andy Hobsbawm says, "It is not where we are or where we come from that is important, but what we care about."[1] According to the Henley Centre (2009), 60 percent of Britons say they have less in common with their neighbors than with those who share their interests.[2] For many of us in fashion studies, this is certainly the case. Through social media, it is possible for us to find a community of like-minded people, even if we cannot find next door.

The beginning of my own professional career coinciding roughly with the late era of Myspace and the birth of Facebook, I have always had the benefit of being able to easily find others with like-professional interests online. Sava Saheli Singh noted, "Media such as wikis, blogs, and Twitter have the power to generate such communities where they are otherwise not available … it turns out that peers and, indeed, friends can be found simply by writing interesting things on the Internet."[3] In the past couple years, though, especially with the mass adoption of Instagram as the social platform of choice *du jour*, it feels as though something has once again changed for the better. Academics interested in fashion, both professionally and personally, are finding each other on Instagram and sharing everything from research and conservation projects to conference style tips in numbers never before seen. Without the community of fashion and textiles academics on Instagram, Facebook, and Twitter, many of us would feel much less connected to the discipline and would have missed out on important conversations and opportunities.

4 Blogging, Instagram, and Research

Blogging and particularly microblogging (such as on Twitter and Instagram) are now a routine part of our academic work. This chapter considers how fashion-oriented graduate and post-graduate researchers around the world communicate with like-minded scholars via social media, especially Instagram, including (1) conducting research on social media, (2) disseminating research on Instagram, (3) the use of social media in academic conference-related communication, (4) the importance of hashtags for all of this work, (5) instant gratification in fashion scholarship, and finally (6) an extended discussion of style blogging as academic work. Far from frivolous, these online social connections are advancing research and writing in the discipline at a rapid pace and reminding those of us working in the Midwest that we do have like-minded colleagues across the country and around the world.

Conducting Research on Social Media

While it may seem obvious, the first step in conducting research on social media is making the decision to actually become comfortable with and use social media, rather than traditional email-based listserves, as one's major online research laboratory. Many of us do not even use listserves correctly anyway, sending messages intended for the list moderator—such as "please keep me on the list messages"—to the entire list instead, clogging colleagues' email inboxes.[1] Social media, by contrast, is designed for posts to go out to the user's friends and followers as well as be seen by other users interested in the post's hashtags.

The second step in conducting research on social media—or even just finding a community of like-minded scholars—is knowing who to follow. While this will surely change, currently one of the best places to start is the group Fashion Historians Unite! on Facebook. (While Facebook is dying among young people as of the writing of this book, participation in this group is still lively.) Finding accounts to follow is a common problem for those of us new to Instagram, Snapchat, etc., especially for those living and working in rural areas (like myself) or in countries without a large dress and textile scholarly community. And in fact, a February 5, 2017, query to Fashion Historians Unite! asked about the best Instagram accounts to follow. Tal G. Amit, collections manager at the Rose Archive for Fashion and Textiles at Shenkar College in Israel, suggested several of the most commonly followed within the historic dress community, including @artgarments, @the_corsetedbeauty, @documentingfashion_cortauld, @fidmmuseum, @ historicalgarments, @isabellabradfordauthor, and @timothylongfashioncurator.[2] Others, mostly museum professionals, suggested @the_art_of_dress, @fitnyc, @ fitspecialcollections, @museumatfit, @udhctc (the University of Delaware Historic Costume and Textile Collection), and @fox_historic_costume at Drexel University for its "amazing detail shots."[3] The Fox Historic Costume Collection (FHCC) is also a leader in the trend of tailoring content on Instagram around major exhibitions at other institutions. For example, in May 2018, the FHCC account posted images from its own collection dealing with the broadly conceived theme of Catholicism and tagged them #fhccheavenlybodies in conjunction with the *Heavenly Bodies* exhibition at the Metropolitan Museum of Art (and of course the popular Met Gala). The account is also known for posting detail shots of its James Galanos collection, often dripping with sequins (Figure 4.1). Of course, there are numerous other relevant accounts to follow, including the personal accounts of many CSA members and other scholars. While personal accounts may feature fashion-related posts only occasionally, they are a great way to network and keep up-to-date on others' research and evolving interests. It is also just reassuring to see that other academics do things like cook, go away for the weekend, have pets and lives. Check your work life balance.

Instagram and Twitter are also two of the best places to find the best new academic books to read. I'm currently working on a book chapter on data visualization for fashion and textile studies, and I was introduced to the work of Alberto Cairo via the Data Visualization Book Club on Twitter (hashtags #dataviz and #VizBookClub) which is organized by Sophie Sparkes of Tableau software, an online book club that I learned about in turn through the @doingdata Instagram account. I now use the hashtag #dataviz to find sources. According to Singh, "Hashtags remain the most straightforward way to interrogate Twitter because they are the most easily tracked phenomenon on Twitter."[4] Singh's assertion can and should be expanded to include the proliferation of the hashtag's use outside of Twitter—Instagram, Facebook, Tumblr, Pinterest, Reddit, and in all likelihood, the next generation of social media upstarts. A good place to start is by searching

Figure 4.1 *Fall 1991 James Galanos sequined gown, detail shot as seen in an FHCC Instagram post from December 1, 2017, Image courtesy of the Robert and Penny Fox Historic Costume Collection at Drexel University.*

#fashionhistory, #historiccostume, #costumestudies, #dresshistory and all of the possible permutations thereof.

The Wisdom of the Crowd

One way in which social media fosters research is by creating a space in which historians can ask their peers in the field questions about unusual or particularly tricky to date garments or textiles. On the Facebook group Fashion Historians Unite!, Andrea Melvin, curator at the Grand Rapids Public Museum, asked about the possible date and provenance of a robe de style in the museum's collection.[5] The robe de style is a style of the 1920s and early 1930s often associated with Jeanne Lanvin. It went against the boyish flapper silhouette of the day by combining a fitted, slim bodice with a long, full skirt hitting above the ankle (Figure 4.2). Panniers, basket-like undergarments worn on the hip, filled out the skirt and gave the look a nostalgic quality, harkening back to eighteenth-century dress. Without its panniers, the robe de style at the Grand Rapids Public Museum looked a bit deflated, almost like a strange sort of Dior New Look gown from the 1950s, or like a reproduction robe de style produced in the 1950s. But the group quickly reached a consensus that the dress was indeed a robe de style, *c.* 1920s, and that new panniers could be constructed out of PVC tubing if period ones could not be acquired.

On Instagram, University of Minnesota doctoral student @SarahLikesClothes posted an image of a very bright pink waistcoat dated to *c.* 1760–1780 in the Goldstein Museum of Design's catalog. She asked the crowd if such a shocking pink dye could truly be from the mid–late eighteenth century without having undergone some fading due to the fugitive nature of the dye.[6] This time the consensus was that the piece was likely a nineteenth-century reproduction made with chemical dyes. Sarah used many hashtags to help other historians find the post, even if they did not follow her account, including: #museumcollection, #fromthecollection, #historyoffashion, #fashioncuration, #costumehistory, #curatorquestions, #historicsewing, and #georgianjanuary.

Who is the Crowd?

Who is the crowd? The crowd is us. Sometimes when one discusses crowdsourcing with other academics, there is an ebullient sense of excitement at the creation of community and speeding up of the pace of research and its dissemination. Other

Figure 4.2 *Robe de style, as seen in a Facebook post to the group Fashion Historians Unite! by Andrea Melvin, Grand Rapids Public Museum, Grand Rapids, Michigan.*

times, one is painted a distorted picture of the crowd that is part uneducated poseur, part country bumpkin, and part internet troll. Academia's reluctance to adopt social media as a legitimate site for conducting research and publishing early findings may stem from a lack of knowledge on how to vet the authority of social media sources. Logically, however, people who search Instagram or Twitter for #robedestyle are quite likely to be well-versed in the history of dress. Many of those folks will work in museums or college teaching in the field. It is not as if random people just wander onto the comment sections of fashion scholars' Instagram accounts simply to wreak havoc. Daren Brabham has exposed what he calls "the myth of the amateur crowd," finding that those who reply to queries online or edit Wikipedia entries are often trained professionals in the field in question.[7] Thus, the binary dichotomy of crowd versus academes is largely a false one. And, the more academics who buy into the value of the crowd online, the more academic the crowd will become. Ultimately, academics need to embrace the wisdom of the crowd to keep up with the increasingly brisk pace of fashion studies scholarship.

#georgianjanuary

Like many online discursive communities, the costume history community on Instagram has adopted certain thematic hashtags to guide posting in the community. Once a year, in January, various costume history accounts focus their posts on the eighteenth century using the hashtag #georgianjanuary. Each day of January also has a hashtagged theme, for example, #pastels, #jeweltones, and #interiors, and Instagram users participating in Georgian January post images from their own research, from museum collections with which they have worked, or found images. In January 2018, over 3,000 individual posts were tagged with #georgianjanuary on Instagram (the equivalent of about 100 users posting once per day each day in January), giving a glimpse into the size and level of activity of the eighteenth-century fashion community online.

Identifying them with the overall hashtag, #georgianjanuary, is only the first step, as tagging also includes the daily theme's hashtag such as #bluemonday, hashtags such as #fashionhistory or #costumehistory, which serve to identify the community, as well as tags pertaining to the subject matter of the post (e.g., #robealanglaise, #sackbackgown, #annamariagarthwaite). The Georgian January format is also used on Twitter, another hashtag-driven social platform, although Instagram seems to draw more traffic on its Georgian January hashtag as of January 2018. Ultimately, themed community events such as Georgian

January are a useful way to see images, museum objects, and new research directions around a single topic, as well as a means by which to present research in progress in a format seen by many scholars with similar interests.

Citing Social Posts

Doing research on social media of course means citing social media. It is vitally important to cite social media, just as one would cite a book or journal article, not only to give credit to the author's intellectual contribution, but also because social posts are difficult to search for and seldom archived effectively. Confusion surrounds the proper citation of social media posts, and uncertainties about citation practices in social media may (unfortunately) actually lead to under-citation. This confusion is particularly prevalent in the field of fashion studies, a field in which researchers have varying disciplinary backgrounds—we may come from art history, psychology, design, human environmental studies, etc.—and consequently, fashion journals do not all use the same citation style. The *Chicago Manual of Style*, which is commonly used by historians (and is the style in which the citations in this book are done), lags behind the *Modern Language Association* (*MLA*) style in terms of concrete guidelines for the citation of social media. Because it is such a frequently used convention within the discipline, however, CMS is the style on which we will focus.

The 17th edition of the CMS contains guidelines for citing web sources, interviews and personal communication, and public and unpublished materials, but not social posts. Complicating matters, social posts could fall under any of the above categories. Emails, text messages, Facebook and Instagram direct messages, and the like should be treated as personal communications under the *Chicago Manual of Style*. So, too, should comments made between two individuals using their social handles (e.g., @sikarska) on posts on Instagram, Twitter, Facebook, etc. For example:

1. Hannah Crump, Instagram direct message to the author, February 15, 2018.

According to the Purdue Owl, emails (and by extension, other kinds of direct electronic messages) should be included in the footnotes or endnotes, but rarely in the bibliography. Additionally, email addresses (and social media handles) should be omitted.

In the Chicago Style, blog entries are set in quotation marks (as one would the title of a journal article), while blog titles are italicized (as one would a journal title).

2. Stylish Academic, "6 tips for packing a capsule conference travel wardrobe," *Stylish Academic*, last accessed April 21, 2018, https://stylishacademic.com/tips-for-packing-a-capsule-conference-travel-wardrobe/.

The Purdue Owl suggests that "generally, blog entries and comments are cited only as notes. If you frequently cite a blog, however, then you may choose to include it in your bibliography."[8] Podcasts are similar in that the title of the episode is set in quotation marks and the title of the series is italicized, but podcasts also require the addition of the producer, the word "podcast" itself (unless it appears in the title as in the example below, in which case it is not repeated), the audio format (such as MP3), and the running time.

3. Dana Goodin, Jasmine Helm, and Joy Davis, "The History of Fashion Week," *Unravel: A Fashion History Podcast*, MP3, 1:02:43.

As of 2018, the *Chicago Manual of Style* does not yet provide specific guidelines for citing tweets or Instagram or Facebook posts. A general convention is to cite the author's name, the type of post, and the date, such as:

4. Amanda Sikarskie, Instagram post, December 27, 2017.

Such a footnote may be omitted entirely, depending on an editor's preference, if the author's name, the type of post, and the date are included in the body text itself. As with emails and direct messages, the citation should be included in the notes only, and not the bibliography.

In contrast to Chicago, the *MLA* has been quicker to adopt standards for citing social posts and other recent online media, and the 8th edition of the *MLA Handbook* includes guidelines for citing not only emails, websites, blogs, and podcasts, but also YouTube videos, songs, and playlists on Spotify, and significantly, tweets.[9] In the MLA style, the citation for a tweet should begin with the author's Twitter handle (unlike in Chicago), include the full tweet in quotation marks (they are limited to 140 characters, after all), the word "Twitter" italicized, the date, and a timestamp. For example:

5. @Fashion_Curator, "We need your help to conserve & exhibit this late 18th century dress, as part of the #redressingpleasure project," Twitter, November 4, 2017, 1:20 p.m. GMT.

The last accessed date is optional, and often omitted. Finally, note that the entire text of the tweet is given in the footnote or endnote even if the entire tweet is also reproduced in the text of the manuscript itself. The MLA style is used in theatre, language, literary, and cultural studies.

The American Psychological Association (APA) style is the most commonly used in the social sciences (other than history). It lags behind even the *Chicago Manual of Style* in terms of concrete guidelines for the citation of social media. The 6th edition does give instructions for citing blog comments, however.[10] Entries should begin with the author's first initial and last name, if known, the date posted set in parentheses, the title of the post (neither italicized nor set in quotation marks), the phrase "Web log" (or "Web log comment") set in brackets (note that "web log" is used in lieu of the more common term, "blog"), and finally, the url preceded by "Retrieved from." Note the differences between this entry for the blog post on *Stylish Academic* and the one in the Chicago style discussed previously.

6. Stylish Academic, (February 26, 2018) "6 tips for packing a capsule conference travel wardrobe," [Web log] Retrieved from https://stylishacademic.com/tips-for-packing-a-capsule-conference-travel-wardrobe/.

The last accessed date is omitted. Until specific guidelines are published, tweets and Instagram posts should be adapted to this model. Again, note the differences between this citation and the one for Timothy Long's (@Fashion_Curator) tweet in the MLA style above.

7. T. Long, (November 4, 2017), [Tweet] Retrieved from https://twitter.com/Fashion_Curator.

If writing for publication, when in doubt, contact the acquisitions or copy editor of the journal or press and ask their policy on citing social media posts. In 2018, the editorial staff of *Bloomsbury Fashion Business Cases*, for example, referred their contributing authors to easybib.com[11] for instructions on citing Instagram posts. Easybib's suggested format reads: the account holder's name (or username), a title or description of the photograph, the names of any other contributors, if applicable, the date that the image was published on Instagram, the last accessed date, and the post's url on Instagram.[12] Using this longer citation format, my Instagram post from December 27, 2017, referenced above would be cited as follows:

8. Amanda Sikarskie, "Just made the happy discovery that the blonde on the right in this #mathiasalten painting at the @grartmuseum is my mom and aunt in law's #auntviola," December 27, 2017, https://www.instagram.com/p/BdOjrbdDoVI/? taken-by=sikarska.

When doing research on social media sites, be sure to note down all information relevant to the citation at the time of reading, as it may be quite difficult to go back and search for the post later. It can be like looking for a needle in a haystack if the author regularly posts multiple times per day. Additionally, tweets, Instagram, and Facebook posts may be deleted by the author at any time after posting. These two reasons are why last accessed dates are seldom included when citing social posts. Helpfully, though, just because a user deleted a tweet or Instagram post does not mean that a cached version of the post does not exist elsewhere on the internet. Caching sites like the Internet Archive's Wayback Machine[13] are a good place to look if one wishes to cite a post that has been deleted (and did not archive it on their own computer during the research process).

Disseminating Research on Instagram

Instagram is not only a place to conduct research; it is also a useful place to disseminate research in progress or to quickly bounce ideas off of the crowd. This is a post by Caroline Rennolds Milbank @jupeculotte.

> Veiling. At top left Mick Jagger's face draped in yellow silk chiffon photographed by David Bailey for the cover of the 1973 album Goat's Head Soup (surprised I don't have a residual stress injury from removing that exact album from that exact sleeve to place on turntable.) At Exhibitionism: The Rolling Stones I learned that Bailey put a scarf over Jagger's head saying "'I'm going to make you look like Hepburn.' I think he thought I meant Audrey Hepburn, when I actually meant Katharine Hepburn in The African Queen." I think the effect is much more Balenciaga, fall/winter 1950, cinnamon silk draped hat and jagged edged ruffled narrow dress photographed here by Henry Clark. Interestingly The African Queen was released in 1951, a year after Balenciaga showed this afternoon ensemble.[14]

I also saw the Rolling Stones's *Exhibitionism*, but I did not pick up on this small detail, so this post really made me think.

Here's another one. Eleanor Houghton @eleanorhoughtonmilliner asks: "A 2015 catwalk take on an 1840s classic? Good style never dies ... (though I think they made a good call in ditching the bonnet) #dolceandgabbana # fashionplate #fashion #highfashion #catwalk #couture #redrose #floralmotif #florals #floralfabrics."[15] And this is a post that I made showing that both Etro (above) and Gabriela Hearst (below) used vintage images of the Rolling Stones in their mood boards for SS/18. All of these and the hundreds like them on Instagram are great little research nuggets, or research bursts, for lack of a better term.[16] This format is concise and immediate and gets into the hands of the right people. But how to document and get credit for work in this emerging scholarly medium? That is another question for another day.

Conferences: If You Hashtag It, They Will Tweet

Conferences have always been the key networking outlet for academics, but hashtags are redefining the discourse while both documenting it and publishing it outside the insularity of the conference context. So far, we have been dancing around the idea of hashtags: #dataviz, #fashionhistory, #dolceandgabbana, etc. "Hashtags provide an efficient way to parse and filter information and people on Twitter, making it easier to follow conversation, trends and people. A good example of this is hashtag use at conferences."[17] Conference attendees function as social reporters, keeping the disciplinary community, including both those in attendance or those who are absent, abreast of the latest developments at the conference. "Those who can't attend have to be content with following the conference hashtag online—now a fixture of most, if not all, conferences. Those who do attend play the role of reporters: they send out vignettes of conference proceedings, hungrily waiting for the perfect soundbite that will fit 140 characters."[18] "Hungrily" waiting, as a cat regarding a treat in its owner's hand, may be a bit of stretch, but no doubt many academics have observed some of their peers glued to Twitter during a conference session. Personally, I do not like to tweet during a conference session, preferring to take notes or just listen attentively, but I do use Twitter while attending a conference as a sort of carnival barker, trying to attract attendees to my own session. At American Historical Association 2017, I tweeted: "Come to the #teachingfashionstudies panel this a.m. @ 10:30 to hear approaches to teaching fashion in the history classroom! #aha17."[19] Note that I created a hashtag for the panel on which I was presenting: #teachingfashionstudies. Doing so is becoming a standard in social academic discourse, as it fosters real-time conversation about the session. Sava Saheli Singh observes:

> Those who attend also use conference hashtags to identify others who are present—either interesting colleagues to network with or old friends to get a drink with; and to identify themselves as present, to both those in attendance and those following from afar. Doing so immediately confirms the tweeter's membership to the community that is represented by the conference and hashtag, thus increasing visibility within the community. Conference hashtags are also a great way to identify and follow other members of the community.[20]

If you hashtag it, they will tweet.

The Importance of Hashtags

Fashion-oriented academics on Instagram use various hashtags to identify themselves (especially in selfies), including #stylishacademic, #academicchic, and #ilooklikeaprofessor. Some hashtags used by historians of fashion, though, are a means by which to apply key texts and theories from the field to a particular image, inviting an open conversation with other scholars. For example, the hashtag #GeorgSimmel, which has been used to refer to Simmel's seminal article "Fashion" (1904), was recently used by a recent FIT alum, fashion historian Vanessa Rosales, in a post about the bomber jacket trend of Spring/Summer 2016.[21]

Beyond fashion and related disciplines, there are certain hashtags that are used by academics generally, across all fields of study, to denote academic discursive communities. Singh lists several, including: #ScholarSunday (the academic equivalent of #FollowFriday, though in my own experience, I have seen fashion scholars using the more generic #FollowFriday instead), #phdlife, and #phdchat, a hashtag started by British scholar Nasima Riazat.[22] I tend to use #academiclife on Instagram to tag posts about how I am dressed for conferences, the first day of the semester, etc. For example, in lieu of using the rather unattractive lanyards that inevitably accompany conference name badges, I always bring at least one necklace with a long chain to a conference so I can use the necklace as an unconventional choice in lieu of the standard lanyard. I did this at the American Historical Association's 2017 meeting in Denver, and posted a photograph on Instagram with the caption: "A necklace chain makes a chic alternative to that boring conference lanyard [elephant emoji] #academicfashion #stylishacademic #styletip #aha17."[23] #Academicfashion and #stylishacademic are both hashtags that mark the post as they bring interest to the academic fashion studies community, while the hashtag #styletip goes beyond academia, reaching out to anyone who is simply looking for pointers on personal style. #aha17 was the official hashtag for the conference, and I used the elephant emoji because my necklace has an elephant charm on it. "As with most social media platforms, Twitter and hashtags work for those who invest time in them."[24] As more academics use social media to post scholarship, or to engage fellow scholars, being vigilant about crediting the intellectual contributions or others becomes increasingly important, and informal contributions are now much easier to find and document.

Emojis in Academic Communication

Hashtags are one discursive tool used by academics on social media—emojis are another. Limited scholarship exists on emojis and what it does is often dated, referring to emojis as "emoticons."[25] This is a shame, as emojis now play an important role in daily life through both our personal and academic communication. Far from "dumbing down" communication between academics on social media or via text message, the use of emojis in academic communication reinforces our collegiality and even our humanity. We are not above the use of emojis up here in our ivory tower. Furthermore, the use of a pictorial character set does not imply that this visual language lacks substance. In fact, some of the earliest, richest, and most difficult to decipher languages are pictographic, including Sumerian cuneiform and Egyptian hieroglyphics.

Emojis also foster the internationalization of fashion studies research. I follow Danish, Dutch, French, Russian, Spanish, and Ukrainian language fashion and textile history accounts on Instagram, and while I can read the French, the use of emojis in a post often helps me to make sense of the others. As a pictographic language, emojis are quite at home on image-based Instagram, and the universality of their meanings is making emojis the new *lingua franca*.

A potential culprit (beyond the stigma that they are lowbrow) for the snail's pace at which emojis are making their way into academic scholarship (as opposed to informal communication between academics) is their proprietary nature. Generally speaking, emojis are the intellectual property of Apple, Android, and other telecommunications companies. An open source set of emojis has been created by Emoji One, however, and is available on the Emojipedia's Emojidex (Figure 4.3). The dress-related emojis are similar to those found in proprietary sets furnished on mobile devices. Just like proprietary emoji sets, they include smileys and people, animals and nature, food and drink, activities, travel and places, objects, and symbol emojis.

Of course, high heeled shoes and hats are not the only used when discussing fashion. Hearts of various colors are used to show appreciation of a particular object or exhibit featured in a post, with the choice of color usually correlating to the predominant color of an object, for example, green hearts for a green dress. To

Figure 4.3 *Open source unicode emojis from the Emojidex.*

express particular esteem for an object or to emphasize admiration for curatorial or conservation work, stars, bombs, explosions, unicorns, the red "100," and the like may be used.

Flag emojis may be employed to denote the country of origin of the objects or designer, such as the use of the Union Jack for a post about an exhibition of fashions from Swinging London. Nature-related objects such as palm trees, cacti, flowers, and waves also help to establish a sense of place as with the location of a photo shoot or the provenance of a museum object. Emojis can also add a sense of the time period to a post. For example, flowers could denote a garden location for the debut of a new collection, or could be read as "flower power," indicating that the objects are from the 1960s or 1970s. Or indeed, flower emojis may simply refer to a floral print fabric, irrespective of time or place. In addition to flowers, many other emojis—various nature emojis described above, sailboats, leopards, penguins, etc.—also may be used to call attention to the print on a novelty printed fabric.

The fact that a single emoji, such as the pink or yellow flower, can take on so many different meanings depending on the context of the post shows that the language of emojis, far from dumbing down communication between academics, can actually add complexity and subtlety in a way that written discourse often sorely needs. For example, although the peach emoji is commonly used to refer to a bum, in fashion history discourse, the peach can also signify bottom-enhancing silhouettes, such as the bustle. Emojis also facilitate intercultural, cross-language communication in a variety of ways. In her poem, "emoji in die skriptorium," South African writer Bibi Slippers mentions several emojis, including *dolfyn* (dolphin), *pizza*, and *pynappel* (pineapple). Because these words are cognates to several European languages.

Perhaps most complex of all are the emojis that represent human actions, expressions, and emotions. In the context of academic communication, the strong arm (reminiscent of Rosie the Riveter) and the hands "raising the roof" are frequently used to congratulate another on the work, much as the bomb or red 100 might be. The blushing face, in turn, is used when one's own work has been congratulated. This conveys a sense of humbleness as well as the genuine honor one feels when others appreciate one's research or curatorial or conservation efforts. As with personal communication in general, the laughing-so-hard-I-am-crying emoji may be employed by academics to describe any variety of humorous work-related situations. I remember seeing it used when museums were filled with visitors playing Pokemon Go, for example. In contrast, the generic smiley face is seldom used to express emotion, and instead, like one of the uses for the flower emojis, connotes the 1960s and 1970s. Importantly, with the addition of a rainbow of skin tones for the human emojis—a much needed supplement to the

Simpsonesque standard yellow—designers, models, and academics of color can now better express their work and experiences through emojis.

The Semiotic Power of Emojis

In case you are not yet convinced of the utility in employing emojis in academic communication, I suggest that emojis have a particular kind of semiotic power, especially when used in fashion studies discourse. In his essay, "Blue Is in Fashion This Year: A Note on Research into Signifying Units in Fashion Clothing," Roland Barthes reflected:

> When I read in a fashion magazine that the accessory makes springtime, that this women's suit (of which I have a photograph in front of me) has a young and slinky look, or that blue is in fashion this year, I cannot but see a semiotic structure in these suggestions: in every case, and whatever the metaphorical detours taken by the wording, I see imposed upon me a link of equivalence between a concept (spring, youth, fashion this year) and a form (the accessory, this suit, the color blue), between a signified and a signifier.[26]

Semiotic theory is often presented as a signifier, an object such as a garment, and a signified, such as the word for the garment. So, for example, the signifier could be an actual, corporeal dress and the signified world then be the word "dress." According to Barthes:

> Signifiers are always part of a physical world which is the clothing content, the fragment of bodily space occupied by the clothing item (a women's suit, a pleat, a clip brooch, gilt buttons, etc.); whereas the signifieds (romantic, nonchalant, cocktail party, countryside, skiing, feminine youth, etc.) are given to me necessarily via the written word, via a literature (that is poor literature in no way changes its status).[27]

Thus, while "dress" is necessarily a signified for a dress, so too can be many other words, such as "heartbreaker," "shimmery," "scandal," and countless others.

This principle can be extrapolated onto the use of emojis. The dress emoji is necessarily a signified for an actual dress, but so too can be the red 100, the heart, the bomb, the explosion, the unicorn, and many other emojis. But can emojis, which make up an image-based rather than text-based language, truly function as signifieds? Although he did not live to see the days of emoticons, I can confidently state that Barthes thought so. He wrote, "Obviously it is easier to bring into my inventory those links which are entirely verbalized, those links where the signifier is a commentary on the image and not the image itself, because in such links the signified and the signifier belong—at least in the practical sense—to the same language."[28] Emojis have not only great communicative power, but also the propensity to confound the uncritical or dismissive, because their visual language is closer than the written word to the visual language of the physical world.

What would Barthes have made of emojis, and specifically the use (and usefulness) of emojis in talking about fashion? Barthes described a kind of liminal space, which he called a "halfway house" between the signifier and the signified: "This [that signifieds are not necessarily given via written text] amounts to saying that, once in their final state, the signifier and the signified do not belong to the same language. This is a crucial distortion, which places fashion within those decoupled, dualized structures that I first tried to describe in a previous essay ['Mythologies,' 1957]. Now, the duplicity of a system, set up, as it were, as a halfway house between a language (clothing forms) and a meta-language (the literature of fashion), requires our method to apply a double description: the study of the signifieds (for example the utopian world they sketch out) is part of a general mythology of fashion. Conversely, the study of the clothing signifiers belongs to a semiological system, in the strict sense of the word."[29] Perhaps emojis, which are simultaneously visual image and characters comprising a language, can and do serve as the halfway house for which Barthes was looking. The study of emojis in communication about fashion bridges the gap between signifier and signified and simplifies the double description of the semiotic method described by Barthes to a more unified and cohesive system of expression.

Bricolage and Polyvore

All of this academic writing on social media ultimately raises the question of bricolage versus narrative. Do digesting and citing tweets and Instagrams lead toward increasing levels of bricolage in academic writing (and is that a bad thing?) "As we construct arguments, we patch together ideas of our peers, trained by the practices of graduate education ('What is the contribution of this week's book?') and the ethics of citation ('Where did I read about that theory?'). In this discourse community, a peer's polished argument is labile feedstock."[30] The key term here is polished.

Social shopping site Polyvore was in some ways evocative of the bricolage that so often characterizes the process of academic writing. "Polyvore" means a consumer of many and varied articles. It is fitting for the website, as its platform allows users to browse and create collections of objects from numerous retailers at once. Academic writers are polyvores, too, consuming the prose of colleagues and creating our own collections of words and ideas from among them. "Equivalent to the bricoleur and 'quilt-maker,' described by Denzin and Lincoln as someone who assembles and combines tools and techniques of research and 'stitches, edits, and puts slices of reality together' (2005, 3), Caroline Evans used the metaphor of ragpicking to describe her approach to the analysis of experimental fashion design in the 1990s, which she conceptualized as a 'case study of what to do with a method' (Evans 2003, 11)."[31] In spring 2018, Polyvore was bought by Montreal-based fashion retailer Ssense and was shut down by their new owner without fanfare on Thursday, April 5, 2018.[32] Users were not notified of the impending shutdown and thousands of users lost not only their accounts, but also all of their mood board sets and saved images, as well. I always backed mine up on my phone and cloud storage, but many users were not in the habit of doing that. The unfortunate end of Polyvore's story is a testimony to how ephemeral the internet really is. Applications and websites with thousands or even millions of users can be taken down in the blink of an eye, accounts deleted. Setbacks like this make the job of researching fashion in a digital age all the more difficult, and create gaps in knowledge and artistic production that current and future archivists will likely be unable to fill.

Instant Gratification in Fashion Scholarship

On Thursday, October 19, the Museum of Modern Art (MoMA) in New York City hosted a symposium on sustainability and instant gratification in the fashion world called "Fashion is Kale," a play, of course, on American fashion designer Elizabeth Hawes's seminal book: *Fashion Is Spinach*. This was remarkable to me because a case study in this very book, which was drafted but not yet published at the time was called "Fashion is Kale." (I have subsequently changed the name of the case study to "Coding Fashion Is Spinach." See the end of Part 3: Visualizing.) Clearly, the time for updating spinach has come.

The mere fact that scholars working in total isolation from one another on two different projects both came up with the title, "Fashion is Kale," is pretty interesting. But even more interesting, I think, is the manner (and speed) with which I learned of this other use of "Fashion is Kale." Living outside the New York area, I was unlikely to see a flyer or hear about it via word of mouth. I am not on the MoMA's mailing list, nor did I see a post about the symposium on any of the museum's social media feeds—not even their Instagram. No, I learned of this symposium and its incredibly familiar title because I happened to see the Fashion Law Institute's posts about it that night. Even in 2015, I would not have found out about something like this until weeks or months later, if ever. Instagram truly does make for instant gratification in scholarship.

Style Blogging

It has been said that the communal spirit and collective consciousness of the 1960s died at the Altamont Speedway on December 7, 1969. But perhaps it simply went into hibernation, to be awakened from its dormancy in the twenty-first century by bloggers. Ideas about mass media put forward in the 1960s, such as Marshall McLuhan's "global village" and Andy Warhol's 1968 prediction that "in the future everyone will be world-famous for 15 minutes," do seem to have finally come to pass in the world of fashion blogging.[33] Peter McNeil and Sanda Miller write, "It immediately becomes obvious why 'blogging' is such a marvelous tool for those passionate about fashion, for what can be more exciting than creating a 'fashion diary.'"[34]

Fashion blogging subverts the expert paradigm (while leaving room for fashion experts to emerge as popular bloggers) and serves as a means of identity construction, both for the amateur and for the academic style blogger.

> Graduating from a Ph.D. program leaves a scholar without an advisor or fellow students to read his or her work. A blog can serve a purpose similar to a writing group, as it pressures one to write regularly, meet deadlines, and explore a work in progress through the eyes of others. Faculty can turn to each other for feedback, of course, where suitable expertise exists nearby, but colleagues are often too overburdened with classes, committees, and family to provide regular input, and after earning doctoral degrees, many scholars find themselves in a series of transient positions, such as postdoctoral and visiting positions, with little opportunity to join a discourse community with peers.[35]

My own experience after receiving my doctorate in 2011 has been a series of visiting assistant professor and lecturer positions. Blogging takes on an increased importance for so-called independent scholars because as with microblogging on Instagram, Twitter, and other social media sites, "being identified with a particular community means one gets to avail of what that community has to offer: jobs, writing opportunities, collaborations, and more."[36] Without the community of fashion and textiles academics on Instagram, Facebook, and Twitter, I would have felt much less connected to the discipline and would have missed out on important conversations and opportunities. That is because: "Media such as wikis, blogs, and Twitter have the power to generate such communities where they are otherwise not available … it turns out that peers and, indeed, friends can be found simply by writing interesting things on the Internet."[37] Above all,

> A well-maintained blog has the potential to provide a crowd for crowdsourcing, a forum for validation or advice, and a kind of collegiality that is no less real for being expressed in type. In this respect, the so-called blogosphere can be seen as a set of continual, overlapping conferences or symposia in an unusually large and friendly institution … Quite apart from the publicity value of having one's name easily associable with well-written and immediately available scholarly-looking content, these are good reasons to blog.[38]

Blogs are also another way—in addition to Instagram, Twitter, and Facebook groups—in which fashion journalists network with fashion academics.

Street Style

True "street style" photography—the kind that has become the fascination of bloggers by contrast—resembles ethnographic documents, with the subjects static, posed, seen head on, and very aware of the camera. This style of photography has its roots not only in anthropology, but more significantly in projects documenting fashion as participant observation in the punk zines of the 1970s, and perhaps most notably in the collaboration of founding editor Terry Jones and photographer Steve Johnston at *i–D* magazine, documenting the safety pin and mohican-sporting youth of the British punk scene. One of the most famous practitioners of the genre is the late Bill Cunningham. In *Street Style*, anthropologist Brent Luvaas describes Cunningham as follows: "Bill Cunningham is a decidedly likeable choice for 'the original street style photographer,' and his status as such goes nearly unquestioned in the blogosphere today. He is famously unpretentious and unassuming, wears a generic blue rain coat to some of the most upscale and exclusive of events."[39] Of course, images capturing something akin to street style have been around much longer than Cunningham's shots of Fifth Avenue or *i–D*'s images of punks in Chelsea.

Many of the earliest photographs—daguerreotypes dating back to the late 1830s—depict the streets of Paris. These can hardly be considered "street style" images, however, as the streets are seemingly devoid of people due to long exposure times. Some of the most famous and arresting photographic images in the history of the street are those created by muckraking journalists of grimy street urchins. Although many of these images were made in New York City, they are a world away from "On the Street." The same goes for Dorothea Lange's "Migrant Mother," one of the most iconic images in the history of American visual culture. Her ragged clothing and prematurely wrinkled brow captured as she and her children huddle by the side of a California state highway at the height of the Dust Bowl and the Great Depression tell the viewer neither about the mother's personal style nor about American fashion in the 1930s.

Up until the 1970s, documentary images made of clothes worn "on the street" were largely either images of traditional costume worn by folk or non-Western cultures (anthropology) or images of the indigent created by journalists. Clearly, for documentary photographers, the meaning of the street has changed and expanded over time. In his book *Street Style*, anthropologist Brent Luvaas asks:

> But what exactly gets to count as 'the street'? Any whose everyday reality does 'the street' represent? Are grand Parisian boulevards 'the street?' Are shopping malls in Dubai? Are Main Street, United States (where most Americans live) and 5th Avenue, New York (where Cunningham tends to shoot) equal in claiming rights to the title? Is 15th Street in Chelsea, just down the block from Milk Studios after a runway event during Mercedes Benz New York Fashion Week 'the street'? I hope so, because I have spotted street style photographers—including [Scott] Schuman and Cunningham—shooting models, still in runway make-up, in front of open warehouse spaces and garages on that block. These shots later appear on their blogs and in their columns, labelled, of course, as 'on the street.' Clearly, in these cases, the everyday reality that the street is meant to represent is not the reality of most Americans.[40]

Probably the closest historical precedent for the glittering genre of street style photography comes not from photography at all, but from realist and impressionist painting of the 1860s and 1870s. The street was a particularly interesting place for Parisians living during the French Second Empire as, in 1853, Emperor Napoleon III tasked urban planner Baron Haussmann with remaking the city, transforming its narrow, winding medieval streets into straight, broad modern boulevards. Napoleon's aim was chiefly political—he feared popular rebellion (and with good reason, considering the events of 1789, 1830, and 1848) and wanted streets that were difficult for citizens to barricade and easy for the French army to move open (a slight oversight: these new roads were also more convenient for the German army to use—they invaded the city in 1870).

Its political motivations aside, the true legacy of the Haussmannization of Paris was that it became a city of walks and strolls. "Planners working under Haussmann 'sought to make the city a place where people could move and breathe freely, a city of flowing arteries and veins through which people streamed likely healthy corpuscles' (Sennett 1996, 256). The streets became conduits of movement, conductors of flow. Their purpose was to facilitate motion."[41] One of the chief figures moving about these new streets was the flâneur, the professional people-watcher of modern Paris who looked upon their fellow Parisians with a mix of curiosity and artistic detachment. Indeed, contemporary chronicler Bezin wrote: "The only, the true sovereign of Paris I will name for you: he is the flâneur."[42] Artist-flâneurs like Edouard Manet painted the social elites of modern Paris as seen out and about on the streets, in the bars and café-concerts, at the racetracks and the opera, often including every detail of their fashionable frippery. According to Proust, "With Manet the eye played such a big role that Paris has never known a flâneur like him nor a flâneur strolling more usefully."[43] This dispassionate, but keen, observation of the clothes worn by others as they walk the city streets began in the nineteenth-century Paris, crystallized in street style publications on both sides of the Atlantic in the 1970s.

> Of course, not everyone had the time, luxury, or disposition to be a flâneur. It took a certain bohemian decadence and a certain bourgeois privilege. 'The attitude of the flâneur,' wrote Benjamin, is 'the epitome of the attitude of the middle classes during the Second Empire' (Benjamin 2002, 420). Their brand of consumption occurred through observation. Their brand of participation consisted largely of seeing.[44]

In the present day, the eye of the flâneur exists as a social media phenomenon in which bloggers clamor to capture the most interesting looks of their city, such as in the popular blog, *Shoes of New York*.[45]

Blogging as Research Method

For anthropologist Brent Luvaas, his medium—the street style blog—is his research method. Addressing the attempt to classify his blog, *Urban Fieldnotes*, Luvaas writes, "Call it a meta-street-style blog. Call it an open-access platform for visual anthropological research. Or just call it a street style blog, because street style blogs are already sufficiently 'meta' and 'anthropological' to encompass these alternative classifications."[46] In addition to the blog, Luvaas uses a mixed-methods approach to his research including auto-ethnography, interviews, participant observation (at New York Fashion Week), photography, and textual analysis.[47]

Related to the street style phenomenon, but focused inward, rather than outward, is the blog as fashion diary, a day-by-day collection of selfies documenting the style of the blog owner, often hashtagged #ootd (outfit of the day). There is a longstanding precedent for this, too, in a particular kind of self-portraiture in which the artists present themselves at an everyday task while wearing their best clothes. A famous self-portrait by Dutch baroque artist Judith Leyster comes to mind.

Academic #ootds and the Simmelian Dandy

There are a lot of great academic style blogs out there to follow: *Chic in Academia, Notebooks on Cities and Clothes, Stylish Academic, Academic Simplicity, Big Data Gal, Black Girl Scientist, Collard Studies, Dr. D. Hodge, History in High Heels*, etc. Minh-Ha T. Pham discusses how style blogs function at length in *Asians Wear Clothes on the Internet: Race, Gender, and the Work of Personal Style Blogging* noting: "Broadly speaking, personal style blogs represent an individual's taste … Clothes on personal style blogs communicate a personal style of dress as well as a style of identity and life. They constitute what Joanne Entwistle terms 'situated bodily practices.'"[48] Compare to street style blogs such as *The Sartorialist*[49] and Instagram blog *Shoes of New York*, and to fashion news aggregate blogs such as *Business of Fashion*[50] and *The Cut*.[51] *The Blonde Salad* (Chiara Ferragni) is an example of a personal style blog that has elevated its young owner to cult, and then to celebrity, status.[52]

Academic personal style blogs differ from a blog like *The Blonde Salad* in that they must balance beauty, ideal photography, and chic clothing with the realities of an academic career and a (primarily) academic audience. Academic style blogs show suits and dresses to wear for teaching, committee meetings, and conferences, off-duty looks for nights on the town, and even loungewear looks for grading exams and papers; plus, all of the other images that inevitably surface on a lifestyle blog: chic eats, gardening, travel, pets, and the like. Some academics eschew or intentionally subvert traditional Western notions of beauty and femininity in their style blogs altogether, although this is not the norm.

Georg Simmel noted that introverted people often like to use fashion as a mask (or a suit of armor, or a security blanket—all are apt metaphors in their own way). According to Schermer and Jary, "Modesty and shyness, lest they betray a peculiarity of their innermost self, makes some delicate natures seek the refuge in the disguise of fashion and its leveling effect."[53] Friends often ask me why I wear such outlandish fur coats or enormous statement necklaces. My answer is: I don't like to draw attention to myself, so I distract people with my clothes. "This is in line with the triviality of expression and small talk whereby sensitive and modest people hide their individual 'soul' by deception."[54]

Simmel also theorized the importance of the dandy as a mask in fashion, a complex, subaltern character one may play. Henry Schermer and David Jary note, "In Simmel's discussion the dandy is a complex special case of leading and being led, of 'superordination and subordination.'"[55] But who exactly is a dandy? Schermer and Jary cite the Teddy Boys, the Mods, and the Rockers as examples of dandies in the Simmelian sense.[56] Nik Cohn, pop journalist of the day, wrote:

> The Edwardian look … lasted til about 1954, by which time it had been taken up and caricatured by the Teddy Boys, who made it so disreputable that even homosexuals were embarrassed to wear it. Nothing could have been more ironic: having started as an upper class defense, Edwardiana now formed the basis for the first great detonation of working class fashion.[57]

Neo-Edwardian dress had largely been a Tory reaction against postwar austerity and the rise of the welfare state.[58] Fashion obeys and exemplifies the Hegelian dialectic, and thus the importance of the dandy is that he or she embodies both halves of the dialectic, providing synthesis.

In subaltern groups, the appearance of the dandy may be read as a barometer for democracy.

> An essential feature of democratic group life is that it operates in direct opposition to this polarity in the case of fashion [such as elite vs. middle class, modest vs. immodest, etc.]. For Simmel, the majority-minority dichotomy has a presence in the constellation of fashion. With the introduction of the dandy the concept of minority and mainstream becomes further relativized: the dandy is a minority within a majority.[59]

Stylish academics are one of these dandy subaltern groups. Academics who communicate with other academics on Instagram and Snapchat in part by posting selfies of their #ootd are neither the elites setting the trends, nor are we the middle class blindly walking into a major retailer and buying the clothes for sale there because they seem "trendy." Like the Teddy Boys and the Mods, the fashion-conscious intelligentsia both lead and follow. It is not a coincidence that education, research, science, and the arts are—like dandies themselves—other such barometer of democracy.

Fashion Blogger Poses and Normative Chic

In her seminal blog post "The Circus of Fashion," Suzy Menkes wrote, "The world changed when fashion instead of being a monologue, became a conversation."[60] Some scholars, however, feel that that conversation is still effectively a monologue, that while the "Circus of Fashion" may be a chorus of many voices, they often seem to be singing the same tune. As Pham writes:

> The final image of Menkes's article illustrates what real fashion people look like, according to Menkes and the New York Times Magazine editors. The image shows three white European fashion editors: Emmanuelle Alt (Vogue Paris), Virginie Mouzat (French Vanity Fair), and Ludivine Poiblance (Interview). Above the image is a caption that reads: 'The opposite of look-at-me fashion: leave it to the French to master understated chic.'[61]

The year 2016 saw a litany of blog posts on how French "girls" use Instagram better than everyone else, for example.

Interestingly, Minh-Ha T. Pham points out that, contrary to the plethora of fashion-related social media that exists today, "the fashion industry was slow to embrace social media. With their peer-to-peer communications and its tolerance, if not outright welcoming, of the amateur opinion, social media and commerce are structurally opposed to the fashion industry's top-down, hierarchical, and highly guarded organization of taste and value."[62] This reluctance on the part of the fashion establishment to embrace new voices is due to the perceived naivete of amateur fashion bloggers. Writing on the role of newcomers as over-night influencers in the blogosphere and fashion business, *Vogue Italia* editor Franca Sozzani asks:

> Why are they so credited? Why do they sit in the front row? Why does the Chamber of Italian Fashion thinks [*sic*] so highly of them ... These aren't people

who have been working in fashion too long to end up criticizing everything, the shows, and they don't have a background in fashion so they are not conditioned by their knowledge or interests. Their comments are naïf and enthusiastic. They don't hold a real importance in the business.[63]

This fashion blogger world of this industry insider echo chamber is what Pham calls "normative chic."[64]

While amateur fashion bloggers in one sense stand against the normative chic of the industry's social media, there is still a marked standardization and normativity in fashion blogging. This is perhaps most keenly seen in fashion blogger poses. "Spend any amount of time looking at the variety of fashion blogs, and a set of recurring poses becomes apparent."[65] Pham has documented several of these poses including pigeon-toed, the shoulder roll, one hand on hip (the teapot), and both hands on hips (the sugar bowl), as well as a preference for "far-away gazes" and "oblique glances."[66]

> Broadly, fashion blogger poses are a set of photographic poses circulating in the fashion blogosphere (and beyond) that emphasize vernacular styles of fashion embodiment. They are antithetical to the dramatic, often exaggerated poses that characterize fashion model poses in print editorials and runways … The images and practices of professional modeling reinforce fashion's aspirational culture: consumers are meant to admire but never attain fashion models' high glamour. This is the work of fashion models. Their job is to embody the aspirational looks and fantasies that drive consumer desire and spending … In contrast, fashion bloggers' embodied vernacular styles are aesthetics of inclusion, compatible with the digital economy's social character. Fashion blogger poses are vernacular styles of embodiment that are used to indicate a genuinely fashionable subject. Set in everyday spaces and public nonplaces, fashion blogger poses are in situ poses that suggest fashion's embeddedness in individual's everyday life rather than its being sequestered in corporate fashion's highly guarded spaces.[67]

Simple, rather than dramatic, poses and locations ranging from academic offices to classrooms to campus quads and landmarks (a far cry from the runway or exotic, often tropical or desert shoot locations) represent the everyday life of the academic who both aspires to a certain fashionability and fashion notoriety and is also proud and confident in their own privileged (albeit less fashionable) spaces into which only years of academic training can grant entry.

Academic Style Blogging as Academic Work

Pham notes:

> Personal style blogging overlaps with women's work in almost every way. Just as women's work is traditionally associated with the unpaid and social labors related to liberalism's private sphere—domestic labor, child care, and reproductive labor—so personal style blogging is typically unwaged and related to the private sphere of self-fashioning. Conventionally understood as unskilled work, women's work—housekeeping, child care, sewing, cooking, and self-styling—is thought to be the natural domain of women and girls. The technological, aesthetic, and ideological construction of bloggers' real style serves at once to reinforce the naturalization of feminine skills and knowledge and to rationalize their devaluation.[68]

Perhaps this is why academic style blogs and bloggers are so interesting. These women have achieved many traditionally masculine social accolades—a life (at least partially) focused on career and an advanced degree (and indeed, many academic style bloggers come from STEM disciplines, rather than the arts and humanities, or the old home economics fields). And yet, in their online lives, they do a traditionally feminine form of work (unpaid self-styling) that is much at odds with their paid and usually highly respected work in academia.

According to Pham:

> Women's work is also defined by its focus on the production and management of emotions. Bloggers' relationships to their audiences are characterized not by social distance (as is the case between fashion models and fashion consumers) [or between academia—the so-called 'ivory tower,' and the general public] but by what Jennifer Terry describes as remote intimacies—social and affective links sustained through media and communication technologies.[69]

Male academics, on the other hand, seem to be conspicuously absent from the community of style-minded academics on Instagram. (Or perhaps I cannot find many of them because I am not "friends" with them. Probably quite a bit of the former, with a tinge of the latter.) Fashion historian Noel McLaughlin noticed a lack of interest in personal style among males in academia as well, writing:

> At the risk of causing offense, academia has never been renowned as a Mecca of male fashion. But, if anything, male dress in the academy has been caricatured as a

> 'fashion disaster-zone' of tweed jackets and elbow patches, ill-fitting, worn corduroy trousers and Hush Puppies (or their more modern equivalents) ... Male academics have liked to see themselves (much in the manner of Michelangelo's David) as having their minds on 'higher' things than the flippancy and vagaries of fashion.[70]

There is also a larger historical explanation for the avoidance of fashion blogging by many male academics. As Fred David noted, "Men's dress became the primary visual medium for intoning the rejection of 'corrupt' aristocratic claims to elegance, opulence, leisure, and amatory adventure ... Men's dress became more simple, coarse, unchangeable, and sombre, sartorial tendencies that in many respects survive to the present."[71] The personal style blog *Academic Simplicity* on Instagram is an example of a female academic performing the "simple" and "unchangeable" dress that Davis and others have associated with male fashion.

Besides following individuals, there are several institutional accounts for fashion scholars to follow: museums such as the Costume Institute at the Metropolitan Museum of Art, Los Angeles County Museum of Art, Museum at FIT, Victoria & Albert Museum; magazines such as *Harper's Bazaar* and *Vogue*, as well as less well-known mags like *Nylon* and *Schön*; and colleges and universities—Central Saint Martins, Fashion Institute of Technology, Parsons – The New School, Savannah College of Art & Design (SCAD), among others. The most worthwhile blogs out there offer analysis versus opinion—*Fashion Studies Journal, Stylish Academic*, and *Unravel: A Time Travel Podcast.*

Fashion Blogger Ethics and the Role of the Independent Blogger

One of the pitfalls of academic fashion blogging is the blurred line between scholars, fashion journalists and influencers, and the loss of true fashion criticism that results when bloggers write with compensation in mind. Successful fashion blogs can generate not only book sales, but also free clothing, fashion show tickets, sponsorships, and other forms in-kind compensation. This quest for fame, designer gifts, and trips to fashion weeks has permeated academic fashion blogs to a much lesser extent than fashion blogging as a whole, partially because most academics have training in critical theory of some sort, but more importantly because academics tend to set their caps at a different prize: book contracts. "Many bloggers are—or were—perceptive and succinct in their comments. But with the aim now to receive trophy gifts and paid-for trips to the next round of shows, only the rarest bloggers could be seen as critic in its original meaning of visual and cultural arbiter."[72] This ethical dilemma, which pits sponsorship against independent thought and criticism is well-summed up in this quip about a fashion blogger at Stockholm Fashion Week: "We once read with great expectation the pronouncement of a world famous fashion blogger who had arrived at Stockholm Fashion Week, only to discover that the insight for the day was regarding the high quality of the bathroom toiletries in the undoubtedly free hotel room in which (s)he was staying."[73] With the ease and speed of publication and multiplicity of voices allowed by blogging culture, now more than ever writing needs to be about something (more substantive than free toiletries) and it needs to mean something. The next chapter explores the critical reading of blog and other social media posts, and the application of critical theory to such media texts, because writing about fashion without critical, interpretive thought behind it is just opinion. As eminent fashion curator and critic Valerie Steele quipped, "Everyone's got opinions, but so what? If you want opinions, just ask a cab driver."[74]

5 Critical Reading of Social Media Texts

Many graduate and post-graduate researchers will be familiar with the concept of critical reading, the application of theory to the reading of a written, visual, or material text. Gaining a working understanding of various schools of critical theory—feminist and post-feminist, Marxist, post-colonial, psychoanalytic, semiotic, and the like—forms the basis of much of the work done at the coursework stage in graduate studies in the humanities. Happily, this theory-based training in understanding more traditional types of texts comes in very handy in making sense of a more recent type of text: posts to social media, such as tweets, Facebook statuses, and Instagram posts.

Applied Theory

In contrast to the difficulties many encounter in finding text and images in databases, most of us are quite accustomed to finding text and images in our various social feeds, whether on Twitter, Instagram, or elsewhere—in fact, we are bombarded with them on a daily basis. Following major design houses, models, fashion magazines, upscale retailers, relevant museums, and the art and fashion sections of national newspapers on social media is the best way not only to keep abreast of news in the industry and stay current on the latest runway shows and ready-to-wear collections, but it is also a data set to mine for potential research topics. In fact, I chose the controversy about whether or not cleavage is "out" (discussed later in this chapter) by burrowing back in my own Facebook feed.

Francesca Granata explores in her essay, "Fitting Sources—Tailoring Methods," the work of Belgian designer Martin Margiela through what she calls "applied theory," mixing theories and methods from not only fashion studies, but also critical theory, cultural history, feminist theory, film studies, and material culture.[1] Later in this chapter, we will use a similar applied theory approach to understanding

Jeremy Scott's "Capsule Collection" for Moschino, drawing upon fashion studies, hermeneutics, Marxist theory, psychology, and social history. The use of multiple critical theories in a single analysis represents another kind of maximalism in research. Some of these theoretical frameworks include: Psychoanalysis, Marxism, Feminism, Queer Theory, Postcolonial Theory, Linguistic Theory, Structuralism and Post-structuralism, Deconstruction, and Postmodernism. A researcher, for example, can employ both Marxist and post-colonial theory in the same interpretation of a text (or work of art or fashion object, etc.).

Hermeneutics

Hermeneutics is one of the oldest strategies for critical reading. Dating from antiquity and possibly stemming etymologically from Hermes, the Olympian messenger god who communicated between the other gods and mortals, hermeneutics was used by Plato and Aristotle and later throughout the Middle Ages for the interpretation of biblical and classical texts. Hermeneutics experienced a revival during the Renaissance, when it became a method more broadly for interpreting texts based on the understanding and context or frame of reference in which the reader is embedded as well as that of the author or artist. In his essay, "Still/Moving: Digital Imaging and Medical Hermeneutics," Scott Curtis defines hermeneutics as, "the theory and method of interpretation, especially of the Bible."[2] Later, "Other theorists expanded the notion of hermeneutics to include other types of 'texts,' each type requiring a different kind or number of 'hermeneutic circles.'"[3] Texts that can be interpreted through hermeneutics are widely varying and extremely broad, including fashion and textiles, the main topic of this book, and social media posts, the main topic of the chapter. No matter what the type of text, however, all hermeneutic circles have in common the notion of a dialectic; that is, there must be a reader along with the text because, in this view, the text only has meaning when interpreted by the reader. The hermeneutic circle, sometimes referred to as the "hermeneutic cycle" or the "hermeneutic spiral," is simply the process of repeated interaction with a text by the reader in which the reader's interpretation becomes more mature/complete/whole because of the previous readings and interpretations. This sounds complicated, but it is actually quite simple. As we'll discuss in the next chapter, on data visualization, it is often helpful to visualize complex concepts or large data sets. The hermeneutic spiral can be understood through the visual metaphor of figure skating, specifically the inside forward spiral.[4] The skater (or the reader of the text) commences the spiral and then builds inward circular momentum (Figure 5.1).

Figure 5.1 *The hermeneutic circle, visualized with ice skating, from* Skating with Bron Meyer *(1921).*

Hermeneutics … and Cleavage

Let us take the example of a particular text and its readership: an article that appeared in the December 2016 issue of *Vogue* UK entitled, "Desperately Seeking Cleavage."[5] The author, Kathleen Baird-Murray, asks if cleavage is "over" in light of the popularity of higher neckline looks such as the Gucci pussy bow blouse (which had recently been worn by future American first lady Melania Trump to one of the presidential debates), to much controversy in another dialectic of interpretation. A hermeneutic interpretation of this article might seek to understand what the author means by the idea of cleavage being over versus what the reader might infer from that statement. Baird-Murray's article, predictably, received much coverage in the online press and much reaction in comments sections and on social media.

A *Bustle* article by Lara Rutherford-Morison responding to the story quoted many women who had taken to Twitter to voice their annoyance with the article, having interpreted Baird-Murray's comments to mean that large breasts were now out of fashion (breasts of course not being something a woman can just store away until they come back into fashion again like a pair of neon tights).[6] One Twitter user tweeted: "I'm glad Vogue has declared the cleavage over because it gives me ample time to get rid of my old boobs and get new ones from Topshop." Another wrote: "'Cleavage is over!' Vogue declares. Suddenly, billions of breasts leap off of their 'owners' whilst screaming in agony." Baird-Murray herself took to Twitter to refute these interpretations offered by her readers, tweeting, "Just to be clear: @BritishVogue cleavage story is not about breast size, large or small, being 'in' or 'out'." and "It's saying that fashion designers are creating more natural, comfortable clothes . . . that focus on other erogenous zones than just the cleavage. #readthewholestory @BritishVogue."

Why did readers of *Vogue* interpret the article differently than the author intended? While it is likely that many of those posting about the article online never actually read the article—they only read the headline or read about the article on *Bustle, Buzzfeed*, or another online media outlet—even those who had read the article might interpret the author's meaning to be that breasts were indeed "out." These readers' interpretations were made early in the hermeneutic process, at the first grasp or first contact with the text. Repeated close inspection of the text, global inspection of the text, or even the reading of related texts would likely have led to different interpretations. Deeper interrogation of the text over time would lead the reader to consider the context of the culture and time in which the author was writing. In 2016, the rise of interest in Muslim fashion and the hijab specifically, and modest fashion generally, as evidenced by the New York University symposium on the subject and the inclusion of hijabs in some mainstream ready-to-wear collections, contributed to a climate in which fashion designers and journalists were interested in styles that show less cleavage, such as the pussy bow blouse, a mainstay of woman's day dress during the more conservative 1950s. Close reading of Baird-Murray's article might also incline the reader to consider the nature of fashion history as a series of pendulum swings from modest to immodest and back again (such as from the mini skirt of the 1960s to the maxi dress of the 1970s to the bubble skirt of the 1980s).

This cyclical process of close reading and interpretation is hermeneutics in a nutshell. Without it, the readers are just ranting about their own limited interpretation on Twitter, insensible to the limitations of their view, or worse, presenting such a limited interpretation of a text in an assignment or manuscript for publication. Hermeneutics is so broad, yet so foundational to the critical interpretation of texts, that there are many sub-fields of the praxis based on different cultural theories, such as Marxist hermeneutics and psychoanalytic hermeneutics. Here the metaphor of maximalism from Chapter 1—of mixing seemingly incongruous prints into a highly variegated yet cohesive whole—continues. At its most basic, hermeneutics of fashion is how fashion is interpreted and analyzed in different times and places based on cultural, social, political, moral, religious, and linguistic norms. This includes everything from popularity to moral outrage.

Scholarly Communication, Professionalism, and Social Media Controversy

So profound are the influences of these echo chambers and cliques that uncritical, judgmental posts even make their way into scholarly social media fora. On November 7, 2016, Katherine Hill Winters felt compelled to post the following on Fashion Historians Unite!, which remains to this day: "Hi All! Please remember that this is a scholarly and professional group. We support one another and work to perpetuate scholarship in the field of fashion and textile history. That means, this is not a forum for personal opinions. Only kindness is spoken here and posts shall remain professional. Anything otherwise, will be removed. Anyone making negative, aggressive or inappropriate comments aimed towards another person, or looking to provoke debate, will be removed from the group without warning. Thanks for being here and for keeping this a positive environment!"[7] Posts about Melania Trump's sartorial choices—most of which were hardly motivated by fashion scholarship—had much to do with this. Using critical theory can go a long way toward avoiding making such unscholarly posts and comments. Critical theory can also help us to read others' social media posts in a more thoughtful manner.

Social Media Outrages: Women in Politics Wear Clothes on the Internet

Unfortunately, some things posted on social media, even within the fashion studies community, are meant simply to polarize, provoke, or outrage. Let's briefly survey three such outrages as seen on Facebook, Twitter, and the comments section of the *Daily Mail*'s Femail. One such social media outrage was the Victoria & Albert Museum's decision not to accession Prime Minister Margaret Thatcher's wardrobe. In her essay, "Museums as Fashion Media," Fiona Anderson writes, "Museum displays are no more or less objective or contrived than a runway show or a fashion photograph."[8] To understand the decision by the staff of the V&A that the bulk of Thatcher's wardrobe did not fit within the parameters of the collecting policy, it is important to note not only the subjectivity inherent in the curatorial process, but also the history of the Textile and Dress Department at the museum. According to Anderson,

> The history of the role of dress within the V&A has been well documented by Lou Taylor in 'Doing the laundry' (Taylor 1998), in which she notes that the museum has always collected dress, yet only in a minor way until the 1950s. Taylor attributes this to the fact that: 'In the eyes of male museum staff, fashionable dress still echoed notions of vulgar commerciality and valueless, ephemeral, feminine style (Taylor, 1998: 34).'[9]

This accent on historical, rather than contemporary dress, was to continue at the V&A until 1971,

> when 'the exhibition "Fashion: An Anthology" organised by Sir Cecil Beaton at the request of then director Sir John Pope Hennessey' firmly established the role of the Museum as a collector and exhibitor of contemporary fashion (interview with Valerie Mendes, 1/3/00). Since that time the collection of dress has grown according to the Textile and Dress Department's policy to 'collect design which leads.'[10]

In the case of Thatcher, it was not the design but the woman who leads. Or at least, that is what conventional wisdom would have us believe.

Reportage on Thatcher from the period in which she was prime minister, however, is rife with sartorial commentary. She also referenced her own dress sense, hair, and accessories in quite a calculated way in her own speeches. In a speech given in 1976, for example, Margaret Thatcher declared, "I stand before you tonight in my green chiffon evening gown, my face softly made up, my fair hair gently waved. The Iron Lady of the Western World? Me? A Cold War warrior? Well, yes."[11] Paul Johnson, historian and former editor of the *New Statesman*, remembered her thus: "I don't recall ever seeing her wear trousers. She took more trouble over her hair than any woman I have met. It was gold, very fine, very soft. When washed, combed and set it was magnificent."[12] Fashion designer

Marc Jacobs even said that the inspiration behind his Autumn/Winter 2004–2005 collection was "all about finding Margaret Thatcher sexy."[13] Far from being a dowdy politician with no dress sense, Thatcher can actually be read as something of a style icon today.

According to Robb Young, author of *Power Dressing*, "During her three terms as prime minister, Margaret Thatcher became arguably the most powerful woman in the world, and it was her take on power dressing that became a key template for women rising in the political and professional ranks."[14] Thatcher was not just a style icon for political and professional women in the 1980s, however. Young notes, "She governed Britain for a decade and came to embody the style of her times, standing out as a rare politician among such popular culture references of the 1980s as Boy George, Madonna, the cast of *Dynasty* and the Versace and Armani labels."[15] She rose above politics in her dress and personal image to become a popular culture icon.

Kira Jolliffe and Bay Garnett wrote in the *Cheap Date Guide to Style*: "No one used to give a hoot about [luxury] bags, but now people go to Topshop and spend £50 on an outfit, then go and spend £900 on a celebrity-endorsed, large bag with Prada written on it. Having the latest, posh power bag gives an overriding identity to the owner, that of 'player' and defiance."[16] This veneration of the power bag likely dates to the 1980s, when Margaret Thatcher used handbags as sartorial (and almost physical) weapons. Young notes that "the Oxford English Dictionary credits the coining of the verb 'to handbag' as being a humorous reference to Thatcher's relentless ministerial style,"[17] and "in 2000 Thatcher donated one of her handbags to an online charity auction, and it sold for £100,000. She later made a statement, 'My handbags did good service in Cabinet and I am pleased they are still having the right effect.'"[18] Cynthia Crawford, Thatcher's personal assistant and long-time style adviser, went on the record as saying: "We always have half a dozen [bags] on the go. They get quite a bashing."[19]

> Thatcher bought her clothes in bulk shopping trips from well-known British companies—both on the high street and from such then-popular upmarket boutique labels as Mansfield, Jean Muir, and Susan Small—chosen partly in recognition of the growing achievements of the British fashion industry … The prime minister's little Salvatore Ferragamo handbag, a repository of lipstick and speech cue cards, became the stuff of legend after Thatcher reportedly slammed it on to the table at a European Economic Community (EEC) summit in 1984, at which she demanded a £1 billion rebate from British contributions made to the EEC budget.[20]

Crawford was thus quite literal about the bags getting a bashing.

Margaret Thatcher's death was heavily anticipated on social media. In her book, *Responding to Margaret Thatcher's Death*, Louisa Hadley looks at responses to Thatcher's death through social media channels, especially Twitter. Martin Belam, for example, posted a pie chart on Twitter in December 2012 (Thatcher did not pass until April of the following year) entitled, "What Twitter will look like on the day that Thatcher dies." The largest segments of the graph, split evenly at around 25 percent each, were "People mourning Thatcher's death" and "People gloating about Thatcher's death." Not far behind was "Young people asking 'Who is Thatcher?'," while the smallest segment was "Leftie in-fighting."[21]

Another such social media outrage is the fact that the internet community became so upset about Prime Minister Theresa May's leather trousers and leopard print heels. "If, immediately after the British elections of 2010, you had asked the average person on the street about Theresa May, more often than not the hesitant reply would have been: 'Isn't she the one with the funky shoes?'"[22] It was as much the Fourth Estate as May's sartorial choices themselves that fed the public this image. In an article cheekily entitled, "A Tory Wet Dream Comes True in May," Laurie Penny described the new Home Secretary Theresa May thus: "Posh, spiky-heeled and stern with a staggeringly intolerant agenda, she bespeaks a type of kinky discipline that just longs to kick naughty little boys and girls into shape and make us behave."[23] *The Daily Mail*'s headline was a bit more tasteful, though perhaps quite a bit more condescending: "Kitten-heeled Theresa May Opts for Flats on First Day as Home Secretary."[24]

> For well-off women in the Conservative strongholds, May offers a bit of pizazz to the staid look of twinsets, matronly suits and court heels usually favoured by their local MPs. So influential did her shoes become that some boutiques couldn't keep enough stock of the models she was seen wearing. (She often selects shoes from mid-market chain Russell & Bromley.) … May definitely hit the style mark with her constituents in Maidenhead, Berkshire: country floral and paisley prints given a modern edge with sleek lines, polished trench coats, expensive shabby-chic separates and a formal wardrobe that ventures from intrepid cocktail dresses to a British East Indies Company-era nostalgia for the exotic … Pointy pony-skin stilettos, leopard-print wellington boots and rainbow wedges have succeeded in providing May with a degree of notoriety, but, without a strong personality to back them up, she has simply been outshone by her shoes. Seen through the prism of this flamboyant footwear menagerie and against the backdrop of her conservative ways, May's roar of idiosyncrasy felt more like a muffled cry.[25]

Throughout her tenure as home secretary, headlines such as "Theresa May looks FAB in her 'Thunderbirds' jacket"[26] and "Theresa May, what did you think you looked like in that strapless dress? Please stop!"[27] kept the focus off her policies and on her dress sense. And social media followed suit.

A third social media controversy related to a woman in politics occurred days after then-presidential candidate Donald Trump revealed to have made remarks about groping women, when his wife Melania wore a pink Gucci "pussy bow" blouse to the presidential debate, a sartorial pun not lost on the internet. Fashion studies academics took to social media to opine what her curious choice of clothing might have meant, and discursive networks devoted to fashion quickly adopted the trending hashtag: #pussybow. Was Melania Trump using dress as a form on nonverbal communication aimed at US presidential nominee Hillary Clinton when she wore a Gucci "pussy bow" blouse, or was her sartorial choice merely a coincidence?

Trump is certainly no stranger to referencing past first ladies through dress. Melania Trump's Alice blue Ralph Lauren coat dress, which she wore to her husband's inauguration, for example, seems to have been inspired by a pink coat dress designed by Oleg Cassini for First Lady Jacqueline Kennedy to wear to President John Fitzgerald Kennedy's inaugural.[28] Many academics responded to Mrs. Trump's inaugural coat dress with charges of fashion plagiarism and disdain that seemed more related to feelings about the new president than to the coat dress itself. Studying the language used to discuss clothing worn by such a contentious figure as Melania Trump reveals both the bias and the professionalism that exists and co-exists when academics take to social media. According to Singh, "It is important to keep in mind, however, that there are possible negative effects of using social media platforms generally and hashtags specifically, such as creating echo chambers and cliques, and causing pigeonholing."[29] We have briefly surveyed three recent fashion-related social media outrages but, of course, we could go on almost indefinitely in this manner. Perhaps no academic is completely immune from allowing their personal beliefs to color their perceptions of what should be professional costume-related posts on social media. The case study that follows offers advice for looking past these personal biases and critically reading the content of social posts using a hermeneutic strategy.

Case Study: Reading the Moschino "Capsule Collection"

The "Capsule Collection" was Moschino's Spring/Summer 2017 collection. It was not, however, a capsule collection in the sense that the fashion business usually uses the term. Susie Faux, owner of London Boutique Wardrobe, coined the term "capsule collection" in the 1970s to describe the core of one's wardrobe, the indispensable pieces that will not quickly go out of style and can be worn from season to season. In the 1980s, Donna Karan expanded the term. According to Business of Fashion's glossary,

> Capsule Collections were originally popularised by Donna Karan in the 1980s. The idea was to create a capsule wardrobe that features only the most essential or influential pieces from a collection. A capsule collection is essentially a condensed version of a designer's vision, often limited edition, which transcends seasons and trends by being functional—read commercial. They often focus on construction and delivering key looks, without the styling and theatrics of a show.[30]

At face value, Moschino's Capsule Collection provides the opposite, the convolution of retail therapy and drug therapy in ironically outlandish clothing and accessories that were clearly meant to be of the fashion moment, rather than timeless and practical. There is a double-meaning of capsule collection here—a collection of core of timeless pieces (which it arguably is not) and a collection using capsules, or pills, as motif and inspiration.

The social media for the Capsule Collection used the hashtag #JustSayMoschiNO, a play on the "just say no" to drugs campaign (Figure 5.2). The pill emoji was also used in many of Moschino's posts about the collection. But some people posted who wanted to #justsaynotomoschino or #justsaymoschinothanks. For example, David Armstrong wrote on Twitter: "An early contender for the most moronic, insensitive and plain stupid marketing campaign of the year."[31] Still, many other Twitter users defended the Capsule Collection, such as Jennifer Depew, who tweeted, "#justsayno to deadly Rx painkillers and say yes to fashion #justsaymoschino."[32] By applying a hermeneutic research methodology to social posts about Moschino's Capsule Collection using the hashtag #JustSayMoschiNO, I was able to arrive at an understanding of the collection as both a reflection of the contemporary moral and social climate and a reflection of a past, which largely embraced prescription opiate use and later associated opiates with creativity and celebrity. The question is not "Did Jeremy Scott go too far this time?," but rather why in American society we fear that he might have.

In her discussion of the practice of hermeneutic art history, Anne D'Alleva urges readers to explore their own process of interpretation in order to arrive at a fuller, less biased understanding. The questions she poses to readers are helpful to consider before arriving at conclusions about controversial topics or topics about which one already has strong opinions. I have selected three of these questions for the purpose of this case study:

#JustSayMoschiNO

#JustSayNoToMoschino
#JustSayMoschiNoThanks

Figure 5.2 *#JustSayMoschiNO, #JustSayNoToMoschino, and #JustSayMoschiNoThanks hashtags as seen on Twitter, Image created by Amada Sikarskie.*

1. What questions am I asking? Why am I asking them?
2. In what ways do my questions stem from my previous understandings of this work or its context? In what ways are these questions very much of my moment? How do my questions, or my process of interpretation, differ from others at other points in time?
3. How can I reframe my understanding so as to be able to see this work of art or issue as part of other wholes, or as a whole rather than a part?[33]

I jotted down my initial answers to these questions in response to an Instagram post about Moschino's controversial "Capsule Collection":

1. What inspired Jeremy Scott to use prescription drug use (and abuse) as the theme for his new collection? Will people think he has gone too far this time? Has he? Prescription drug abuse does not represent or result from any kind of moral failing, though many people think that it does. I am making the assumption here that some people will find this collection immoral, or at the very least, that people will worry that a glorification or fetishization of prescription drug abuse will inspire young people to seek out these pills.
2. Jeremy Scott has long sought to create controversy and embraced the shock value of his work. I am, on the whole, a fan of Scott's work, however. His Gold show (1997) was one of the very truly maximalist fashion collections in the era when minimalism still reigned—it was dismissed by fashion editors at *Vogue* and other magazines as a result. My concern—even in light of my regard for Scott as a designer—that he may have indeed now gone too far is a reflection of the current vilification of opiate use in the United States. In

other times, however, prescription of such drugs was widely accepted for the treatment of minor aches and pains from headaches to menopause.

3. Clearly, Scott's Capsule Collection does not exist in a vacuum and is part of a larger whole.

Opiates: An Historical Background

Opiates have been used since at least the Middle Ages as a painkiller and to treat a variety of medical conditions. Their ability to produce a state of euphoria made them popular with doctors and patients alike for centuries.[34] In the nineteenth century, they were most commonly prescribed to women. As Barry Spunt notes in his history of opioid addiction in *Heroin and Music in New York City*, "Before heroin, the typical opiate user was a middle-aged, middle-class, white woman who had become habituated to opiates through self-medication, as a result of the widespread medical custom of prescribing opiates for menstrual relief and menopausal discomforts. Even without a prescription, opiates were easy to obtain."[35] Although Spunt is writing about opiate use in the 1800s here, he could just as easily be describing opiate use today.

Heroin Chic

Illegal drugs have long been associated with fashion and popular culture in both positive and negative lights. In the 1960s, songs such as the Rolling Stones's "Mother's Little Helper" and the popular novel (and subsequent film) such as the *Valley of the Dolls* simultaneously glorified the use and abuse of prescription drugs and showed their potentially disastrous impacts. Heroin chic may sound very much like a relic of the 1990s—President Clinton specifically attacked heroin chic in fashion modeling in a speech given on November 10, 1997,[36] but the reality is that prescription and street opiate addiction far outpace that of twenty years ago, and this phenomenon cuts across all classes: the elite, the middle class, and the poor. Moschino, without being coy, is just presenting us with what we already know, and inviting us to wear the pills like a scarlet letter "A." But unlike Hester Prynne, today's fashion conscious need not worry for, as Simmel theorized, shame has no place in fashion.

According to Barry Spunt's *Heroin and Music in New York City*, "The drug research literature supports the notion of a link between subculture, identity, and heroin use."[37] Further adding to the fashionability of assorted drugs over time is their allure among creative types—artists, musicians, and the like. "History shows that many very creative people have used, and abused, various types of drugs, including opiates, and that drugs have helped in the creative process. For example, during the Romantic Age of the early to mid-1800s, many artists, writers, and composers drew artistic inspiration from opium."[38] Given the centuries-old practice of over-prescribing opiates to women and the predilection toward drugs of all types among those in the creative professions, it is no wonder that Jeremy Scott knew that novelty prints of pills would sell in the fashion world. Isn't Scott just showing us what we already know? In this historical light, how should we read and interpret social media posts about the Capsule Collection?

Popular Criticism of "Fashionable" Drug Use

While collective memory associates heroin with the rock and roll acts of the 1960s and into the 1970s, one of the first musical subcultures specifically associated with heroin use was bebop. According to Spunt, "Among the beboppers of the 1940s and '50s, it was 'hip' to use heroin."[39] Indeed, Spunt's description of the bebop subculture reads very much like a description of the fashion world in the 1990s might. "The bebop ethos was an alternative and subversive one. The central goals were creativity, spontaneous pleasure, freedom, and excitement."[40] Just like today, there were many—including celebrities—that spoke out against the drug use of the bebop set. Louis Armstrong called opiates "ungodly shit" and song and dance man Cab Calloway said, "I know that the drug menace in music is very real, and that unless immediate steps are taken it will lead to the deterioration of a splendid art."[41] In rap parlance, "dope [which has long been slang for heroin] essentially means excellent, top-quality, and cool."[42] Sociologist and quilt historian Marybeth Stalp has documented quiltmakers referring to their (often very large) collections of fabric using a drug vernacular, as their "stash" or "habit," and to themselves as quilt or fabric "addicts."[43] Similarly, most people in the West have encountered a french fry, potato chip, cookie, or other junk food amusingly marketed as "crack" to indicate that the product is uncommonly tasty.

Among fashion bloggers on Instagram, the drug-related term "hustler" is currently in vogue in generic statements of positivity such as, "I'm following my dreams and getting my hustle on." Barry Spunt defines what actually constitutes "hustling" as follows: "'Hustling' has long been a part of street life; the hustler has been described as a 'generic figure who occupies a central position in the symbolic space of the black American ghetto.' On the streets, being a successful dealer equates with being a resourceful hustler, and resourceful hustlers are looked up to and respected."[44] The language of illicit drug use has (seemingly benevolently) permeated contemporary popular language in myriad ways—from music to blogging, food, and even quilting. And yet, when people *see* images of pills on a handbag or a jacket, some take to social media in righteous indignation. What is accepted in language, it seems, need to be seen as socially acceptable in a visual medium like fashion. Perhaps this is because while popular musicians have been playing songs about drugs for decades, fashion designers arrived much later at the concept of openly using drugs as subject matter. In the case of Yves Saint Laurent's "Opium" fragrance, we do not actually see the drug, and our imaginations are left to complete the image. A more apt historical precedent for the Capsule Collection was the nudie suit worn by cosmic Americana musician Gram Parsons, which featured appliquéd emblems of poppies (the botanical source of opium), as well as marijuana leaves and a variety of pills.

Simmel and Psychoanalytic Readings

We can apply many different lenses to interpret a single phenomenon, each of which helps us to understand them from a different angle. Although we just explored an Instagram post about the Capsule Collection using a hermeneutic methodology, for example, Marxist and psychoanalytic critical readings may be made of the same post as well. Simmel relied not just on Marxist hermeneutics, but also on psychoanalytic hermeneutics in his interpretation of the sociology of fashion. He wrote: "The tendency toward imitation characterizes a stage of [early childhood] development in which desire for expedient personal activity is present, but from which the capacity for possessing the individual acquirements is absent."[45] Children are only capable of living in the moment until they construct a past for themselves through imitation—needing to hear their favorite story read aloud every night without alteration, needing to wear their purple socks this Tuesday because they wore them last Tuesday, etc. Simmel argued that through imitation, "the individual is freed from the worry of choosing and appears simply as a creature of the group, as a vessel of the social contents."[46] Beyond fashion in dress, the process of imitation and reiteration of trends in thought in the echo chambers that circles of acquaintances create for themselves in social media is another example of the individual as vessel for the social. Are the various posts about the Capsule Collection stemming from individual thought or the subsumption of the individual into a vessel for mass thought (which almost always exists at the beginning of the hermeneutic spiral)?

Here we come to the crucial difference between fashion and personal style. Simmel calls the fashionable individual the "imitator" and the stylish person the "teleological individual," explaining, "the imitator is the passive individual, who believes in social similarity and adapts himself to existing elements; the teleological individual, on the other hand, is ever experimenting, always restlessly striving and he relies on his own personal conviction."[47] Can the fashion of the Capsule Collection be worn with style? This is a question that one might ask on the way to making a critical (hermeneutic), rather than a judgmental, interpretation of the collection.

Simmel and Marxist Readings: Modesty, Class, and Imitation

German sociologist Georg Simmel wrote extensively on fashion, including the role of modesty and shame in fashion. Simmel argued that "all feeling of shame rests upon isolation of the individual; it arises whenever stress is laid upon the ego, whenever attention of a circle is drawn to such an individual—in reality or only in his imagination. By reason of its peculiar inner structure, fashion furnishes a departure of the individual, which is always looked upon as proper. No matter how extravagant the form of appearance or manner of expression, as long as it is fashionable, it is protected against those painful reflections which the individual otherwise experiences when he becomes the object of attention." Put succinctly, there is no shame in fashion.

Many social theorists writing in the twentieth century perceived that urban modernity was speeding up the dialectic of fashion. Schermer and Jary summarize this: "In Walter Benjamin's phrase, fashion is the 'tireless help-maiden of modernity' and it 'can postpone progress' by prescribing rituals in which a 'fetish commodity' can be worshipped. In *The Fashion System* (1965), the semiotician Roland Barthes similarly suggests that fashion often has an 'idealistic bourgeois emphasis.'"[48] This dialectical process is continuing to accelerate in the digital age, and likes, hearts, and upvotes are among the new fetish objects.

Like Benjamin and Barthes, Simmel's view of fashion is that it is inherently dialectical, a series of pendulum swings, such as from immodest to modest and back again.[49]

> On the one hand the lower classes are difficult to put in motion and they develop slowly. A very clear and instructive example of this may be found in the attitude of the lower classes in England towards the Danish and Norman conquests. On the whole the changes brought about affected the upper classes only; in the lower classes we find such a degree of fidelity that the whole continuity of English life which was retained through all those national vicissitudes rests entirely upon the persistence and immovable conservatism of the lower classes ... The highest classes, as everyone knows, are the most conservative, and frequently enough they are even archaic. They dread every motion and change, not because they have an antipathy for the contents or because the latter are injurious to them, but simply because it is change and because they regard every modification of the whole, as suspicious and dangerous. No change can bring them additional power, and every change can give them something to fear, but nothing to hope for. The real variability of historical life is therefore vested in the middle classes, and for this reason the history of social and cultural movements has fallen into an entirely different pace since the *tiers état* assumed control.[50]

The role of class is foundational to Simmel's Marxist hermeneutic interpretation of fashion. "Absent in classless societies [if there is such a thing], in class societies fashion tends to flow from elites to the imitating middle class, but before class differences are eliminated, the elite move to a new, more fashionable mode."[51] Fashion is driven by the aspirational middle class, not by the upper class. For every $10,000 statement bag, there must be a thousand $200 handbag charms. Just as it aspires to the $10,000 statement bag, the middle class also aspires to the druggy chic of some elites, all while finding it immoral. "Kate and Johnny were the chicest, druggiest couple since Keith Richards and Anita Pallenberg, the epitome of cool in a *Trainspotting* culture."[52] But, as noted earlier, there is no shame in fashion.

Ultimately, reading cultural theory stemming from disciplines such as philosophy, anthropology, and sociology can help the reader advance along the hermeneutic spiral to form more cogent interpretations of the text. In doing critical reading of social media posts about fashion, the reader is performing a kind of metahermeneutics, interpreting both the original text (e.g., the fashion collection or piece of fashion journalism) *and* the social post, which is itself another reader's interpretation of the original text. The next chapter concerns itself with much more quantitative data about fashion, although data visualizations, as we will see, still leave much room for interpretation by the reader and for creative research on the part of the maker.

PART 3

Visualizing

The fashion world is starting to recognize data visualization as an important tool quite compatible with the visual, data-driven nature of the fashion business. Giorgia Lupi's data visualization to close out the *Items: Is Fashion Modern?* exhibition at the Museum of Modern Art is a conspicuous example of this. Collaborations such as this one suggest that the time is right for a *data visualization turn* in fashion studies. Known simply as #dataviz on social media, data visualization is a method of visual communication that uses information design to make large, complex, and/or multi-faceted data sets readily intelligible for a reader. For those without a background in technology, data visualization need not be intimidating.

Dear Data

Just as emojis are a universal language, so too is data. As Giorgia Lupi and Stefanie Posavec showed in their *Dear Data* project, data is a form of academic communication. They wrote: "In our correspondence, we didn't speak English or Italian—we spoke data."[1] Although one often associates both academic communication and data visualization—the subject of the following chapter of this book—with the digital, communicating with and through data need not be high tech. In the *Dear Data* project, for example, Lupi and Posavec hand drew data visualizations explaining the details of their everyday lives on postcards, and for fifty-two weeks, (snail) mailed them to each other across the Atlantic.

As we have seen, dress is an essential aspect of not only an academic's personal life, but also their professional self-fashioning, and communicating this identity through dress is a form of academic work. Lupi and Posavec devoted the sixteenth week of their correspondence to the theme of "our closets," or as Posavec, writing from the UK noted, "wardrobes." Lupi and Posavec explained, "This week Giogia and Stefanie decided to take an 'archaeological' approach to getting to know each other. Just once in the week, they would analyze their closets (or wardrobes!) and categorize and quantify them. They wanted to see beyond tracking activities and into how their personalities are expressed."[2] In researching their own clothing, they asked many questions, such as: "What do I actually wear?" "What should I get rid of?" "How many dresses of the same type?" and "What am I ashamed to own?"[3] For her data visualization postcard, Lupi used blue for stripes, yellow for patterns, and red for clothing that she had not worn in the past year.[4] There is a great deal of red in the graphic, and Lupi notes that after visualizing her closet in this way, she did a massive clean-out and decluttering.[5]

Posavec used many more colors, indicating special occasion clothing, dressier professional attire, casual professional attire, street wear that counts as professional attire [this category is pretty much the whole of my own closet], party and club wear, thermal wear, outer wear, exercise wear, loungewear downgraded from professional/casual wear, loungewear downgraded from exercise wear, free loungewear (conference tees!), and finally loungewear actually purchased as loungewear.[6] Also unlike Lupi's visualization, Posavec did not order the colors as they actually appeared in her wardrobe as, "embarrassingly, all Stefanie's clothing during this survey was crammed into a filing cabinet!"[7] (This situation is no doubt familiar to many early career academics who move frequently.) Clearly, data visualization fosters both informal academic communication about dress and research on dress. But what are data visualizations, and how does one go about making one? This is the subject of the chapter that follows.

6 Data Visualization

Data is a rather ubiquitous product of our daily lives. As Giorgia Lupi and Stefanie Posavec note in *Dear Data*, "Besides finding data in the world around us, we are all creating data just by living: our purchases, our movements through the city, our explorations across the internet, all contribute to the 'data trail' we leave in our wake as we move through life."[1] You may even create data visualizations on a regular basis, and simply not think of it as such. For example, last winter, while considering how to pack for a vacation in Florida, I used emojis to create a note on my phone showing a plan for the number of each kind of item I needed to pack: four dresses; two bathing suits; three shirts; two pairs of pants; four sets of pajamas (the kimono emoji); one pair each of sandals, dress shoes, and comfortable walking shoes; one pair of sunglasses; two handbags; and make-up. The end result is a simple (and very easy to make) data visualization (Figure 6.1).

Researchers create data visualizations for many different kinds of data, spanning a broad range of academic subjects. For example, scholars doing work as fans, and fans doing work as scholars—individuals who cultural critic Henry Jenkins has termed "aca-fans"—often create data visualizations to further the understanding of their favorite musical group or celebrity.[2] Jeffrey Roessner observed this phenomenon among the Beatles fans. Roessner defines data visualization in fan communities as follows: "The most striking examples of liminal fan scholarship of the Beatles involve data visualization—that is, taking existing information available from other sources (either in print or online) [or, I would add, generating new information through original research], asking new questions of it, and then presenting the results in graphic form."[3] What data about the Beatles benefits from being "visualized"? (A professor or colleague might easily ask the same question regarding data about fashion.) Roessner notes, "Work that falls under this category [data visualization] includes, for example, graphs that display the average tempo of particular songs or entire albums. Other popular charts reveal the frequency of words that occur on particular Beatles songs, albums, or in their entire oeuvre."[4] The possibilities for data visualization in fashion and textiles are equally, if not more, broad. Preference for particular cuts and fabrics over time, changing hems and waistlines, frequency of particular types of objects in

Figure 6.1 *Data Visualization: Packing list for Florida created using emojis, Amanda Sikarskie.*

museum collections, patterns of language usage in fashion criticism, journalism, and marketing are all potential uses of data visualization in fashion studies. Before we model some of these fashion- and textile-based visualizations, it is useful to have some background on data visualization—its history, the various types of visualizations, what constitutes a successful visualization, and the rudiments of how to make one.

The History of Visualization and its Practitioners

In his essay, "Visualizations and Historical Arguments," John Theibault notes that images have been used to supplement written text or explicate concepts for centuries, giving the example of medieval illuminated manuscripts.[5] While cliometric, climactic, and so-called big history are currently on the rise, social history, of which the history of dress and textiles are a part, has stagnated somewhat in comparison. Theibault suggests that "many explanations have been offered for the relative decline of social history since its heyday in the 1970s. A failure of imagination in the integration of visualizations with text-based arguments may have contributed to the decline."[6] By incorporating visualizations, fashion historians, who often have a creative eye for color and pattern, may begin to turn the tide in this.

Edward Tufte, one of the fathers of modern data visualization—a scholar who was writing on the subject before the digital age, referred to visualizations in his more recent 2006 book, *Beautiful Evidence* as "mapped pictures," defining them thus: "*Mapped pictures* combine representation images with scales, diagrams, overlays, numbers, words, and images."[7] Tufte gives the example of applied text denoting the given names of various pet dogs over a photograph of the dogs.[8] While such an example may seem so simple that it hardly qualifies as "data visualization," Theibault defines "visualization" as follows: "When the term visualization is used today, it usually refers to an image that is derived from processing information—often, but not always, statistical information—and that presents the information more efficiently than regular text could."[9] The field of data visualization is truly a broad tent, encompassing visual presentations of information from the most basic to the most complex. Thus, a computer is not required to create a visualization, although computers do make it much easier. "Scholars quickly recognized the potential of computers to help process information and display the results in an easily interpreted format."[10] While many do consider Tufte's minimalist, engineer's vision of data visualization to be something akin to gospel, designer Nigel Holmes's more maximalist approach continues to have a following. As Alberto Cairo has noted, "There has always been a fundamental clash in information graphics and visualization between those who favor a rational, scientific approach to the profession, emphasizing functionality, and those who consider themselves 'artists,' placing emphasis on emotions and aesthetics."[11] Combining the philosophies of Tufte and Holmes represents a mixed-methods approach to the field of data visualization.

Today, one of the giants of the field of data visualization is information designer Alberto Cairo, whose book, *The Functional Art: An Introduction to Information Graphics and Visualizations* (2013), is essential reading for anyone seriously contemplating a large data visualization project. According to Cairo, "A cherished notion of Tufte's is a principle of efficiency: A visual design project is good if it communicates a lot with a little."[12] Cairo advocates a mixed-methods approach, combining the scientific and artistic aspects of data visualization: "No matter what style you choose—whether you decide to follow Tufte and become a minimalist or adopt a friendlier approach—always take advantage of the space you have available to seek depth within reasonable limits. After that, worry about how to make the presentation prettier."[13] In terms of influences, going back much farther than Tufte, in *The Functional Art*, Cairo cites Chicago School architect and early practitioner of the skyscraper Louis Sullivan as one of the grandfathers of all the design disciplines, for both good and ill.

Sullivan wrote in "The Tall Office Building Artistically Considered" that "form ever follows function. This is the law."[14] Cairo argues that we misunderstand Sullivan's notion that forms follow function, and that generations of artists and designers have used this perversion of his maxim to their own ends.[15] This is much like the Victorians' willful misinterpretation of the ancient phrase "the blood of the covenant is thicker than the water of the womb" as "blood is thicker than water," a pleasant sentiment much in line with Victorian ideals of the cult of domesticity, but meaning the exact opposite of the original idea.

Lupi and Posavec opt for more of an artisanal, sort of "slow food" conceptualization of data visualization. "We prefer to approach data in a slower, more analogue way."[16] Primarily interested in the role of the human element in data, Lupi and Posavec write, "Instead of using data just to become more efficient [such as, to do scholarship more efficiently], we argue we can use data to become more humane and to connect with ourselves and others at a deeper level."[17] The discussion of data visualization in the pages that follows largely combines Cairo and Lupi's and Posavec's approaches to data. Before proceeding to a discussion of how to actually make a data visualization, it is important to understand the qualities that data visualizations possess (and try to balance), as well as the various types of visualizations.

The Visualization Wheel

Alberto Cairo argues that successful data visualizations are: truthful, beautiful, insightful, functional, and enlightening.[18] To create a visualization that embodies these five qualities, it can be helpful to begin with what Cairo calls the "visualization wheel." The visualization wheel is a meta-visualization (that is, a visualization explaining data visualization itself) created by Cairo to aid in the creation and evaluation of data visualizations and infographics. It follows the same principle as the color wheel, with opposite qualities arranged in a circle around a central point (Figure 6.2). In the visualization wheel, these opposites are a series of axes including: abstraction and figuration, functionality and decoration, density and lightness, multidimensionality and unidimensionality, originality and familiarity,

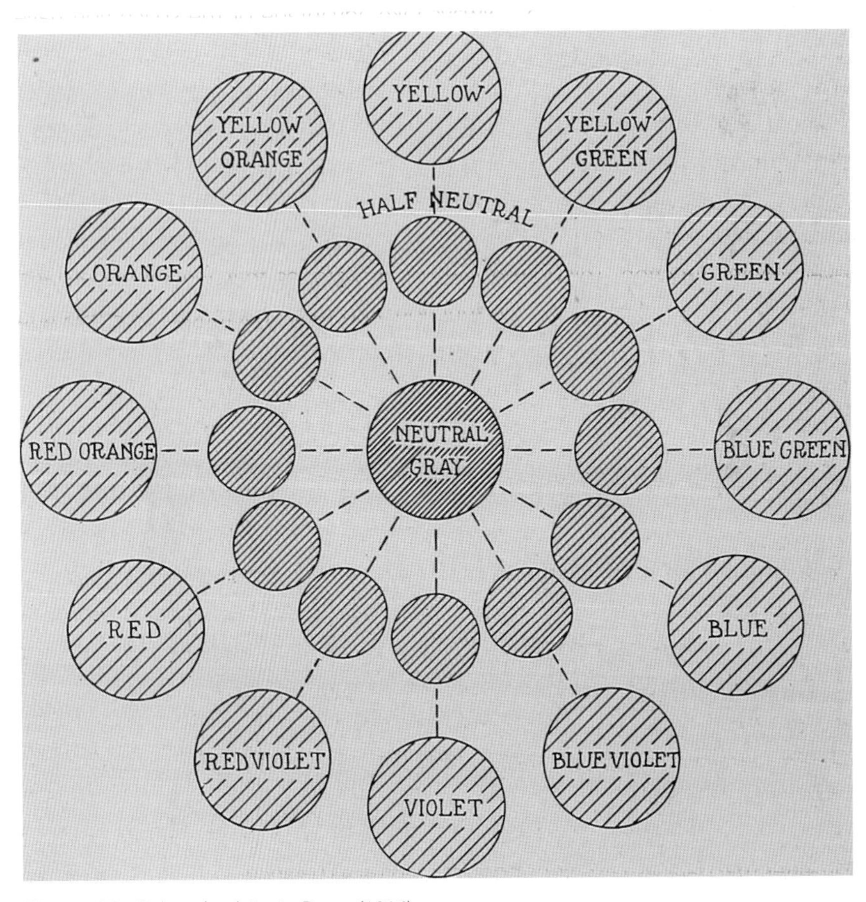

Figure 6.2 *Color wheel,* Art in Dress *(1916).*

Data Visualization

and novelty and redundancy.[19] Along each of these continua, the first value given is more complex and deeper, while the second value given is more intelligible and shallower. Every data visualization falls on a point (albeit a subjectively determined one) along each of these axes.

The trick in creating a successful data visualization is striking a balance so that it is intelligible enough for the reader to comprehend, but complex enough to be really meaningful. To return to our discussion of the hermeneutic spiral from the previous chapter, visualizations cannot be too abstract, dense, or unfamiliar, or the reader will be unable to progress along the spiral toward a critical interpretation of the data. At the other end of the spectrum, if a visualization is too decorative, light on data, or familiar, there will be little that even merits the reader's time and interpretation. When in doubt, lean toward information density.

Density and Transparency

When creating a visualization, balancing density and transparency is crucial. According to Theibault, "The key dimensions of a visualization are the density and the transparency [what Cairo calls lightness] of its information. Density is the sheer amount of useful information that the visualization conveys, and transparency is the ease with which the information can be understood by the reader."[20] The most information-rich visualization is useless if its complexity renders it illegible to the reader. (My husband has often complained, for example, that the Taco Bell drive through menu is too visually dense, reading about as clearly as a Jackson Pollock painting!)

Sometimes the data in a visualization is so lacking in transparency that the resulting image is indeed a work of art (these are the sorts of visualizations that Edward Tufte abhors, but that fascinate Nigel Holmes).

> Bloomsbury, WC1, is a postal district of London: the area of grey Georgian houses, straight streets, long terraces and leafy squares, pubs, restaurants, small publishers and specialist bookshops around the elegant British Museum and Senate House. It was also, as Woolf implies, something more: the name of a cultural climate, a social and intellectual grouping, that challenged the age, asserted the spirit of art, and had a massive impact on the culture, arts and manners of modern Britain.[21]

Photographer Adriane Little's *Mapping Mrs. Dalloway* series (2016) visualizes recurring words in the writing of Virginia Woolf as a text-free bubble chart (see multidimensional visualizations in the following section) superimposed over her own photographs of the city of London. The resulting images abstract and obscure the data, all while heightening its beauty.

The Importance of Color

Color is crucial in visualizing data. Theibault notes that one of the most critical elements in producing a data visualization is the "challenge of balancing honesty in visual rhetoric with clarity and visual persuasiveness."[22] Color can reinforce (or challenge) political and gender biases and stereotypes (pink for girls and blue for boys, "red" states and "blue" states, etc.). The way a reader understands color is also based on their mood at the time and their long-held personal preferences. Besides properties such as hue, saturation, and temperature (warm or cool) of colors, think about social and cultural symbolism and associations.

In her book, *Visualizing Culture: Analyzing the Cultural Aesthetics of the Web*, Roxanne O'Connell urges the reader to think in terms of color palettes, not individual colors, when designing a visualization or other graphic content for the Web.[23] O'Connell suggests creating a mood board for color before beginning a project using adjectives such as "dark, muted, bright, clean, soft, etc.," or a phrase such as "spring has sprung" or "have a nice day."[24] A mood board can be created using a social image aggregating site such as Pinterest or Polyvore.[25] I made this example for the phrase "have a nice day" using Polyvore. Using the color wheel can be helpful in creating a color mood board, as well.

Data Visualization Ethics

Color is also one of the easiest ways to do harm with a data visualization, that is, to create a visualization that misleads the reader. According to Stephanie Evergreen, author of *Effective Data Visualization* (2017), "At best data visualization errors are unintentional mistakes that lead to misinformation. At worst, they are purposeful manipulations designed to influence the story a graph can tell. Elements like the scale of the axis or the size and shape of the graph can distort data and produce interpretation errors."[26] Cairo urges information designers to avoid the temptation of dumbing down the data. Never underestimate the reader's intelligence, even if you are creating visualizations to be used outside the academic context (such as for fashion journalism). Cairo cites Charlotte's Web author E.B. White's book on writing, *The Elements of Style*: "No one can write decently who is distrustful of the reader's intelligence, or whose attitude is patronizing."[27] This is a good golden rule for the field of data visualization.

Types of Visualizations

1. Angela Zoss, of the Duke University Libraries, has put together a very thorough and helpful introductory guide to data visualization. The full list of visualization sub-types Zoss described, fifty in all, was inspired by B. Schneiderman's 1996 paper, "The Eyes Have It: A Task by Data Type Taxonomy for Information Visualizations"[28] and is available on the Duke University Libraries website,[29] so I won't try to reinvent the wheel here. Rather, after explaining the main types or families of data visualization, this discussion will focus on those most useful for various applications in fashion and textile studies.
2. D/Linear: Linear visualizations are rare. While data sets organized along a single dimension (such as "sunglasses worn by Karl Lagerfeld") are quite commonplace in all disciplines, including fashion studies, such a data set amounts to a list, and is simply listed as text rather than visualized. When a visual attribute, such as color—or in this case, shape—is integral to the one-dimensional data set, that data may be rendered as a visualization instead of a list, as with this example of the various theoretical types of UFOs (Figure 6.3).

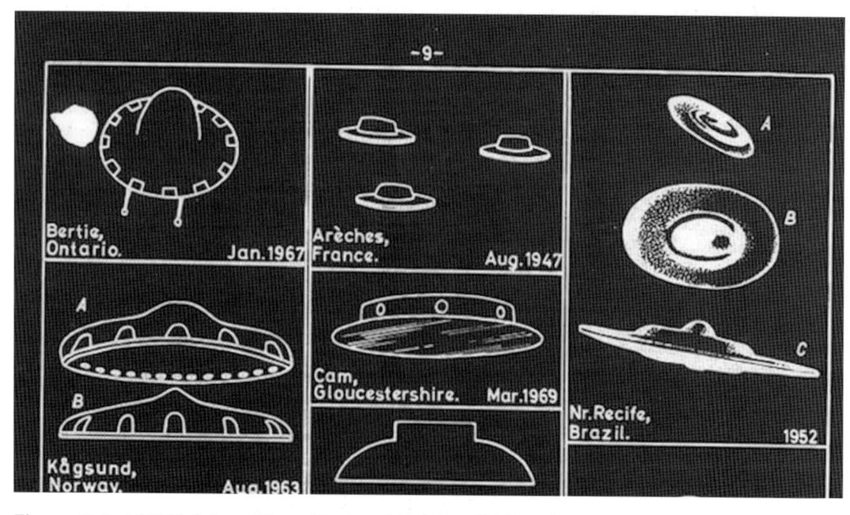

Figure 6.3 *UFO Sightings Chart, National Archives UK (1969).*

3. D/Planar: Most visualizations along two dimensions contain at least one data set that is geo-spatial in nature, and are thus rendered as maps. As an example: two data sets, both of which are spatial in nature, the so-called hippie trail from London to Bombay of the 1960s and 1970s and the points of origin of various Pakistani and northwest Indian *ralli* quilts, would be best visualized in one map.
4. D/Volumetric: 3D visualizations are mostly used in the hard sciences for studying surface and volume. Such visualizations can be used to study complex garment construction and couture techniques, however. Work done by curators and conservators at the Costume Institute at the Metropolitan Museum of Art to understand how Charles James created his incredibly complex patterns for *Charles James: Beyond Fashion* is a good example of this.
5. Temporal: Temporal visualizations, such as timelines, show changes of patterns in data over time, such as this graph showing the change in perception over time of what color constitutes the "new black."
6. Multidimensional: Multidimensional visualizations show proportion across demographic, economic, temporal, and other categories. When one thinks of data visualization, one is generally thinking of multidimensional visualization. Common charts and graphs with which most everyone is familiar, such as pie charts, histograms (bar graphs), and more recently, word and tag clouds, are multidimensional visualizations, as are more complex charts such as bubble charts, spider charts, and box and whiskers plots, and elaborate variations of these such as beeswarm and violin plots. Some types of multidimensional data visualizations are infrequently used due to high information density and low legibility.
7. Tree/Hierarchical: Various tree visualizations, including dendograms, radial trees, and tree maps, among others, visualize a hierarchy of data. Family trees are a common example. Although genealogical data do happen over time, births, marriages, and deaths are usually plotted on hierarchical trees rather than on timelines to show how the primary datum (the descendant) is related to the rest of the data set (the ancestors), or vice versa.
8. Network: Networks are complex visualizations that show the interconnected relationship of a variety of data sets or matrices. Tube or subway maps, such as this map of the London Underground, are a commonplace example of a network visualization (Figure 6.4).

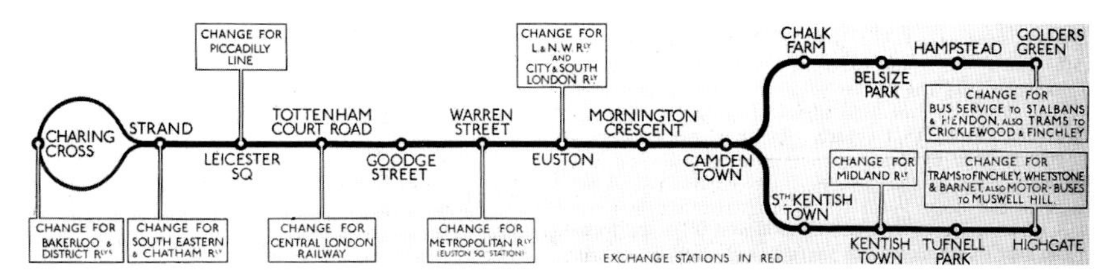

Figure 6.4 *London Underground Map,* Electric Railway Journal *(1908).*

The Visualization Process

It can be difficult to know where to begin the process of creating a data visualization. Cairo outlines a six-step process as follows (abridged from the original):

1. Define the focus of the graphic, what story you want to tell, and the key points to be made.
2. Gather as much information as you can about the topic you are covering.
3. Choose the best graphic form.
4. Complete your research.
5. Think about the visual style.
6. If you've been sketching offline, move the design to a computer.[30]

Even if you are working with a data set for academic purposes, it can be all too easy to skip over research steps 1–4 and commence from step 5, fantasizing about the colors, fonts, and the type of visualization that you will use. Do not let yourself fall into this trap. Do the research and create the data set first, and then play around with how best to visualize it.

Sketching is a crucial step in the process of data visualization. Moritz Stefaner, who has created visualizations of large data sets for organizations such as FIFA and Skype, said in an interview with Alberto Cairo: "I want to stress the importance of early sketches. If you are on the wrong track but you have only invested a day in them, then you are fine. You can easily throw them away and start over. But if you are on the wrong track and have invested six weeks in wonderfully rendered sketches, then you are in trouble."[31] Whether you sketch with paper and pen, or on the computer using an Adobe Creative Cloud product, or Tableau as Stefaner does, do not try to create a finished visualization without creating a mock-up sketch that you are satisfied with first.

Single Number Visualizations

In 2010, when I was working at the Quilt Index[32] as a research assistant, I worked with the programmers on staff to create a listing of the 200 most common quilt patterns (of over 4,000 unique patterns and 70,101 individual quilts) recorded on the Index. After each pattern name, I have included the number of quilts of that pattern that appeared on the Quilt Index as of May 1, 2017. The ten most common patterns are bolded.

Acorn (36)	Morning Star (477)
Airplane (var. aeroplane, airship, aircraft) (45)	Mosaic (467)
Album (1,054)	Necktie (157)
Attic Window (78)	New York Beauty (117)
Autograph (75)	Nine Patch **(2,674)**
Bachelor's Puzzle (28)	Nosegay (51)
Baltimore Album (61)	Oak Leaf (277)
Barn Raising (440)	Octagon (68)
Basket **(1,736)**	Ohio Rose (var. tree) (95)
Bear's Paw (var. claw, foot, tracks) (255)	Ohio Star (var. whirly gig) (431)
Big Dipper (26)	Old Maid's Puzzle (var. ramble, fancy, patience) (138)
Blazing Star (var. blazing sun, splendor) (309)	One Patch (621)
Block **(2,514)**	Orange Peel (162)
Bow Tie (556)	Orchid (39)
Broderie Perse (62)	Pansy (121)
Broken Dishes (247)	Peony (var. piney) (135)
Butterfly (572)	Periwinkle (100)
Cactus (94)	Philadelphia Pavement (var. patch, beauty) (42)
Cake Stand (95)	Pickle Dish (var. pickel dish) (51)
Calamanco (37)	Pictorial (116)
Capital T (18)	Pineapple (419)
Carolina Lily (var. rose, tulip) (186)	Pine Tree (179)
Carpenter's Wheel (var. square, star) (122)	Pinwheel (694)
Cathedral Window (var. cathedral glass, church window) (195)	Poinsettia (54)

(Continued)

Centennial (260)	Pomegranate (var. love apple) (97)
Century of Progress (26)	Poppy (119)
Charm (99)	Postage Stamp (var. square) (388)
Cherry Basket (var. cherry clusters, berry basket, fruit basket) (169)	Prairie Star (99)
Chevron (28)	Princess Feather (var. princess plume, prince's feather) (186)
Chimney Sweep (var. chimney block) (300)	Puritan Star (57)
Chips & Whetstones (57)	Puss in the Corner (147)
Chrysanthemum (32)	Pyramids (194)
Churn Dash (var. churn fly) (319)	Rail Fence (214)
Clamshell (20)	Railroad Crossing (31)
Clay's Choice (21)	Rainbow (383)
Cockscomb (131)	Redwork (279)
Compass (263)	Rising Sun (184)
Corn and Beans (var. corn crib) (72)	Rob Peter to Pay Paul (104)
Courthouse Square (451)	Rocky Mountain (68)
Crazy Quilt **(5,070)**	Rocky Road to California (60)
Cross Stitch (203)	Rocky Road to Kansas (22)
Crown of Thorns (170)	Rolling Star (87)
Dahlia (194)	Rolling Stone (87)
Daisy (184)	Roman Stripe (var. way, zig zag) (138)
Delectable Mountain (117)	Rose of Sharon (353)
Devil's Claws (var. footprints, puzzle, crossroads) (34)	Rose **(1,860)**
Diamond Field (425)	Rosebud (54)
Dogwood (104)	Sailboat (62)
Dolly Madison's Star (var. Dolly Madison's workbox, workshop) (20)	Sage Bud (var. sage bird) (33)
Double Irish Chain (var. ring, rose) (755)	Sampler (1,473)
Double T (155)	
Double Wedding Ring (1,549)	Sawtooth (452)
Double X (143)	Schoolhouse (75)
	Scrap Quilt **(2,834)**
Dresden Plate (var. platter, saucer, star, rose) (1,414)	Seven Sisters (91)
Drunkard's Path (var. trail, road, walk) (509)	Signature Quilt (539)
Duck and Ducklings (var. goose and goslings) (24)	Shoo Fly (296)

Dutch Girl (var. Dutch doll) (145)	Sister's Choice (30)
Dutchman's Puzzle (var. wheel, breeches) (41)	Six Pointed Star (202)
Economy (75)	Snail's Trail (64)
Eight Pointed Star (865)	Snowball (321)
Fan (1,171)	Snowflake (152)
Feathered Star (327)	Spider Web (var. spider den) (175)
Flower Basket (393)	Spool (83)
Flower Garden **(2,278)**	Square in a Square (251)
Flower Pot (95)	Star of Bethlehem (var. star of: the east, David, the Magi, the milky way) (492)
Flowering Almond (4)	Steps to the Altar (30)
Flying Geese (var. flock of geese, flying birds, flying mallards) (461)	Storm at Sea (23)
Flying Swallow (15)	Strawberry (34)
Fool's Puzzle (18)	Streak of Lightning (142)
	String Quilt (545)
Fox and Geese (55)	Strip Quilt (781)
Friendship (1,288)	Sugar Loaf (51)
Goose in the Pond (79)	Sunbonnet Sue (793)
Goose Tracks (88)	Sunburst (320)
Grandmother's Fan (379)	Sunflower (403)
Grandmother's Flower Garden **(1,715)**	Sunshine and Shadow (324)
Handy Andy (var. Overall Bill, Sam, Andy) (98)	Swastika (61)
Hawaiian Flag (82)	Texas Star (206)
Hearts & Gizzards (var. & darts, & pomegranates) (185)	Thousand Pyramids (var. thousand triangles) (71)
Hen and Chicks (27)	Thrifty (24)
Hexagon (673)	Tiger Lily (15)
Hit or Miss (var. hit and miss) (209)	Tree of Life (198)
Hole in the Barn Door (130)	Tree of Paradise (83)
Honeycomb (143)	Triangles (549)
Hour Glass (194)	Trip around the World (694)
Improved Nine Patch (127)	Triple Irish Chain (239)
Irish Chain (1,515)	Tulip (1,019)
Jacob's Ladder (255)	Tumbling Blocks (var. diamonds, hexagon, star) (320)

(Continued)

Joseph's Coat (var. coat of many colors) (66)	Turkey Tracks (var. turkey trot) (174)
Kaleidoscope (58)	Ulu (Breadfruit) (82)
Kansas Star (20)	Variable Star (237)
Kansas Sunflower (18)	Virginia Reel (49)
Kansas Troubles (29)	Virginia Star (26)
Lady of the Lake (91)	Wagon Wheel (43)
Laurel Wreath (49)	Wandering Foot (53)
LeMoyne Star (493)	Washington Sidewalk (26)
Lincoln's Platform (10)	Water Lily (39)
Liliuokalani's Fans and Kahilis (45)	Weathervane (30)
Log Cabin (var. straight furrow, sunshine and shadow) **(3,026)**	Wedding Ring **(1,854)**
Lone Star (1,300)	Wheel of Fortune (var. chance, life, mystery, time) (127)
Lover's Knot (var. lover's chain, true lover's knot) (111)	Whig Rose (var. democrat, Roosevelt rose) (216)
Maltese Cross (57)	Whig's Defeat (56)
Maple Leaf (204)	White House Steps (40)
Mariner's Compass (var. mariner's star) (224)	Whitework (50)
Martha Washington's Flower Garden (121)	Wholecloth (50)
Mayflower (31)	Wild Goose Chase (var. wild geese) (264)
Medallion (717)	Windmill (257)
Melon Patch (23)	World's Fair (34)
Milky Way (28)	Yankee Puzzle (var. yankee charm, doodle, star) (38)
Missouri Daisy (var. dahlia, rose, sunflower, belle) (40)	Young Man's Fancy (var. gentleman's fancy) (33)
Mist of Kaala (20)	Yo Yo (298)
Monkey Wrench (279)	Zig-Zag (110)
Morning Glory (85)	

To visualize this data set from the Quilt Index in a format other than a list, I began with a single number visualization. The most basic data visualization is the single integer, percentage, fraction, or ratio presented impactfully. Single number visualizations make sense if one single number is significant enough to tell the story (or rather, *a* story) of the data set. Evergreen quips: "Seriously, if you want people to remember just one number, just show them the number, really big."[33] In the example of frequency of quilt patterns appearing in the Quilt Index database, I had expected, given my familiarity with quilt history, that crazy quilts would be so much more common than even the second most frequent pattern. What I did not expect, however, was the ten most common quilt patterns—Crazy (5,070), Log Cabin (3,026), Scrap (2,834), Nine Patch (2,674), Block (2,514), Flower Garden (2,278), Rose (1,860), Wedding Ring (1,854), Basket (1,736), and Grandmother's Flower Garden (1,715)—would make up such a large percentage of the approximately 70,000 quilts on the Index: 36 percent. This percentage was so impressive to me—that out of over 4,000 unique quilt patterns, 36 percent are made up by just ten patterns—that it makes sense to visualize this number in this way (Figure 6.5).

Icon Arrays

An alternative to the single large number variation is the icon array. Evergreen defines icon arrays as: "Those visuals where one shape—sometimes a square, circle, or little dude—is repeated usually 10, 100, or 1,000 times and then some of the icons are color coded to represent a percentage or proportion."[34] If I had wanted to emphasize the fact that crazy quilts, with 5,070 individual examples, are by far the single most common pattern on the Quilt Index, I could have created a crazy quilt icon and repeated it many times (such as one icon per every 100 quilt records), but icon arrays are generally much more complicated to make, much more visually noisy, less striking, and less legible and impactful for the reader. Icon arrays are best attempted by those with very strong drawing and graphic design skills. Evergreen points out that "icon styles that don't look alike or appear too much like clip art can misrepresent your professionalism."[35] This icon array representing the cost of a wedding in New York City and its environs, for example, was done entirely with one clip art image. Furthermore, in this case, I decided that the percentage of the ten most common quilt patterns was a more interesting bit of data than the number of the single most common pattern. In data visualization, always let the type of datum dictate the best type of visualization (Figure 6.6).

The Cleveland-McGill Scale

When one thinks of visualizing a data set, often a basic bar graph or pie chart comes to mind. Pie charts are colorful, easy to make online, and when done right (for the right kind of data set) they are readily legible. There are several free,

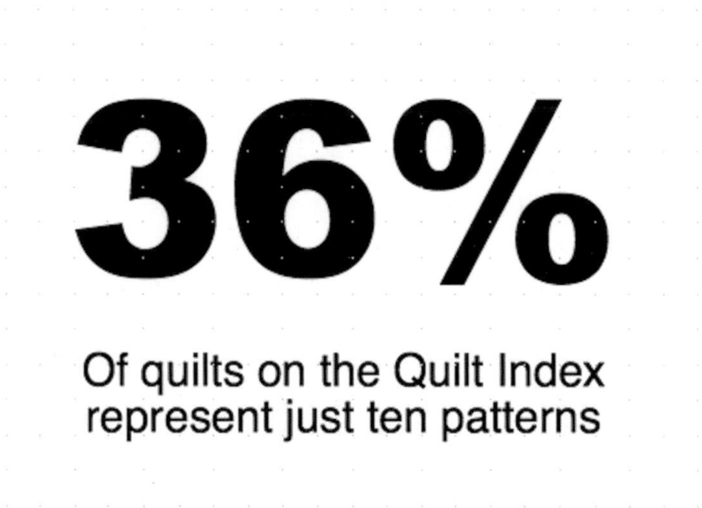

36%

Of quilts on the Quilt Index represent just ten patterns

Figure 6.5 *Single number visualization of the ten most common quilt patterns on the Quilt Index, Amanda Sikarskie.*

Figure 6.6 *Data visualization: The cost of a wedding, Amanda Sikarskie.*

easy-to-use websites to make such visualizations. Most word processing software packages also provide the tools to create simple data visualizations such as pie charts and bar graphs, and indeed many of the visualizations depicted in this chapter were made in Libre Office, a donation-based, open source program. Sometimes simple is indeed best, but how can I know that this is a good way to visualize the data? The first and most important metric is your own instinct. Does it look good? Does it readily communicate what it is supposed to? If not, what is wrong with it? Another approach to judge the success of a visualization is to show it to family and friends outside of your own academic discipline.

One of the best ways is to use the Cleveland-McGill scale. Created by William Cleveland and Robert McGill, two statisticians at AT&T Bell, in 1984, the scale ranks various visual perceptive tasks from those that allow the viewer to make more generic judgments to those that allow for more accurate judgments about the data. At the base of the scale, allowing the reader to make only the most generic judgments about a data set, is color saturation. Progressing up the scale toward allowing for more accuracy in making judgments about the data, in order, are: shading, curvature, volume, area (e.g., bubble charts), position along a nonaligned scale, and finally, position along a common scale (as in a bar graph)—the perceptive task that Cleveland and McGill argue allows for the most accurate judgments about a data set by a reader. A pie chart uses area and angle, but then positions these features along a common scale—the radial axis of the circle or pie. While this scale does not mean that visualizations using perceptive tasks lower on the scale are not useful or valid, the Cleveland-McGill scale does help to explain the general effectiveness and continued popularity of the humble pie chart and bar graph.

Gestalt Theory

Gestalt theory in a nutshell is the idea that the brain is made to detect patterns and that when confronted with a group of objects or images, the brain will aggregate them into a pattern based on the nature of the objects or images, both collectively and individually. The brain detects size, orientation (landscape or portrait), and color and shade pre-attentively—that is, before the viewer has even had time to process what they have seen.[36] While color saturation and shading are not very important on the Cleveland-McGill scale, they are of critical importance in Gestalt theory. Also key in Gestalt theory are connectedness (such as lines connecting forms), continuity, proximity, and similarity. Proximity is particularly important in the spacing of individual bars in a bar graph. As Cairo notes, "Objects close to each other will be perceived as belonging to a group."[37] Similarity—or the lack thereof—is crucial in conveying meaning for most types of data visualizations. "Objects that look alike will be identified as parts of a group."[38] It is a simple concept, so much so that it seems self-evident, but many a visualization has gone wrong because unlike data were made to look too similar, thus (unintentionally) inviting the reader to compare them, and vice versa.

Pie Charts

Trusting and following one's hunches is a good practice in data visualization, especially in a project's early stages. Returning to the example of patterns appearing in the Quilt Index database, instinct stopped me at the rough sketch stage from going any further. On the whole, 200 items, most of which represent tiny proportions of the whole, are simply too much data to visualize in a pie chart format. With a medium-sized data set of 200 items, these graphs and charts from school days work less well (I say "medium-sized" because scholars working with big data, very large data sets, can have hundreds of thousands or millions of unique items in a data set). So instead, I chose to make a pie chart of the same datum from the single number visualization example—the percentage of quilts on the Index made up by just those ten most common quilt patterns. This chart is quite legible and tells a truthful story of the most commonly occurring data, but unfortunately, these frequently made quilt patterns are only the tip of the iceberg. While the viewer can see that some numerous other patterns must make up the other 64 percent of the quilts on the Index, I needed a type of visualization that would allow me to clearly compare the relational size of the 200 quilt patterns all at once. More useful for visualizing this data set of popular quilt patterns is a tag cloud, which allows items that occur with greater frequency to have greater visual weight. To make one requires a little bit of mathematics (Figure 6.7).

Bad Pie Charts and Donut Charts

While there is an enduring preference for pie charts, they can be used badly. In fact, Evergreen avoids using them, if possible. She argues that "pie charts and donut charts get a bad rap—and for a good reason. That's graphing by angle and curvature, respectively, and we humans don't interpret those properties all too well."[39] This humorous pie chart visualizing the public reaction to the death of the pop artist Prince is an exaggerated example of a bad pie chart. Hundred

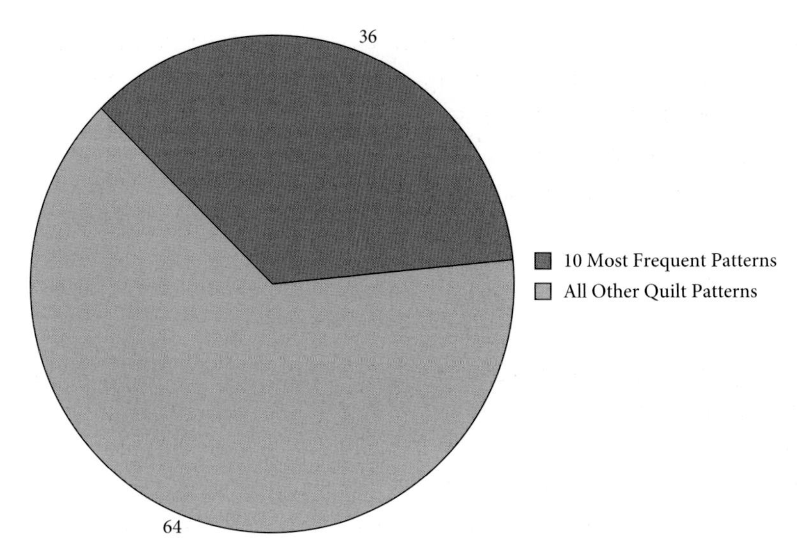

Figure 6.7 *Pie chart: Quilt Index, Amanda Sikarskie.*

percent of people represented in this fictitious survey were "sad," so the chart is nothing more than a light purple circle (Figure 6.8). Donut charts should really only be used to highlight one key number or statistic, as in the previous example. She continues, "The typical (typically bad) donut chart looks like a cousin of the traditional pie chart, with one major difference. The middle of the pie is gone. The middle of the pie … where the angle is established, which is what humans would look at to try to determine wedge size, proportion, and data."[40] Look at the pie chart of the percentage of occurrence of the ten most common patterns in the Quilt Index database, and your eye should linger heavily on the center of the pie, that key piece that is missing in a donut chart. While both pie charts and donut charts leave room for reader error by relying on visual perception skills, word clouds can be more straightforward for the reader.

Word Clouds

Word clouds, or tag clouds, are another type of visualization that is quite easy to make online using browser-based applications such as Wordle[41] and WordyUp.[42] Stephanie Evergreen defines word clouds as "a visual display of the most frequently used words in a given set of data, with a fun font and some eye candy color scheme."[43] Word clouds are great for those who are more linguistic, rather than visual or number-minded. Given that my background in fashion and textiles is as a historian rather than as a designer, I feel more

Figure 6.8 *Pie chart: Prince death reaction, Amanda Sikarskie.*

comfortable manipulating words than I do objects or forms. Perhaps this is why word clouds have always appealed to me. Word clouds are, however, the Rodney Dangerfields of the data visualization community, not getting as much respect as they deserve. Evergreen recalls: "My friend Humphrey Costello referred to word clouds as 'dog vomit.' Others have called them the mullet of the Internet."[44] This is partly because they focus on the low- to mid-level perceptive tasks of volume or area (and many of them intentionally confound direction, a higher-level perceptive task, as an aesthetic choice). But also, as Evergreen notes: "It is important to keep in mind that the purpose of a word cloud is not really to generate insight. It is to display the most frequently used words."[45] The reader needs to engage with a word cloud for a while to draw insights out of it. Unlike some other types of visualizations, they do not yield their full meanings immediately. This is likely one of the reasons that many people do not like them. We live in a fast-paced society in which immediacy is prized. People want meaning, and they want it now.

Word clouds can be created using word processing software, such as this example visualizing the popularity of various flavors of macarons. A 2014 Huffington Post article ranked the popularity of various flavors of macarons as follows[46]:

15. Rose
14. Vanilla
13. Lavender
12. Apricot
11. Hazelnut
10. Orange blossom
9. Salted Caramel
8. Chocolate
7. Lemon
6. Strawberry
5. Almond
4. Coffee
3. Passionfruit
2. Raspberry
1. Pistachio

To create a word cloud, I simply varied the font size for each data item, starting at 54 pt. font for pistachio and going down to the next lowest font size for each item on the list. Using word processing software also allows for maximum flexibility in the choice of color; in this case, the color of each word reflects the color that one might associate with the flavor (Figure 6.9). Word clouds can

Lavender Coffee Pistachio
Passionfruit Salted Caramel
Almond Strawberry Hazlenut Chocolate
Orange Blossom Rose Raspberry Apricot

Figure 6.9 *Word cloud data visualization: Macarons, Amanda Sikarskie.*

Figure 6.10 *Number cloud data visualization: Angel numbers, Amanda Sikarskie.*

also be combined with drawings or images, as in this example visualizing the belief in various angel numbers (Figure 6.10). To get the traditional look of a word cloud, however, a program designed specifically to generate word clouds should be used. While there are several web-based programs that generate word clouds, two of the most popular are Wordle and WordyUp. Wordle is free, while WordyUp is a subscription-based service requiring a fee. WordyUp does group words into clusters that appeared together when entered, however. For example, WordyUp would keep "Thierry Mugler" and "Mugler Circle" together in the visualization. This adds an additional layer of meaning to the word cloud, which, depending on the nature of the project, might make the subscription fee worth the cost.

A word cloud can be a useful way to visualize one's preconceptions or misconceptions about a data set. As someone who has studied quilt history, I was fairly confident that I could guess many of the ten most common patterns before I even ran the numbers. I chose: Baltimore Album (61), Crazy Quilt (5070), Double Wedding Ring (1549), Dresden Plate (1414), Grandmothers Flower Garden (1715), Irish Chain (1515), Log Cabin (3026), Lone Star (1300), Nine Patch (2674), and Sunbonnet Sue (793). While most of my hypotheses were on point, one quilt pattern, Baltimore Album, was not even close to the top ten, with a paltry 61 examples on the Quilt Index. Baltimore Album quilts are much researched and exhibited, but it seems that scholarly interest in them does not correlate to their commonness. Many date from the 1840s, so their relatively old age probably accounts for their scarcity.

At any rate, I made the word cloud using the advanced (and still free) version of Wordle.[47] The advanced version allows the user to weight the words based on how frequently they appear in the text or database. To do this, one simply enters into the text box in Wordle the word or phrase, followed by a colon, and the number of appearances made by the word. Use no spaces, no commas in the number values, and avoid other punctuation such as apostrophes or hyphens in the words and phrases themselves. For example:

Baltimore Album:61
Crazy Quilt:5070
Double Wedding Ring:1549
Dresden Plate:1414
Grandmothers Flower Garden:1715
Irish Chain:1515
Log Cabin:3026
Lone Star:1300
Nine Patch:2674
Sunbonnet Sue:793

The finished product does what a pie chart does—just in a different way. Rather than simply giving us a visualization of the percentages, such 36 percent and 64 percent, as fairly uniform pie pieces, the word cloud visually represents the frequency with which the quilts patterns occur by varying the font size of the word proportionally. Because those top ten, such as crazy quilt and nine patch, represent so much of the whole of the data set, their size is larger in relation to the other patterns, giving us the same visual cue as the pie chart that these few patterns are of paramount magnitude in the data set. Sunbonnet Sue, with only 793 records on the Quilt Index, appears quite small next to the others, and Baltimore Album, with its 61 records, is in a font so small that it is almost invisible to the human eye! The tiny horizontal line above the left side of the "u" in Crazy Quilt is actually the phrase "Baltimore Album." Such a minuscule rendering visually makes the point that, contrary to my hypothesis, Baltimore Album quilts are very much in the minority of all quilt records on the Quilt Index (Figure 6.11).

Figure 6.11 *Tag cloud: Common patterns on the Quilt Index, Amanda Sikarskie.*

A Word about 3D Modeling

3D modeling can be considered another type of data visualization. In the fashion world, "modeling" generally refers to the wearing—for demonstration purposes—of the latest designer clothing. The other kind of modeling with which those of us on the historical side of fashion may be less familiar—the creation of a model based on a physical object. Designers, and anyone who uses AutoCAD (a popular and robust computer-aided design program), of course use 3D modeling to render garments and accessories prior to production. 3D modeling files are also used in 3D printing and in online gaming, such as Minecraft and Second Life. 3D modeling also has great potential for teaching in apparel design and historic dress classes, and in the presentation of research in these areas.

Designers take courses devoted solely to learning CAD, so the nuts and bolts of creating and manipulating 3D modeling files, such as polygonal modeling and scanline rendering, cannot be discussed here. For those unfamiliar with CAD, however, there are ways to get your feet wet in 3D modeling. One is Thingverse. Thingverse is a database, but unlike those discussed in Chapter 1, the files contained within the database are not 2D image files (fashion photography, photos of museum objects, scans of documents, etc.), but rather, they are crowdsourced 3D model files created and submitted by the community. Searching the Thingverse database is much like querying any other database, however. The front end of the database is set up for simple keyword searches such as "dress" or "coat." Many of the models on Thingverse are architectural in nature, but many are dress and accessories files as well, such as clothing designed for fit on a 3D scale model of the *Venus de Milo*. All 3D model files on the site are free to download and manipulate.

Having viewed and downloaded 3D model files, a good intermediary step before moving on to the complex world of AutoCAD is a lighter (and free) CAD software program called Tinkercad. If, after downloading and playing around with Tinkercad, 3D modeling still seems like an avenue worth exploring, go ahead and purchase the more robust AutoCAD software (and consider taking a class on it). One nice thing about AutoCAD is that it has a mobile version. In addition to AutoCAD, a couple specialized 3D simulation software programs that have been used to build models for historic costume education include Lectra Modaris (and Lectra Modaris 3D Fit) and Gerber Automark (and Gerber Automark 3D).

Above all, the type of visualization and the software to be used are a function of the nature of the data set and what the researcher wishes to communicate about it. As Cairo writes in *The Functional Art*, "This is one of the most important principles to remember when dealing with infographics and visualizations: The form should be constrained by the functions of your presentation."[48] The desire to use a particular type of visualization or a particular application should never guide this decision-making process; let the data itself dictate the form that the visualization will take.

7 Mapping

Maps are the most specialized, and yet the most familiar, form of data visualization. They are with us from childhood—the Hundred Acre Wood in *Winnie the Pooh*, Middle Earth in *The Lord of the Rings*, Hogwarts on the Marauders' Map in *Harry Potter and the Prisoner of Azkhaban* all come alive through maps. From Piglet's house to Professor Dumbledore's office, reading maps means much more than simply taking in the sum of their parts. Judith Tyner in *The World of Maps: Map Reading and Interpretation for the 21st Century* writes that "map interpretation, rather than focusing on determining distances, elevations, locations, and quantities, brings all of these basic tasks together to paint a picture of the nature of an area, its physical and/or human features."[1] Interpreting maps—to say nothing of making them—gives the map-reader a sense of mastery and control over their environment. It is no coincidence that the entrance of the map—with its affirmational and resounding song of "I'm the map!"—is one of the most energetic and exciting points in each episode of beloved children's television series *Dora the Explorer*. The map—and her ability to read and interpret it—functions as a key source of agency for Dora. Above all, maps help us to recognize, describe, and correlate different patterns,[2] and the ability to interpret them gives us the confidence to make our own way—through unfamiliar terrain, or for scholars, through a data set. "I'm the map!" indeed.

Of the many types of data visualization, mapping is also perhaps the most useful for textile studies. Computer mapping is quite helpful for layering social and economic data[3]—the sorts of data encountered in fashion studies work.

> As statistical analysis become more sophisticated, the visualizations that resulted became more and more central to the argument. In some cases, the visualization made the interpretation possible. These success stories demonstrated the worth of statistical analysis and visualization. Arguably the most notable example is John Snow's map of the incidence of cholera in an 1854 London outbreak, which helped plot the source of that outbreak to a single water pump in the neighborhood. Snow's cholera map showed that visualizations could serve as both narrative and analysis.[4]

While computer applications have leveled the playing field—individuals have been able to make commercial-quality maps at home since the 1990s[5]—map-making for social history properly dates to the nineteenth century, when John Snow revolutionized the practice of history by mapping London's 1854 cholera outbreak.

Reading Maps

Like other types of data visualization, maps are quite powerful. According to Black, "Visual representation in a map is a more effective way to suggest patterns of distribution and causation than talking or writing."[6] Recall that the human brain is always searching for patterns. Maps give the mind and eye what they are looking for, and quickly. Furthermore, like other media discussed thus far in this book—social media posts and other types of data visualizations such as pie charts and word clouds—maps both are immediately legible and require a second (and a third) read to be fully understood. As Black notes, "In one sense, readers can take in the contents of a map at a glance. In another, they have to teach themselves to study maps—as art historians do with paintings [or fashion historians do with dress]—very carefully indeed, and this takes time."[7] Take for example this map of Spitalfields, a neighborhood in London's East End.

The silk industry in Spitalfields was bolstered economically and politically in the eighteenth century by a prevailing mood of protectionism. In 1721, the importation of printed calico was prohibited, and then in 1766, a ban for the import of French silk (which was the primary source of both inspiration and competition for the weavers of Spitalfields) cemented the prosperity of the Huguenot silk weavers: The Spitalfields Acts of 1773. With the free trade reforms of 1826, the silk industry collapsed, almost overnight.

> London can be a grief-inducing city. Everyone loves the London they first knew, whether as the place they grew up or the city they arrived in, and everyone loses it. As the years pass, the city bound with your formative experience changes, bearing less and less resemblance to the place you discovered. Your London is taken from you. Your sense of loss grows until eventually your memory of the London you remember becomes more vivid than the London you see before you and you become a stranger in the place that you know best. This is what London can do to you."[8]

A look at the OpenStreetMap of residential Spitalfields today shows the same street names upon which many of the Huguenot silk weavers of the seventeenth

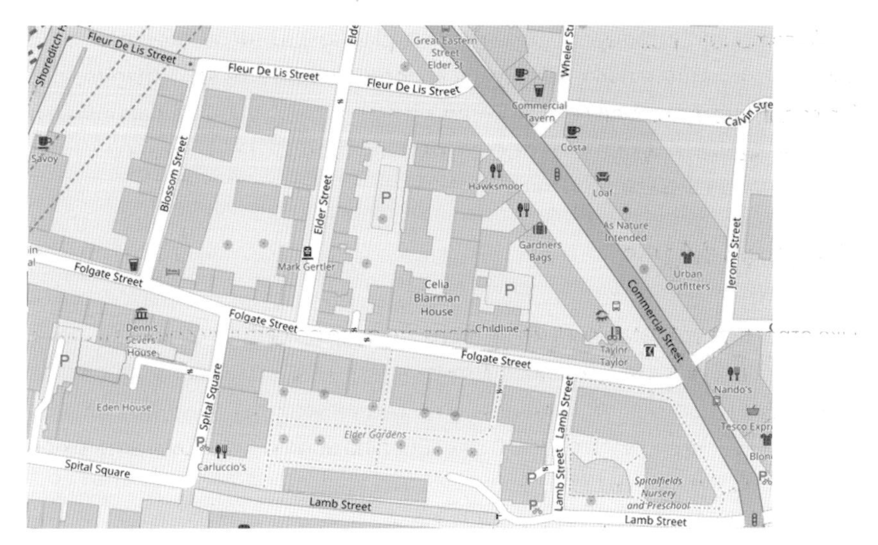

Figure 7.1 *Open Street Map: Spitalfields, London.*

and eighteenth centuries lived—Elder Street, Folgate Street, Lamb Street, etc.—but the neighborhood is decidedly not one that the weavers would recognize. Note the Urban Outfitters, the Nando's, and the Tesco Express (Figure 7.1). Incidentally, the weavers of Spitalfields were never able to reap the benefits of the newly invented Jacquard loom, which was surely to have revolutionized their designs. Still, the silk industry had contributed enormously to the development of modern Britain. Adam Geczy argues that it was the prohibition of Indian printed cotton imports in 1721 that gave rise to the Industrial Revolution.[9] As we will see later in this chapter, this natural process of change over time in the urban landscape makes mapping dress and textile *history* quite difficult with easy-to-use sites such as OpenStreetMap and directions sites like Google Maps. This becomes increasingly the case as the further one is removed from the present time.

Types of Maps

Most maps created to visualize geographic data related to fashion and textiles are thematic, rather than general reference maps. Thematic maps illustrate a particular topic, such as trade, agriculture, or population.[10] A map of the Empire Polo Fields in Indio, California, showing the density of clothing vendors in proximity to the various stages at the Coachella music festival, for example, would be a thematic map. Many of these thematic maps are also historical—that is, maps created in the present to visualize place-based data of the past. (It should be noted that there exists a distinction between these historical maps, and *historic* maps, maps created in the past, but still very much of use to the historian.)

A map indicating dusty areas at Coachella—where one could accidentally soil their designer boots—would be a topographic map, however. Topographic maps emphasize physical features of a terrain, and creating them may be helpful for textile scholars in answering questions related to pre-modern fabric and dye production and trade routes. As Tyner notes, "A topographic map carries a wealth of information. To a large degree, the interpretation of such a map depends on the ability to distinguish many overlapping patterns, one from another."[11] Topographic maps relay information about not only terrain and drainage, but also cultures (e.g., transport, settlements, and economic information) and occupancy (e.g., population density and distribution, economic production, agriculture).[12] A topographic map is used to better understand trade routes of medieval silk later in this chapter.

Projections

All flat, two-dimensional maps, regardless of their type, must also make use of a projection style. The projection is the means by which the cartographer translates the spherical globe into a flat image. Projection styles include conic, azimuthal, and cylindrical (such as the familiar Mercator projection). In map-making, the choice of projection is nearly as important as the type of map itself. This is because each projection produces a different zone of least deformation. Deformation necessarily occurs in the translation of the three-dimensional earth into a two-dimensional map. In *The World of Maps*, Judith Tyner explains deformation occurs when any of the following essential characteristics of the globe become distorted: parallels, meridians, area scale, and distance scale.[13]

The zone of least deformation is thus a privileged space on the map, which is rendered most closely to geo-spatial reality. The cylindrical Mercator was a highly popular projection in the twentieth century, in part because its zone of least deformation falls along the earth's equator. So much of the global population lives close enough to the tropics of Cancer and Capricorn such that most populated areas are not too badly affected in the Mercator projection. Because of their great distortion of the poles, however, "in 1999, the various cartographic organizations got together to recommend against using cylindricals for most purposes—especially education."[14] Given that in the Mercator projection, the Arctic—Alaska, northern Canada, Greenland, Scandinavia, and Russia—and the Antarctic are extremely distorted in a cylindrical projection of the globe, spatial data from one of these places are better served by an azimuthal projection, which places some point on the earth's surface, such as the north or south pole, in the zone of least deformation at the center of the map.

If one wants to put Coachella at the center of the world, an azimuthal projection works quite well. For spatial data not focused around a particular point, azimuthal projections can be quite limiting. Conic projections have largely replaced the Mercator for educational purposes such as the illustration of research. According to Tyner: "They [conic projections] are best for midlatitude areas with east-west extent … The United States is most often shown on a conic."[15] Europe is as well. It is well-noted that all of these map projections have political and philosophical implications. Locations within the zone of least deformation are emphasized and rendered more accurately than others. The longstanding convention of placing north at the top of a flat map or globe minimizes the importance of the Global South and perpetuates colonialism.

Remote Sensing and GIS

For most of the history of map-making, map data were created through exploration and surveying. Now, most geographic data are generated through remote sensing, satellite (and aerial) images created of a place without the map-maker actually being in contact with that place. Whereas before cartographers had to physically explore and measure the earth in order to map it, maps of the most distant locations, harsh climates, and politically unstable regions may be made with satellite data anywhere in the world. Geographic Information Systems (GIS) is one digital program that can turn raw spatial data into maps, though there are many others as well, such as Google Earth.

GIS is often perceived as difficult, yet powerful mapping software. While GIS is certainly used to make maps, it is first and foremost a database application. As Ian Gregory and Paul Ell explain in *Historical GIS*, "What makes it unique is that the GIS combines attribute data, which describe the object, with spatial data, which say where the object is located. Traditionally, attribute data would have been statistical [quantitative] or textual [qualitative]; however, more recently, images, sound, video, and other multi-media formats are used."[16] GIS does indeed have a steep learning curve, although many scholars view GIS as the only mapping software worth using. Gregory and Ell take a more moderate view: "GIS is effectively a spatial database technology concerned with structuring, integrating, visualising and analysing spatially referenced data … It is, however, a huge mistake to equate GIS and mapping as one in the same. If a researcher is simply interested in creating a number of maps as part of a research article, then conventional cartography—probably using a computer—is likely to be the best way to proceed (Knowles, 2000)."[17] For projects on a small scale, with a lot of street-level data, researchers may be better off buying and learning GIS. Writing on his GIS-based project, *Digital Harlem*, Stephen Robertson explains:

> Harlem became the 'Negro Mecca' (a more cosmopolitan place than America's other 'black metropolis,' Chicago), deserving of the title, 'the world's black capital.' … The picture of Harlem that I have presented so far is in line with those you would find setting the scene for most studies of the neighborhood or offering a snapshot in some broader account. After six years of sing digital geospatial tools to study Harlem, I am struck by how much that picture omits and how little sense of the place it conveys … GIS organizes and integrates sources on the basis of their shared geographic location—in this case an urban setting, their street address. Working with addresses involved thinking about Harlem on a much smaller scale than other scholars.[18]

Gregory and Ell offer that "a more positive approach as to what GIS has to offer is simply that it should encourage historians to think more carefully about geography and the impact and importance of location."[19] Free software with a shallow learning curve, such as OpenStreetMap or Google Earth, tends to be best for big picture maps, as seen in the Milanese example featured later in this chapter.

Density, Scale, and Color

Since maps are just a specialized kind of data visualization, the qualities that must be balanced in the creation of any data visualization—abstraction and figuration, functionality and decoration, density and lightness, multidimensionality and unidimensionality, originality and familiarity, and novelty and redundancy[20]—must be balanced in the production of maps as well. Information-density overload can be a particular challenge with maps, but John Theibault suggests that adding a temporal dimension adds density without compromising on transparency. "Complex visualizations based on maps are emerging as part of a 'geospatial turn' in the humanities. One particular way that geospatial information density can increase is by animating it, adding time as another dimension of visualization."[21] The importance of scale is also paramount in mapping projects.

Scale is a fundamental aspect of human visual perception and is often where the battle of legibility and truthfulness in a map is won or lost.

In terms of their production, one area in which maps differ from other forms of data visualization is the importance of color. "The desirability of color is also an issue … Commonly judged essential for illustrations, colour is often used to make maps more striking rather than more informative. Given its cost, colour often yields a surprisingly poor return in scholarly terms, and good black and white may even be preferable."[22] Little or nothing is lost in translation by the reproduction of the maps in this chapter in black and white, for example. Still, while color is of less import to mapping than other visualization techniques, color can perform as a strong supporting character in historical thematic maps. For maps visualizing fashion data of a particular decade—say the 1950s, '60s, '70s, or '80s—the color palette of the map may be chosen to reflect the predominant color palette of the time period. For instance, a map of the global wool trade in the 1970s would be rendered appropriately in rich 1970s hues of gold, moss, and ochre.

When color is of particular import to the people of the location being mapped, however, those colors should be considered for *sensitive* incorporation into the mapping project. For example, ralli quilts made in the deserts of Pakistan and northwest India call to mind a very distinct color palette, as does the desert environment itself. In an essay for the exhibition catalog for *Textiles and Ornaments of India*, which was held at the Museum of Modern Art, New York in 1955, Pupul Jayakar also noted the role of the sun in the appreciation of the textiles of northwest India:

> In the west, we find a great belt stretching from Sind to Baluchistan through Kathiawar and Rajasthan to Gujarat, where the bare stretches of sand, the intolerable heat of the noonday sun, and the fantastic twisted forms of cactus and the thorny babul tree, demand compensation in the deep glowing colors of the resist- and tie-dyed cloths of this area.[23]

"The extravagant and unforgettable colors at first seem to clash before occidental eyes, but they soon assert surprising harmonies."[24] Monroe Wheeler also notes the cultural importance of color in his introduction to *Textiles and Ornaments of India*: "But many a foreign traveler, when asked what has given him the most intense pleasure, will speak of the beauty of the multitudes of people in their fairy-tale raiment, of all colors of the rainbow."[25] Finally, Jayakar noted the role of the desert in the production of color:

> Color was not a pigment applied to the surface; it so permeated the fabric that it became an integral part of the material. A superlative knowledge of color

chemistry and of the rich resources of madder dyeing gave to India's colored cloths a quality of growth and maturing, in which the colors ripened in the sun. The sun was a catalytic agent which constantly acted and reacted upon the minerals, vegetables, and water, so that color came to life in response to the sun's rays; the fading too was like flowers that age in the sun, giving back their color to the energy that gave it birth. Fading was a graceful process of soft tones unutterably beautiful ... the red and the ochre colors of the earth and the green fields of the countryside; in this process no cloth looked drab or ugly but only grew older with the body of the person who wore it.[26]

A map or any other kind of data visualization presenting information about ralli quilts should be made with the "deep, glowing" colors of the region in mind. The participatory turn in mapping opened map-making up to a much broader population, meaning that the honoring of regional and cultural elements such as color in cartography, and maps made from the perspective of the Global South, is all the more likely.

The Participatory Turn in Mapping

In the 1960s, interpersonal communication theory was applied to cartography in the form of the MCM, the Map Communication Model. The MCM was predicated upon the notion that the cartographer and the map user are disparate entities and that the map serves as a go-between. The notion of participatory mapping—that map users can be map makers—is as pivotal a shift in mapping as the shift from topographic to thematic mapping that began in earnest with Snow's work on cholera in the nineteenth century. GIS has been considered the gold standard in mapping software since at least the 1980s, but the best software to use in participatory mapping is much less clear. Plantin defines GIS as "a geo-referenced database associated with software that enables the introduction of queries."[27] GIS allows the user to ask questions of spatial data and visualize the answers (mapping is just another type of data visualization, after all) on a map.

Plantin notes that "GIS are inadequate to show a range of information coming from the population" and points to more user-friendly online mapping software, such as Google Maps, as the best platforms for participatory mapping. "It is not a set of tools and techniques specific to online mapping systems—led by Google Maps—that have made them more successful than GIS and PPGIS, but their ability to facilitate the participation of a very large number of people and their adaptability to different uses."[28] Participatory mapping aims "to gather local knowledge and experiences, following a bottom-up approach to data collection with the concerned populations [WEI 02, p.5],"[29] while "neogeography refers to a number of practices that aim to produce geographical information or applications designed by non-geographers and non-cartographers," adding, "it is not so much about replacing a professional geographical practice, but rather about enriching it."[30] Scholars of fashion studies can become neo-geographers both to be good digital citizens, adding local knowledge of fashion-related locations to online maps for the benefit of all, and to pose and investigate research questions. While GIS is designed to query spatial data, online, participatory maps, such as the OpenStreetMap, are also rich potential research sites and tools.

The OpenStreetMap and Crowdsourced Mapping

The software used by the OpenStreetMap is much easier to use than GIS, making OpenStreetMap a tool that anyone can start using immediately either to plot locations or to use existing map data submitted by other contributors for research purposes. OpenStreetMap works best for fashion scholarship that queries trends or processes in the present day, rather than of long ago. As we saw in the Spitalfields example, while the streets may have the same names and be in the same places, often little else will have remained the same.

One of the main uses of OpenStreetMap for scholars outside fashion studies is the generation of impact of maps on the lives of communities affected by disaster, such as Haiti relief effort mapping after the earthquake (or Houston after the flood), crisis mapping, and disaster management. Scholars create maps that are generative of policy recommendations for state and local government agencies and zoning agencies. This speaks to the credibility of OpenStreetMap. OpenStreetMap is styled as a wiki for maps, with wiki like control. It is edited by crowdsourcing, what geographer Jean-Christophe Plantin calls "volunteered geoinformation" or "participatory geoinformatics."[31] This is community-driven scholarship. Scholars do not need to study the maps as if it were a colony of ants—from above and afar—but rather, can dive in and become a part of the crowd.

Anyone can edit the OpenStreetMap. To add a clothing store, select the location on the map and use one of the following tags: shop=fashion, shop=clothes, or shop=boutique. These tags correlate to a purple shirt icon which appears on the map and plots the location. Tags are key value pairs, not freestanding on the map, but always connected to a node (a point of interest on the map, such as

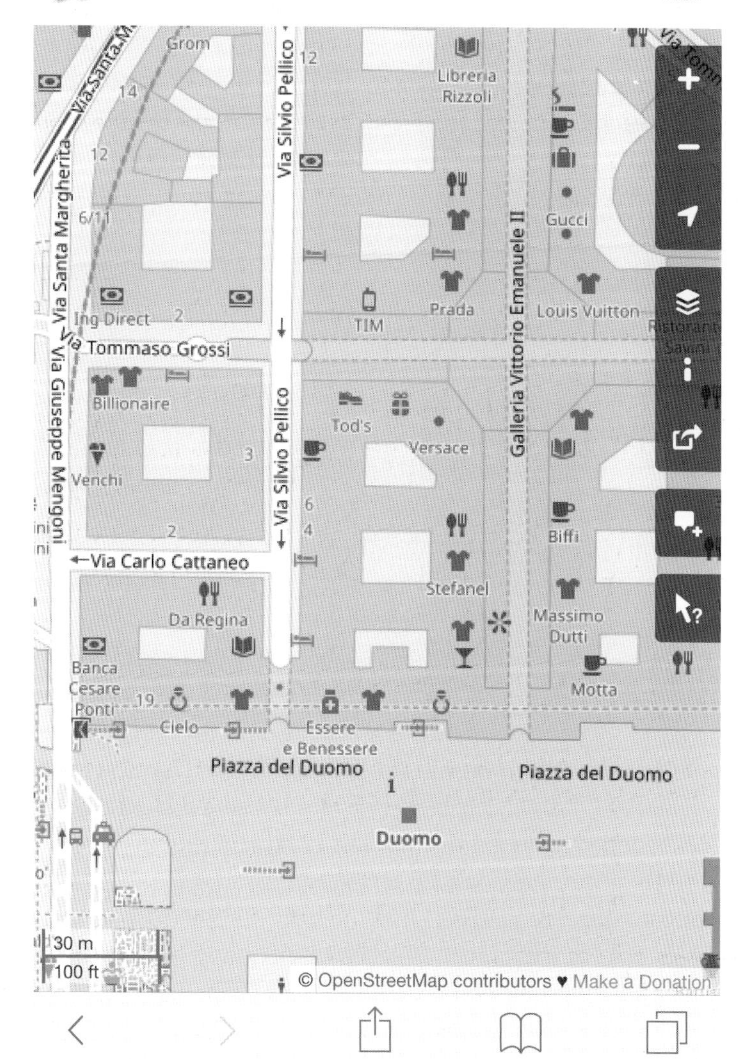

Figure 7.2 *OpenStreetMap: Boutiques of Milan, Italy.*

a shop), a way, or a relation. There has been a proposal within the community to differentiate these tags through different icons, such as a black T-shirt for shop=boutique. These community-generated nomenclatures are known as folksonomies.

Milan, Italy, is of course one of the world fashion capitals, and this view just north of the *Plaza del Duomo* in Milan shows many stores that have been added by OpenStreetMap users, including Prada and Gucci. The map of Milan in this example is a dot distribution or dot density map. It is a one-to-one map, meaning that each T-shirt icon represents the location of only one shop, rather than a one-to-many density map, which would let one icon on the map stand for multiple shops, suggesting the density of retail clothing stores in a particular area (Figure 7.2).

Research informed by OpenStreetMap could investigate topics such as fashion deserts in cities and rural areas. The proximity of such events to other sites within the city or to particular neighborhoods or demographics yields interesting information for researchers. Users interested in fashion can help the OpenStreetMap by mapping pop up shops and other ephemeral fashion events and mapping fashion week events. Futures of the OpenStreetMap include improved accessibility for visually impaired persons, AIs (machine learning) as map editors, offline editing and rendering, investigating geospatial extensions to make it easier for OpenStreetMap data to talk to other databases.

Qualitative and Quantitative Mapping

Like many of the research methods described in this book, thematic maps may be either qualitative or quantitative. Both qualitative and quantitative maps can use point symbols, or dots, to express the density of distribution of a particular feature, such as woolen mills or indigo plants, across the map area. This is called a "simple dot distribution" map,[32] or as I like to think of them: a "polka dot map." Both these kinds of maps also use linear symbols (e.g., roads) and areal symbols, shaded areas of distributions of icons that, like point symbols, show the density of distribution of a particular feature. Although they use the same symbolic language, qualitative and quantitative maps differ in their use of numbers.

Quantitative maps attach a particular number, born out of the data set that the map visualizes, to each symbol, for example: 1 dot = 100 indigo plants, or to return to the example of Coachella: 1 dot = 10 flower crown vendors. There are several specialized types of quantitative thematic maps. Choropleth maps are quantitative maps which feature shaded areas representing numerical values.

Cartograms are maps on which numerical values for distance are scaled against another value, such as time. Qualitative maps, on the other hand, do not provide hard and fast quantities, focusing instead on the general pattern of distribution.

Trade Routes of Viking Silk

Mapping is often done for the purpose of visualization for greater historical understanding, in this case: mapping cities along known trade routes. In her book *Silk for the Vikings*, Marianne Vedeler, an historical archaeologist at the University of Oslo, analyzes the discovery silk at two key Viking sites: the Oseberg ship burial in Norway and Jelling in Denmark (home of the famous runestone of Jelling). Silk was mentioned in the Norse Sagas of the eleventh century, both the word *silki* and *gudvef*. "The term gudvef literarily means 'god-weave,' or a good and costly fabric."[33] Thor Ewing has argued that the terms "silk" and "god-weave" were synonymous.[34] Silk was a highly gendered commodity among the medieval Norse. Silk is most often found in female burials.

Vedeler articulates two main theories explaining the movement of silk via trade routes to Scandinavia in the Middle Ages: "Following the major routes of exchange, the eastern silk could have come to Scandinavia either from the Baltic areas through the Russian waterways, or through trading stations in western Europe."[35] Despite the fact that the Norse discovered silk through interaction with the Byzantines, most silk in medieval Scandinavia was imported not from Constantinople via Western Europe, but via trade routes stretching from the Middle East and Central Asia up through Eastern Europe. Most silk found at the Oseberg site was woven in Central Asia, while only two examples were Byzantine or Mediterranean in origin.[36] Vedeler argues based on this and other archaeological evidence "that the eastern routes along the Russian river systems were probably used for transporting the precious silk during most of the Viking Age."[37] Mario Novak, an archaeologist at the Institute for Archaeological Research, Zagreb, Croatia, notes that the early medieval period in southeastern Europe, roughly from the sixth through the twelfth centuries, was a time of profound political, social, and economic change, yet few written sources survive from this period. This already scant historical record is particularly limiting when dealing with rural areas and marginalized peoples.[38]

Two primary routes made up the network of Russian rivers that served this trade between Central Asia and Scandinavia. The first and more easterly route went north up through the Caspian Sea, along the Volga through the cities of Bulghar and Jaroslavl. The second, more westerly route went north up through the Black

Sea, along the Dnjepr River and passing through Kiev and Novgorod.[39] The route of legendary trader Ibn Fadlands began in Baghdad, passing through Bukhara (a trading post situated near the major cities of Samarkand and Tashkent), before concluding in Bulghar, where goods destined for the Norse could then be sent on up the Volga.[40]

Scandinavian presence in the Volga dates to at least the early 800s, even earlier than the Dnjepr. There were several trade routes connecting the Black Sea and the Caspian Sea, an area dominated by Jewish merchants during the early Middle Ages. Period writing by Muhammad ibn Ishak describes Slavic trade routes in this way: "As for the Slavs, they take fox and beaver skins from the most distant Slav territory and come to the Roman Sea [Black Sea] and the King of Byzantium imposes the duty of ten per cent on them. Then they go by sea to Samkush of the Jews."[41] According to Vedeler, female burials at a fort called Sarskoe Gorodishche, near Rostov, have yielded Scandinavian jewelry from *c.* the 830s, as well as silk of various dates and origins.[42] The archaeological record thus supports a strong trade network through the Dnjepr, even while historical evidence suggests that heavy taxation made trade in the area undesirable. "It has been argued that the establishment of taxation posts along the Dnjepr blocked the trade from Scandinavia from the last decades of the 9th till the mid-10th century. But there is no reason to believe that the Kiev realm would have been interested in hindering Scandinavian trade by tax overload. On the contrary, the keepers of Kiev strongholds were probably interested in encouraging trade along the Dnjepr."[43] This is not to say that trade relations in the region always went smoothly. Prince Oleg of Kiev, for example, attacked Constantinople in the year 907. In the *Primary Chronicle*, a history of Kievan Rus from the ninth to the twelfth centuries, a historian recalls: "The Russes unfurled their sails of brocade and the Slavs their sails of silk, but the wind tore them. Then the Slavs said, 'Let us keep our canvas ones. Silken sails are not made for the Slavs.' So Oleg came to Kiev, bearing palls, gold, fruit and wine, along with every sort of adornment."[44] While these period anecdotes are colorful and interesting, relying solely on the historical record still does not give us a clear picture for the preference of one silk route over the other. Mapping the trade routes of medieval Eastern Europe and Central Asia can help to explain this phenomenon.

Overlaying Data Sets and Mapping Transport History

Jeremy Black argues that, in terms of social history, the history of trade and transport is one of the fields best analyzed through mapping. "It [transport] lends itself readily to mapping: not only routes and volumes, but also changes with what they suggest about shifts in perception of space."[45] Concepts like near and far are relative. Map-making sheds light not only on our perception of space, but also on near and far, Western and non-Western, etc. "The mapping of transport history is greatly dependent on data availability, not least because the quantifiable information also throws light on the qualitative nature of the system."[46] Mapping of trade routes and other transport data-based maps naturally invites mixed-methods research.

Maps in *Silk for the Vikings* show rivers and changes in elevation, but no other physical features, such as forests.[47] As I read Vedeler's book, I wondered: to what extent did physical geography play a role in the preference for one silk route over the other? What would happen if these trade routes were visualized with physical, rather than political, maps? Overlaying terrain onto political, social, and economic in detail maps can help to show the proximity of trade routes to specific physical features of the landscape. Most of us are used to making maps on directions sites and mobile apps such as Google Maps, Apple Maps, and MapQuest. Unfortunately, while these sites are easy to use and generally allow for customization of routes, they are quite limited in mapping global fashion and textiles. Because of ongoing conflicts in the Middle East, these directions sites will not permit the user to create routes through countries such as Afghanistan. Afghanistan and its neighbors were part of the Hippie Trail in the 1960s and 1970s (a much more peaceful for most of the Middle East).

Mapping historical fashion and textiles poses yet another difficulty on these directions sites to which most of us are accustomed. These sites are designed to give driving directions on roadways, but most modern roads simply did not exist hundreds of years ago, even as dirt roads. For much of European history, for example, goods were typically transported from city to city along rivers. But how to map trade routes along rivers? In this case, with the variables of the passage of time, and riparian trade rather than overland, it is sensible to create maps using GIS, or to work with a colleague who can. Another advantage of working with GIS for a project such as this is that "it is possible to superimpose layers of data onto chosen based maps. In former days this could only be done by placing a tracing of one map on top of another, and then only if they were the same scale."[48] To conclude the case of the Viking silk: "When the silk reached the Scandinavian region, it had come a long way from its original areas of production. Some of the original meanings of patterns and colours may have got lost. But as in the production areas, prestige and power were closely connected to silk."[49] Using Russian rivers was likely cheaper and easier than using the route across Western Europe that stretched from Constantinople to Venice and up through France that is so commonly associated with medieval European trade.

Mapping the Discovery of the Hope Diamond

Whereas silk is pliable, smooth but also soft, diamonds are hard, more akin to fire or ice than liquid. Nonetheless, the material trade networks dedicated to the material are just as well illuminated, if not more so, by digital mapping techniques. Surely no material has the capacity to sparkle—and fascinate—like the diamond. And no diamond has fascinated the world more than the Hope Diamond, with its dazzling blue color, whopping 44 ½ carats, and supposed curse. More fascinating on a scholarly level, though, is the location of the Hope Diamond's discovery and its journey from India to France, Britain, and ultimately the United States. The diamond was acquired in India by legendary French explorer and merchant Jean-Baptiste Tavernier. He sold the diamond, which he called "*le beau violet*," to Louis XIV in 1668.[50] The "French Blue" was recut by British gem collector Henry Philip Hope (brother to furniture designer Thomas Hope and friend to King George IV) in the early nineteenth century. It was exhibited at the Crystal Palace in the London Great Exhibition of 1851 and eventually the supposedly cursed stone (now called the "Hope Diamond") was bought by the Cartier brothers in 1910 and taken to America. Today, the diamond resides in the collection of the Smithsonian Institution.

The story of the Hope Diamond following its arrival in Europe is well-known and well-documented. What is much less well-documented are the diamond's origins in India and where Tavernier came to possess the gem. Marco Polo, who had visited India four centuries before Tavernier, wrote that diamonds came from the bellies of eagles near the coastal kingdom of Motupalli.[51] Clearly this is a fantastical account, though it is worth keeping an open mind regarding the potential role of Motupalli in the medieval gem trade. Richard Kurin notes in *Hope Diamond* that Tavernier repeatedly visited the kingdom of Golconda, in India's Deccan Plateau, which was the center of the seventeenth-century diamond trade. Tavernier visited several mines, and Kurin's hypothesis was that Tavernier bought *le beau violet* at the diamond fields of Kollur in 1653, some fifteen years before he sold it to the king of France.[52]

It may seem that such an exercise—mapping a place that no longer exists—is such a rare and exotic task that the average researcher will never have to do it themselves. Consider, though, that places disappear all the time. Place names and geography are in a constant state of flux, such as in the example of Spitalfields, London, given earlier in this chapter. To test his theory, Kurin had to visit Kollur, which was highly problematic, not because of cost or distance (although these factors would certainly prove problematic for many, especially student researchers), but because Kollur was not then found on any map. "The Kollur mine was closed hundreds of years ago—certainly by the mid-eighteenth century—and the population dispersed. There are no listings in contemporary gazeteers. Kollur does not appear on any commonly attainable map."[53] Writing in the early 2000s, Kurin's working method was archival research—pouring over old maps from the seventeenth and eighteenth centuries—and the traveling to India and driving across the Deccan region until he saw a landmark—the crescent-shaped Medusala Mountain[54]—that let him know that he was in the right place. Surely this must have been the adventure of a lifetime, a bit like something out of an *Indiana Jones* film—albeit a lot safer, but such a journey is too costly and impractical for many researchers to make.

Nearly twenty years after Kurin's trip of discovery to Kollur, I wondered if OpenStreetMap might not be a much quicker and easier way to find Kollur which still, incidentally, does not exist on most printed or traditionally published maps. One problem with using OpenStreetMap for historical research is that the site maintains a policy of its geographic data being both real and current: "OpenStreetMap is a place for mapping things that are both *real and current*—it includes millions of buildings, roads, and other details about places. You can map whatever real-world features are interesting to you. What it *doesn't* include is opinionated data like ratings, historical or hypothetical features, and data from copyrighted sources. Unless you have special permission, don't copy from online or paper maps."[55] Nevertheless, it does not mean that OpenStreetMap will not be able to generate a map of the site; it simply means that it will not be labeled as "defunct Kollur diamond mine" or some such. Still, I began by doing a keyword search of "Kollur" on OpenStreetMap (online mapping sites are just another kind of database, after all), but it returned no useful results.

So, to find a map of Kollur on OpenStreetMap, I used a nineteenth-century map of India[56] that I found on the Internet Book Archive and used the city of Hyderabad to the northwest and the Krishna River to the southeast as points of reference—the historical area of diamond mining in the region lying between them (Figure 7.3). Then, I zoomed in on India in the OpenStreetMap until I was looking at the same area. Sure enough, a village named *Kolluru* appears on the map! It is around here that Tavernier first acquired *le beau violet*. Ideally, I would have then edited the OpenStreetMap to add that information to the site, but respecting the website's prohibition on historical (that is, no longer extant)

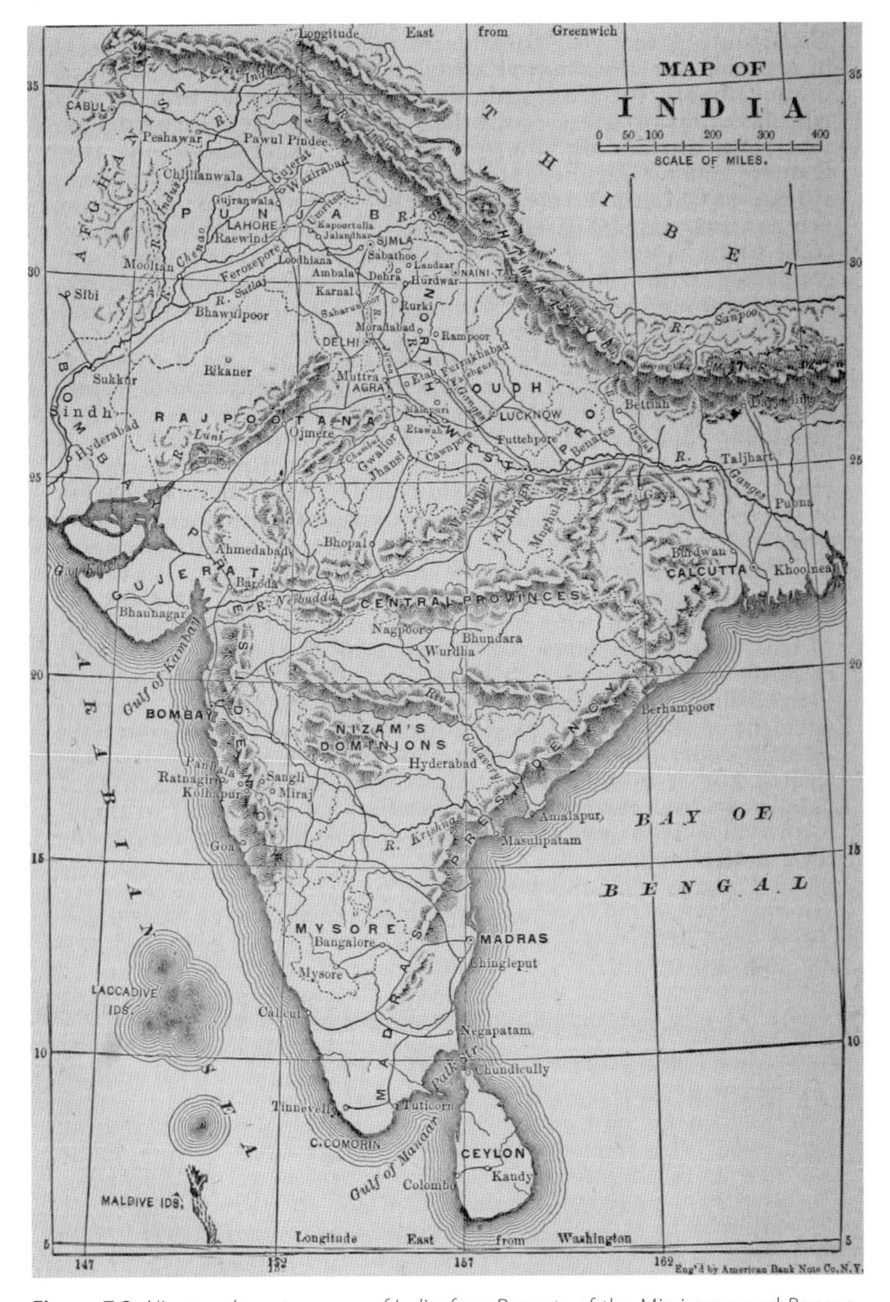

Figure 7.3 *Nineteenth-century map of India, from* Reports of the Missionary and Benevolent Boards and Committees to the General Assembly of the Presbyterian Church in the United States of America *(1891).*

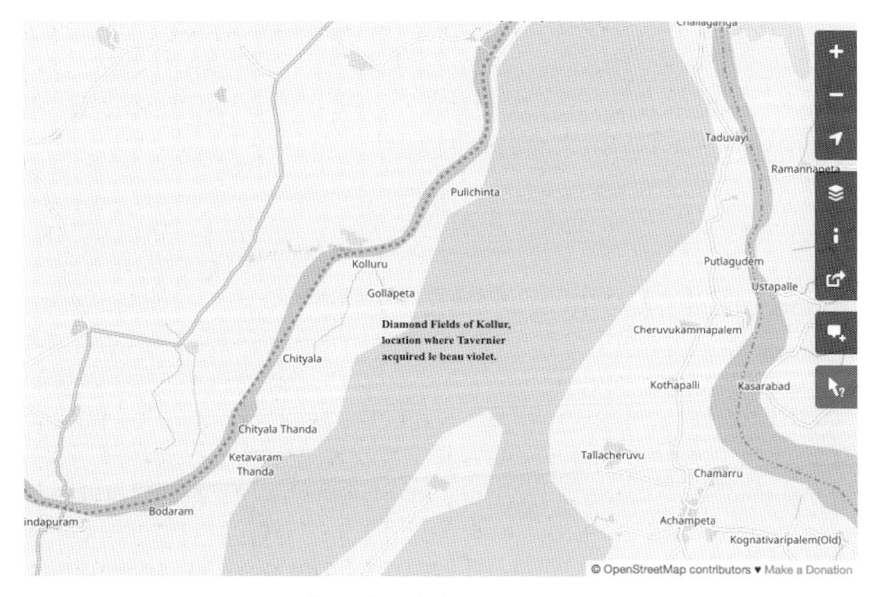

Figure 7.4 *OpenStreetMap: Kollur, with added text by Amanda Sikarskie.*

places, I left it alone. Researchers wishing to use the map in the dissemination of their own research, however, would only need to open a screenshot of the map (which is entirely public domain) in an image editing program, or even in a PDF application, to add the relevant details for publication, as I did here in Apple's Preview (Figure 7.4).

Visualizing Qualitative Data

Thus far, we have focused on visualizing quantitative data—hard and fast numbers such as the frequency of particular quilt patterns in a database or the locations of luxury retail shops in the streets of Milan. The most rudimentary and easy-to-make visualizations—including single number visualizations, pie charts, and word clouds—work well at visualizing this sort of data. For qualitative data, however, such as open-ended survey results, ethnographic data, and subjective data (such as the identification of specific themes in a work of art or literature or a fashion collection), these entry-level visualization techniques can work less well. To visualize survey results, Evergreen recommends a variety of techniques—most of which can be done with a moderate or advanced knowledge of Microsoft Excel or other spreadsheet software, including: bar graphs (both aggregated and diverging), nested area graphs, and lollipop graphs.[57]

Because the purpose of this book is to introduce a variety of digital methods that students and advanced researchers in fashion and textile studies can pick up and use quickly and easily, I needed to find a way—easier, yet still powerful—to visualize subjective data. I found the answer in an unlikely place: in the pages of *On the Road*.

Case Study: Coding *Fashion Is Spinach*

These days, computer programming is often colloquially referred to as "code" or "coding," as with the popular Instagram account *Girls Who Code*. But what does that mean? Coding refers to binary code, the language of zeroes and ones that all computers "speak," to use an anthropomorphism. Early computer programmers, such as Ada Lovelace, the nineteenth-century mathematician who coded the first proto-computers invented by Charles Babbage, would actually read and work in binary language. With only two characters—zero and one—such a language is obviously very difficult for humans to understand, let alone compose in. Even basic mathematics in binary is rather arcane. In *Geek Sublime: The Beauty of Code, the Code of Beauty*, Vikram Chandra explains the four basic rules of binary addition:

$0 + 0 = 0$
$0 + 0 = 1$
$1 + 0 = 1$
$1 + 1 = 0$, and carry the 1[58]

Using this logic, one of my lucky numbers, the decimal number 82, is written in binary as 01010010. Confused? If you are, don't worry. Coding no longer requires the ability to read binary, and as we will see, sometimes, it does not even require a computer at all.

Modern programming languages, therefore, hide the binary code—the machine language—from the programmer. And in the vernacular, coding has come to mean work in any programming language, not just binary. Even though most programmers do not work in binary anymore, binaries are still helpful. And binary codes need not be written as either zero or one, on or off, etc. For example, a binary (non-programming) language could be written using the words "style" and "fashion," or any other words a researcher wished to use. By the process of coding, which in the social sciences means a qualitative research technique in which text is marked up based on key concepts or words or phrases mentioned (another parallel with the digital world—the Web is based on HTML and XML—marked-up text), we can apply Hawes's binary code of fashion and style to her text, *Fashion Is Spinach*, using both coding and code. As Giorgia Lupi and Stefanie Posavec note, "Everything can be mapped, counted, and measured."[59] Even, in this case, *Fashion Is Spinach*.[60]

Coding and Code … with Highlighters

As we have seen in the emoji, pie chart, and word cloud examples, creating a data visualization need not necessarily require any specialized technical knowledge. In fact, you do not need to use a computer, tablet, or smart phone at all (though doing so usually saves a lot of time). Visualizations can be made on paper using colored pencils, pens, or markers, and maybe a ruler, compass, or stencils, as well, for example. London-based information designer Stefanie Posavec took a different approach, filling her copy of Jack Kerouac's *On the Road* with color-coded highlights, each color denoting the frequency with which the author used a particular theme and the degree to which those themes are adjacent to each other in the text. While such a method for visualizing data may seem unconventional, it fits with their artisanal approach to data. Lupi and Posavec write, "We see data as a creative material like paint or paper, an outcome of a very new way of seeing and engaging with our world."[61] As Cairo notes of Posavec's *On the Road*, "When you see them displayed side by side, they work like a visualization that lets you see what key theme each portion of the book deals with."[62] I wonder if my 10th, 11th, and 12th grade literature teacher would be surprised to know that the many hours she had us highlighting passages of *A Farewell to Arms* and *The Great Gatsby* was actually data visualization.

I decided to try this low-tech approach to visualizing literature myself by highlighting the introductory chapter to Elizabeth Hawes's seminal book on fashion, *Fashion Is Spinach:* "The Deformed Thief, Fashion." First, I read the text several times (recall that progression along the hermeneutic spiral requires multiple readings), and then determined the terms that I wished to visualize based on both the frequency with which they appeared in the text and my own interests as a historian and researcher. These are "style," which I highlighted in pink, and "fashion," which I highlighted in green (since Hawes likens it to spinach).[63] This is effectively a colorful visualization of coding, a method of organization of qualitative or quantitative data that social scientists frequently employ (Figure 7.5).

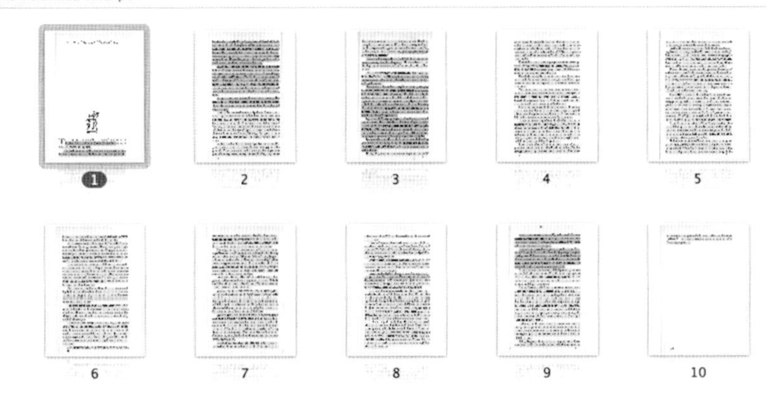

Figure 7.5 *Data visualization:* Fashion Is Kale, *Amanda Sikarskie.*

Document Annotation Methods and Annotation as Method

Preview (Mac) or Adobe Acrobat is perhaps the most obvious choice for highlighting and otherwise annotating PDF files, and many already have it installed on their computer. Using Acrobat for this purpose is very limiting, however, because to change the color of the highlighting, one must actually go into the settings on their computer and change the default highlight color every time a new color is needed. This is obviously too tedious and time-consuming. For Mac users, Preview eliminates this problem by allowing for highlighting in five colors: yellow, green, blue, pink, and purple. I created by visualization of "The Deformed Thief, Fashion" using Preview, highlighting in the regular content view and then switching to the contact sheet view to take the screenshot.

Mendeley is a desktop application that allows users to create a digital library of PDFs, and annotate and organize them in myriad ways. Mendeley is a rich, multi-function, and powerful program, though, and if all one wants to do is highlight a PDF, if might be app overkill. (But by all means, if you wish to create an entire library of well-organized PDF files, download and use Mendeley.) Another good choice for our purpose, creating a data visualization through highlighting, is a mobile one: iAnnotate for iPad and iPhone ($9.99) and Android (no cost). Of course, one can always just print the pages of the PDF out, use actual highlighters, and then arrange the pages and photograph the result. In the end, this is a cheap and possibly the easiest way to go about this task. Even in a digital age, digital need not always be the best method.

The kinds of data visualization that are explored earlier in Chapter 5—single number visualizations, pie charts, word clouds, and the like—all serve primarily to communicate something about the data set to the reader. That is, the researcher makes these visualizations mostly for the audience, rather than for themselves. In this final case on *Fashion Is Spinach*, however, the researcher uses PDF document annotation *as a research method* rather than as a communicative tool. While the finished product of the visualization itself can be so opaque and information dense as to be unhelpful for a reader just approaching the subject, visually marking up text gives researchers new information that can be missed in a text, even with repeated reading.

Why Spinach?: The Binary of Style and Fashion

At this point, readers unfamiliar with Hawes's book may be wondering: Why spinach? There was a fashion for spinach in the 1930s—think Popeye. Food fashions, whether for spinach then for kale now, are highly telling of and are analogous to changing fashions in clothing. Baked Alaska, for example, is as much stuck in the 1970s as a "Night at Studio 54" vinyl record. Hawes's book sets up the dichotomy of made-to-order (which Hawes associates with the concept of style and French couturiers) versus readymade (which she associates with the concept of fashion—used more or less pejoratively—and American designers). Hawes states that there are two kinds of women in the world—those who have their clothes custom-made especially for them by a designer and those who buy ready-made cloths off the rack.[64] Shopping is thus a major occupation of the ready-made type: "Meanwhile, the ready-made lady shops. She too may want a special color to wear in her dining room. She may find that color after two weeks of hunting, or she may never find it, since very possibly 'we are not using it this season.'"[65]

There is almost always an exception to every rule, and in diving right into this literary visualization, I chose to ignore the prescribed order of Alberto Cairo's six-step process, skipping directly ahead to step five, "think about the visual style," exactly the step I had said not to do first. I did this not because I wanted to produce an amazing visualization *per se*, but because I wanted to demonstrate a no-tech visualization style. Some of the more pithy passages from the larger section of the book, coded as green (fashion), are:

> 'They' decide everything. 'They' know whether it is to be pink or green this fall, whether it's to be short skirts, whether you can wear mink.[66]

Fashion gets up those perfectly ghastly ideas, such as accessories should match, and proceeds to give you shoes, gloves, bag, and hat all in the same hideous shade of kelly green which he insists is chic this season whether it turns you yellow or not. Fashion is apt to insist one year that you are nobody if you wear flat heels, and then turn right around and throw thousands of them in your face.[67]

In the past they were able to decree that all of Fifth Avenue was to be purple in a given week. If you didn't get a purple dress in those days, you were jailed.[68]

What the data visualization immediately brings into focus, more than even repeated reading of the text, is the striking contrast in the amount of real estate that Hawes gives over to her discussion of fashion versus the very small quantity that she writes about style, what she sees as an antidote to fashion.

Shopping as Research Method

The problem, if anything, is even more acute today. Walk into any department store, or discount store hawking last season's unsold clothes, and one is immediately struck by the dominance of fashion, those ephemeral trends set months and years in advance by the fashion forecasters. Everything this spring has a sheer or lace cutout in the back between the shoulders. Oh, you find the new sheer and lace cutouts preposterous? Just wait until next season, because they'll be gone, replaced with some new fashion. Want neon tights? Too bad. Those were in fashion two years ago. You'll never find them in a store again (at least not until they come back around again as retro). Try going online.

Plus-size women's clothing suffers particularly from fashion. The clothes are often not the designer's first priority; choices are limited as the lines have fewer products in them. All of our tops with this summer have a deep scoop neck, rhinestone embellishments, and a screen-print of either Paris, London, Rome, or New York. What do you mean that is not exactly what you were looking for? Compounding this is the fact that shops catering solely to sizes 14 or 16 and up tend to cut their tops much too large, the end result of which are blouses that resemble a tent with a hole cut out of the roof for the neck. *Vogue* editor Alexandra Shulman noted, "Loose clothes don't make you look slimmer. Loose clothes look best on beanpoles. If you are larger, huge amounts of material hanging around the place does no favours and won't disguise the fact you are of a fuller figure. Tents are for sleeping in and not for wearing."[69] Not particularly flattering. This leads us back to the world of online shopping. Shopping for designer plus-size clothes online can be an exercise in frustration. Luxury retailers like Net-a-Porter will carry a few pieces in European sizes 48 and 50 (roughly US 16 & 18), but again choice is very limited. The whole, sprawling site might have one swimsuit in an IT 50, for example, an orange bandeau style with a French cut leg. Definitely not what I was looking for. *Peccato.*

High-end designers are guilty of putting fashion before style as well, although they at least can satisfy their own creativity in choosing the themes, cuts, and materials for their collections. All of Dolce & Gabbana's pieces this season are devoted to motherhood. Don't have any kids? Then carrying that "*Te Mamma*" clutch would be decidedly awkward. KTZ is featuring cultural appropriation of American Indian and Canadian First Nations designs this season. If one does not want to go about cosplaying an Inuit shaman, better head to another atelier. The pace of fast fashion is accelerating in our mobile media-saturated world. Smart phones at runway shows mean that the next season's fashions are on Instagram months before they can be bought in the store. Historical, ethnic, and "tribal" forms and motifs come and go with the changing of each season. It was the same in Hawes's day: "They also love to take up 'influences.' Sometimes it's Chinese, other times Mexican. The game those seasons is to try and find the influence in anything but print."[70] What would Elizabeth Hawes do today? Make herself the clothes that she actually wanted, most likely. And for the rest of us, those with rudimentary or completely absent dressmaking skills?

Perhaps thrifting is the answer. In their cult book, *The Cheap Date Guide to Style*, Kira Jolliffe and Bay Garnett suggest shopping at not only thrift stores, but also local school and church bazaars, rummage sales, yard sales, occupational and other specialty shops, and pillaging the wardrobes of family and friends.[71] "We find thrifting infinitely more pleasurable than shopping. It's a relaxed, thrill-of-the-hunt, creative, Bohemian pastime, an archaeological dig, spend-thrifting without too much spending."[72] Jolliffe and Garnett suggest that going online to buy clothes on a second-hand seller's site, like eBay, can be an antidote to fashion (as opposed to personal style), that the internet is a bit like a massive conglomeration of thrift store that one can efficiently scour for a particular type of piece. "Do you have a yen for pink stilettos? On eBay, the most specific thing you can think of could literally be at your fingertips."[73]

Is online shopping the answer, the way in which one can shop according to one's personal sense of style rather than in accordance with fashion? One blogger thinks so. "Mrs. Spinach," who runs the blog fashionisspinach.com, noted in 2014 that the problem of fashion had largely been solved by the democratization of fashion and by the efforts of bloggers.

> But now, the democratization of fashion – sparked, in large part, by a long list of blogs (including a little help from even from Fashionisspinach.com) – has elevated and celebrated creativity over conformity. Anything goes these days – just wear it with confidence. Now, 76 years after the debut of "Fashion is Spinach," it may finally be time for a follow-up with a more positive point of view. How do you feel about "Fashion is Chocolate Cake?"[74]

Is fashion in the early twenty-first century truly chocolate cake, rather than spinach? Elizabeth Hawes did not think so, conjecturing that society might get away from fashion and back to style in around 1,000 years or so.[75] I tend to agree with Hawes.

Conclusions: Responding to the Critique of Minimalism

This book applies digital research tools and methods to the field of fashion and textile studies, but much of the material in each chapter is applicable and transferable to researchers working in any of the humanistic disciplines. At its core, this book represents a new way of doing research on fashion for a new generation of students and scholars. Harriet Walker begins her book *Less Is More: Minimalism in Fashion*, by stating that "any history of fashion in the twentieth century is a history of minimalism."[1] If this is the case, then the study of how fashion is unfolding in the twenty-first century is the story of maximalism. These two impulses in fashion and design—the reductiveness of minimalism and the additivity of maximalism—seem antithetical, two schools of thought locked in the permanent impasse of a never-ending series of pendulum shifts.

Defining maximalism and minimalism is deceptively difficult. Minimalist sculptor of the 1960s Donald Judd described his work as "simple expression of complex thought."[2] Maximalism, by contrast, can be understood as a complex, multi-faceted expression of complex thought. According to Walker, "Decoration and minimalism are not mutually exclusive, but any embellishment should come by way of structure and construction."[3] The maximalist urge, however, rejoices in surface decoration—charms and other attachments, embroidery, and the mixing of mis-matched colors, patterns, and textures. How can such an aesthetic of mixing and multiplicity be helpful in research? Decorative does not equal non-functional. *Complexity* of form or method is equally as elegant as simplicity.

Minimalism has come to be conflated with modernity, which begs the question: is maximalism inherently late modern or post-modern? Harriet Walker describes the turn toward the minimal in the arts writ large in the early twentieth century: "The simplification of dress that occurred in the early decades of the twentieth century is undeniably minimalist *avant la lettre* … Just as modernist authors were abandoning the rhetorical curlicues of Victorian and Edwardian novelists, and the 1920s Bauhaus movement in architecture worked with a clear aim of practicality and pragmatism, early fashion designers sought to reassess the values inherent in womenswear at the time. Modernity at this point necessitated a paring down and a clarifying of line, silhouette, and content."[4] The work of British fiber artist Kate Terry combines these influences, which seem to be diametrically opposed—Minimalist art of the 1960s (which reads as masculine, modern, and clean) and the string art craze of the 1970s (which reads as feminine, old-fashioned, and kitsch). The result is a kind of historicism.

Historicism, however, is one important point of commonality between the two. Harriet Walker notes that while minimalism is often thought to lack referentiality "many minimalist designers take clothing beyond the seasonal cycle of autumn and spring trends and place them in a more historicized context."[5] Walker argues that the kimono is an important point of reference for creating minimalist constructions: "Such historicism finds an influence in Japanese culture, which, through Shintoism and the practice of Zen, preaches an easy harmony between archetypes and prototypes, between the traditional and the modern."[6] Maximalist design is often historical in its points of reference as well, for example, L'Wren Scott's spring 2010 collection inspired by the rococo style of Madame du Barry, a mistress of King Louis XV, or Sarah Burton's 2015 collection for Alexander McQueen inspired by the "bizarre" and "luxuriant" patterns found on seventeenth- and eighteenth-century Spitalfields silks (two of my favorite recent shows). In contrast, "The traditional view of the fashionable minimalist is a rather severe-looking intellectual wearing a shapeless black sack. This might not be too far from the mark; minimalism has a reputation, an archetype even, for being challenging, deliberately academic and rarefied, a fact backed up by the didacticism that has come with some of its incarnations."[7] Whereas minimalism, at least in high fashion, is often academic and arcane, maximalism is popularizing, giving the wearer multiple points of entry into appreciating a garment and the scholar multiple points of entry into research.

It can be argued, however, that maximalism, not minimalism, represents a new kind of intellectualism. Jil Sander commented in 2010, "Minimalism is less brainy today, more hedonistic and instinctive."[8] The conflation of minimalism and intellectualism is further undermined by the trend of the late 1990s toward so-called pretty minimalism, a term coined in *Vogue* (UK) in 1998 describing the marriage of minimalism with a more traditional femininity.[9] One of the longest-standing and most potent arguments against exaggerated complexity in women's fashion is the feminist argument—that simplicity of clothing makes women's lives simpler and thus more productive and liberated. According to Walker, "The story of the ascendance of the modern woman is mirrored by the rise and fall of popular minimalism as a fashionable aesthetic; it could be said that her wardrobe becomes simpler to enable her better to deal with the complexities of her lifestyle and its multiplying demands."[10] But the various "multiplying demands" that this minimal, pared down fashion seeks to accommodate are themselves anti-feminist, or at least ambivalent to feminism—working a forty-hour week *and* taking care of the home and the children, etc. Walker continues: "Interestingly, setbacks on that road to a parity of gender opportunities have also been key to the development of minimalism: the backlash against feminism in the 1950s and 1980s saw a return in fashion to a hyper-feminine look, by Christian Dior and by the likes of Thierry Mugler and Christian Lacroix respectively, but such regressions were inevitably over-turned by a new wave of avant-garde designers working in a more reductive mode."[11] And while "reduction has been a reflex throughout twentieth century fashion, a reactionary aesthetic impulse to create clothes and design more suited to their contexts,"[12] radical *addition* is now en vogue, informed by cultural contexts of increasing globalism, an increasing interest in diversity and pluralism, and the fragmentation of news and entertainment media of the digital age. (As an aside, I personally find Iman and Jerry Hall in Mugler [who was synonymous with maximalism in the 1980s] to be some great looks.) Minimalism or maximalism, androgeny or "High Femininity," a black sack or corsetry and puff ball skirts: in the end, is this all just a matter of personal preference? Or is some deeper philosophical belief at stake here?

The current maximalist aesthetic is clearly informed by the increasing role of globalism and critical diversity in the fashion world. Whether or not the maximalism of the 2010s will be associated with a major setback in women's rights, Dior's New Look has come to be associated with the enforced housewifery and general return to domesticity of the 1950s remains to be seen. Certainly, as of the writing of this book in 2018, women's rights are under threat. With the continued failure to pass the Equal Rights Amendment and the increasing threat of overturning Roe versus Wade in the United States, and the meteoric rise of human trafficking around the world, fueled in part by the refugee crisis, many gender equity issues seem to rest on a knife edge at present. Is it absurd to think that this time of great uncertainty is somehow reflected in the current taste for handbag charms? Perhaps. Or perhaps not.

Harriet Walker identifies a "New Minimalist Revival" beginning around 2007.[13] Indeed, minimalism seems like it should have been a natural and lasting expression of the austerity of the economic downturn that closed out the first decade of the twenty-first century. Instead, this revival was short-lived, replaced by a cacophony of patterns and accessories. In the early 2000s, brown, and then navy, was "the new black." But for the past few years now, prints have been the new black. In her influential 2013 blog post, "The Circus of Fashion," critic Suzy Menkes wrote:

> We were once described as 'black crows' – us fashion folk gathered outside an abandoned, crumbling downtown building in a uniform of Comme des Garçons or Yohi Yamamoto. 'Whose funeral is it?' passers-by would whisper with a mix of hushed caring and ghoulish inquiry, as we lined up for the hip, underground presentations back in the 1990s. Today, the people outside fashion shows are more like peacocks than crows. They pose and preen in their multi-patterned dresses, spidery legs balanced on club-sandwich platform shoes, or in thigh-high boots under sculpted coats blooming with flowers.[14]

In that same year, Italian fashion icon and paragon of maximalism Marta Marzotto passed away, and interviews with friends and family about her in the days that followed signaled that the pendulum shift in fashion back toward maximalism was well underway. "'If you love minimalism, she's not your woman,' says her youngest son, Matteo Marzotto, the former chairman of fashion brands Valentino and Vionnet ... Although some of her peers in conservative Italian society bristle at her maximalist style, it is welcomed in Marrakech, where she and her house incarnates the spirit of this often exuberant, colourful city."[15] During New York Fashion Week 2017, Gigi Hadid walked in the Jeremy Scott show. The look typified the youthfully exuberant maximalism of today—a jacket with wide, glittery lapels, leopard-print bodice, and floral brocade sleeves, paired with pants featuring a very large and slightly cartoonish image of Jesus Christ on each leg. Hadid's wild, long, dishwater blonde hair was everywhere.

For young people today, minimalism is beginning to take on a timbre of self-righteousness, a style for Gen X forty-, and now, fifty-somethings who have the purchasing power for conspicuous consumption, but choose not to exercise it as an aesthetic statement (Figure 8.1). Stella McCartney, for example, who was a paragon of minimalism in the late noughties, has now gone full maximalist with *horror vacui* feline print brocades in her "Stella McCatney" collection. And younger designers like blogger-turned designer Chiara Ferragni (aka The Blonde Salad) are putting glitter and pictorial leather embellishments on practically everything.

Perhaps maximalism is a reaction against contemporary trends born of the austerity of the first generation of modern youth who will likely never have it as good as their parents—the tiny house movement, decluttering, cheap and disposable "fast fashion," and the primacy of the experience economy over the ownership economy. Maybe sometimes, today's youth, just like the Greatest Generation and the Baby Boomers before them, really do just want MORE.

Figure 8.1 *A look from LA swim week 2018 in which maximalism meets retro futurism. https://www.flickr.com/photos/prophotobomb/35671107463/in/photolist-Wm8Kuc-C5Nkoo-VLD-vBq-YNbKZ9-VPzi24-UJZDwf-XzzdxM-Y7nH91-Y4CJ9n-GNpMsE-ULoGQN-HQxFmq-23RsZW9-Yb9Ugk-BnaykX-Gp8urB-VsydCS-Gp7qrK-25YxjcZ-UJJAws-VqVTYL-qF9ctH-Y6XaXJ-VPzzjz-Y7kDeS-Uz4TAD-UK1ahh-QeJH8U-24W3XL4-VLmwKw-UK16o5-VLD6JW-24W3XeT-24z9Dae-YbPkfn-29jZrjG-Cpx8JY-BR5iDA-HQGiaJ-XNaS8S-HQGsqh-W3JRLk-YqWPob-VqVCkm-CbkoD9-23dsCy7-YN4beh-Cbfm6y-ZfRkX1-2aSJKCX.*

Post-script: Maximalist Muse: A Conversation with Kristen Bateman

Around the time that I began writing this book in earnest, I was interviewed by Kristen Bateman for an article about Anna Magnani for *Vogue*: "Anna Magnani, the Most Important Italian Film Star You've Never Heard Of."[1] Mid-century Italian Neo-Realist film was all about the gritty realities of everyday life. These films were created in opposition to the escapism and glamor of old Hollywood. Consequently, costuming in these films eschewed the monochromatic silk or satin evening wear staples, the pearls, and the diamonds that one might associate with leading ladies of the 1940s and 1950s. But that does not mean that Neo-Realist costuming was boring. The characters that Magnani played often displayed an idiosyncratic dress sense, pairing geometric prints and more bohemian than luxe jewelry—like velvet chokers—in a way that we might read today as maximalistic, or at least proto-maximalistic, a bit like a "lite" version of Gucci under Alessandro Michelle.

In the days and weeks after we corresponded, I began to think of this new, digital, mixed bag approach to research that I hoped to document and make manifest through this book as a kind of maximalism that has a parallel in fashion, both historically and in the fashion of the present. That experience ended up being hugely formative in terms of my thinking about mixed-methods research. Reproduced here is my conversation with Kristen.

Kristen: Thanks again for agreeing to give me some quotes for my Anna Magnani article. When it came to her costumes on screen, how did you think she was different than other 1940s/50s/60s actresses who may be more well-known (Sophia Loren, etc.)? How do you think she was the same—or what aesthetic traits do you think she shared with other Italian actresses on screen if any?

Amanda: The 1950s was such a glamorous decade for Hollywood, but Italian neorealist cinema was much grittier, exploring the inner lives of working-class characters. Many of the costumes from Italian films of the '40s and '50s still have a decidedly sexy quality about them, though, because of the way they accentuated women's bodies. The actresses of this period, Sophia Loren, Anna Magnani, even Anita Pallenberg in the 1960s, had this beautiful way of being sexy by keeping their clothes on, by emphasizing their bodies while leaving something to the imagination.

In terms of how Magnani was different, Loren embraced the '50s glamor, while Magnani's style was more the salt of the earth type. On-screen, Magnani tended to be cast as the strong, hot-blooded peasant woman, roles that didn't lend themselves to glamor. But Magnani brought the glamor just by virtue of her magnetism, her body, and the way she carried herself.

Donatella Versace once said, "On a hanger, no dress is sexy. It's just fabric on a hanger."[2] That is, it's the woman's body that really brings the sex appeal, not the clothes. Anna Magnani typified this. For example in the pivotal scene in *Bellissima* (1951), she wore a simple geometric print day dress, or in *The Secret of Santa Vittoria* (1969), a film set during World War II in which the inhabitants of an Italian village are trying to hide a million bottles of wine from the Germans, Magnani wears the simplest peasant costume. These clothes probably wouldn't look sexy on most women, but she looks amazing in them (and at the age of 61!).

Off-screen, Magnani was more the salt of the earth as well. Whereas her contemporaries might have been accessorizing with diamonds or pearls, she was just as likely to go for a simple velvet choker. Chokers are hugely popular right now, and we think of them as such a '90s thing, but the choker was a signature piece for Magnani back in the 1950s.

Kristen: Looking at her costumes on screen and the way she dresses in photos, what sort of historical moments do you see her using as references, if any?

Amanda: One of her most iconic costumes was the dress she wore in *La carrozza d'oro* (The Golden Coach) (1952). She plays the leading lady of an itinerant *commedia dell'arte* troupe in eighteenth-century Peru, and she wears this incredible harlequin-patterned dress that's part of eighteenth-century period piece and at the same time, like something straight out of Picasso's Rose Period (which has been called his circus period). The dress is so colorful and flamboyant that it really should be over the top, but Magnani had such presence and confidence that she carried it off. Magnani was made for channeling the eighteenth century. The tight-fitted bodices and low necklines were perfect for her.

Kristen: How do you think the time during which she was working in Italy (specifically the fashion scene in Italy, during the time she was working) affected the way she was styled on screen?

Amanda: Magnani was working during one of the most pivotal moments in Italian fashion. By 1950, there was this deep polarization between the elegance of French fashion and the casual chic of American fashion, with many people looking for some sort of happy medium between the two. When Giorgini staged what many consider to be the first Italian high fashion show in 1951, he set the tone for Italian fashion as casually elegant … and of course, sexy. You see this marriage of casual wear with impeccable tailoring in a lot of Magnani's costuming.

Kristen: In fashion history, can you think of other actresses, style influencers, or designers who have taken inspiration from Magnani's style directly, or the similar aesthetic movement that she was a part of?

Amanda: In terms of individual designers: Miuccia Prada for starters, in terms of individual pieces (she herself has been known to wear a choker that she bought from Anna Magnani's estate), in the styling of models, but also in terms of her approach to style—that clothes can be sexy without being obvious about it.

Versace has been influenced by the inherent womanly sexiness and the self-assured independence of the Italian actresses of this period. Dolce & Gabbana, too. When I saw the D&G Fall/Winter 2015/2016 "Viva la Mamma" collection, I was immediately reminded of Anna Magnani. Not in the way that the clothes were cut—Magnani tended to wear lower necklines and more figure-hugging pieces—but just in the idea behind the collection. Her only son lost the use of his legs to polio at a very young age, and she really used her career, leveraged her beauty and talent, to be sure that he would always have medical and financial support. She's as much an icon of motherhood as she is a fashion icon and I think a lot of women find that inspirational as well.

In terms of a larger aesthetic movement: Anna Magnani is a great symbol for women today of aging gracefully and the idea that one can be beautiful at any age. Acting into her 60s, she was quite forward thinking in her approach to aging and comfortable in her own skin, famously saying, "Please don't retouch my wrinkles. It took me so long to earn them."

Fin.

Glossary

areal symbol: In mapping, a symbol proportional to the quantity of a data value in a particular region.

artificial intelligence: The ability of machines to emulate thinking, such as by learning or problem solving.

big data: Data sets so large that they must be analyzed by computers, rather than human-read. Such large data sets often have the potential to shed light on the human condition.

blogosphere: Aggregate term for the numerous blogs on the Web.

Boolean queries: Search language that allows the researcher to search multiple keywords at once using the operators AND, OR, and NOT.

bubble chart: A type of chart that visualizes a three-dimensional data set by the plotting of circles in respect to X-Y axis values and the size of the circles themselves.

cartogram: Often visually distorted thematic map showing a discrete variable, such as population, in lieu of area or distance.

Cleveland-McGill Scale: Hierarchy of graphical perception devised by William Cleveland and Robert McGill showing which cognitive tasks take precedence in the reading of a data visualization.

code: Higher-level programming languages understood by computers. "Code," the preferred term in common parlance, is a shortened version of "source code."

coding: Categorization of either qualitative or quantitative data for the purposes of analysis in research.

computer vision: The branch of machine learning dealing with the ways in which computers process, analyze, and understand digital images.

content-based image retrieval (CBIR): Computer vision method in which the computer performs searches based on the visual content of a digital image.

Creative Commons: A non-profit organization fostering the legal sharing or creative works through a set of standards for licensing and attribution.

crowdsourcing: Knowledge or creative work sourced by soliciting the opinions or skills of other internet users, often within discursive communities.

cylindrical projection: A projection of the globe as if placed onto a cylinder and then unfurled into a flat map.

database: A data set held digitally and organized using a metadata scheme.

data set: Like or related items of information that can be studied or visualized using one or more variables.

data visualization: The graphical communication of data, often encoded in charts or graphs.

discursive community: On the Web, individuals who share a common discourse, often signified through the use of particular hashtagged words or phrases.

document annotation: Notes, such as clarifications or coding, attached to a text either through additional, superimposed text or visually through colors or symbols.

donut chart: Much-maligned in the data visualization community, a pie chart with its center removed.

Dublin Core: International, interoperable standards for the creation of metadata schemes first adopted in Dublin, Ohio.

echo chamber: A closed system, such as a network of like-minded people on social media, in which community beliefs are constantly upheld and other views are absent or immediately shut down.

emoji: Pictograms used in digital communication expressing emotion (previously known as "emoticons") or standing in for or emphasizing words for animals, plants, colors, weather phenomena, clothing, etc.

fashion blogger poses: A more relaxed system of modeling poses used by fashion bloggers to model online. These poses contrast the more severe or exaggerated poses employed by professional print and runway models.

folksonomy: A crowdsourced system of categorizing digital images and other content by tagging, in a manner similar to a metadata scheme.

geospatial turn: A turn in the digital humanities, and the humanities in general, toward location-specific scholarship, often enabled by GIS.

Geographic Information Systems (GIS): Software for acquiring, processing, and cataloging place-based data.

hashtag: Words or phrases preceded by the pound symbol online to denote particular topics and facilitate their searching.

hex code: Hexadecimal strings of letters and numbers preceded by the pound symbol that signify a particular color as it is rendered and represented by computers.

icon array: A type of data visualization in which a shape, or icon, is repeated a number of times to proportionally represent a much larger quantity.

information density: In data visualization, the amount of information packed into an information graphic.

information transparency: In data visualization, the relative legibility, or ease of understanding, of an information graphic.

linear visualization: A data visualization that visualizes data across one dimension only; effectively, a list.

linked open data (LOD): Linked data licensed to be shared and reused for free.

lollipop plot: A type of graph showing the relationship between two variables, one of which being a number.

machine learning: The field of artificial intelligence dedicated to fostering the ability of computers to learn concepts without having been programmed to do so.

Map Communication Model: In cartography, the belief is that the primary role of the map is to communicate information from the mapmaker to the map reader.

metadata: Metadata simply means "data about data," especially data about objects in databases, and is the term that museums and libraries use for information about an object in their collection.

metadata scheme: The combined metadata fields for describing an object in a database, such as the maker or designer, provenance location, year of production, and other pertinent data, such as copyright and licensing information.

mixed-methods research: A school of research methods combining the use of qualitative and quantitative techniques in a single study.

mood board: Found images, often accompanied by fabric or color swatches and text, arranged on a wall, posterboard, or digitally for purposes of research or creative inspiration.

multidimensional visualization: Data visualizations utilizing more than two variables (e.g., more than just the X-Y axis).

neogeography: Literally, the "new geography"; geography that takes into account volunteered geographic information.

nested area graph: Also called a "stacked proportional area chart," a type of data visualization used for showing relationships between the parts and the whole based on a changing variable.

network visualization: A data visualization showing the relationships by connection of items in a data set.

open access: Research or educational media distributed for no charge online.

pie chart: A round data visualization divided into slices (as a pie in pastry) to show the proportional quantities of items in a small data set.

public domain: Descriptor for material not under copyright because it belongs to the public as a whole.

qualitative methods: Research methods, such as participant observation and focus groups, used to gather non-numerical data.

quantitative methods: Research methods, such as surveys, used to gather numerical data.

query by example (QBE): A visual language for searching databases by means of a sample image.

remote sensing: Data gathering done above the earth by satellite or aircraft, used in disciplines such as climatology, geography, geology, meteorology, oceanography, etc.

research burst: Term developed in 2017 by Holly Kent and Amanda Sikarskie for the posting of research in progress on Instagram.

reverse image search: Related to query by example, but instead of querying like images in a database, reverse image searches query like images across the entire internet.

search engine optimization (SEO): A process or method for raising the profile of a website in a browser-based search engine's results.

single number visualization: A graphic visualizing a single key number in a data set to emphasize its importance.

spiders: Spiders, also known as "web crawlers," are bots that systematically crawl the World Wide Web in order to index it for searching or other purposes.

street style: Dress as it is worn by fashionable people in the streets, as opposed to fashion as it is styled for runway shows.

temporal visualization: Data visualization in which time is the key variable illustrated.

user-generated content (UGC): Any content, such as text, images, or audio-visual media, created by users of a particular website or service, and uploaded freely for the benefit of all. User-generated content may be solicited by the staff of the website or service or uploaded spontaneously by the user.

volumetric visualization: A two-dimensional rendering or projection of a three-dimensional data set.

volunteered geographic information: A form of user-generated content encompassing user-gathered or user-submitted geographic data.

word cloud: Also known as a "tag cloud," a type of data visualization showing the proportion of occurrence of words or phrases in a text-based data set.

3D modeling: The use of a computer application to create a mathematical rendering of the three-dimensional surface of an object.

Notes

Introduction

1. Amy Larocca and Rebecca Ramsey, "How Maximalism Is Changing the Shape of Fashion," *The Cut*, February 12, 2016, Last accessed May 21, 2018, https://www.thecut.com/2016/02/trends-maximalist-toolbox.html.
2. "Starchitect": a portmanteau of "star" and "architect," referring to one of the contemporary giants of the field of architecture.
3. Heike Jenss, ed., *Fashion Studies: Research Methods, Sites and Practices*, London: Bloomsbury, 2016, 3.
4. Jonathan Faiers, "Dress Thinking: Disciplines and Interdisciplinarity," in Charlotte Nicklas and Annebella Pollens, eds., *Dress History: New Directions in Theory and Practice*, London: Bloomsbury, 2015, 16.
5. Jenss, 138–139.
6. Jenss, 11.
7. Susan B. Kaiser and Denise Nicole Green, "Mixing Qualitative and Quantitative Methods in Fashion Studies: Philosophical Underpinnings and Multiple Masculinities," in Heike Jenss, ed., *Fashion Studies: Research Methods, Sites, and Practices*, London: Bloomsbury, 2016, 162.
8. Rebecca Coleman and Jessica Ringrose, *Deleuze and Research Methodologies*, Edinburgh: Edinburgh University Press, 2013, 5.
9. Coleman and Ringrose, 5.
10. John Brewer and Albert Hunter, *Foundations of Multimethod Research: Synthesizing Styles*, Thousand Oaks, CA: Sage Publications, 2006, 56.
11. This is my distilled and simplified version of a much more complex chart on page 191 of David E. Gray's *Doing Research in the Real World*.
12. Carolyn S. Ridenour and Isador Newman, *Mixed Methods Research: Exploring the Interactive Continuum*, Carbondale: Southern Illinois University Press, 2008, 1.
13. David E. Gray, *Doing Research in the Real World*, 2nd ed., Los Angeles, CA: Sage Publications, 2009, 197.
14. Jane Elliott, *Using Narrative in Social Research: Qualitative and Quantitative Approaches*, Thousand Oaks, CA: Sage Publications, 2005, 171.
15. Brewer and Hunter, 53.
16. Margaret Eichler, *Nonsexist Research Methods*, London: Routledge, 1987, 5.
17. Eichler, 8.
18. Jenss, 12.
19. Jenss, 12.
20. Kathleen Baird-Murray, "Desperately Seeking Cleavage," *Vogue* (UK), December 2016.

21 Sian Boyle and Josh White, "Victoria and Albert Museum Spurns Offer of Maggie's Frocks Saying They Lack 'Technical Quality' and Only Have 'Social Value,'" *The Daily Mail*, November 2, 2015, Last accessed May 21, 2018, http://www.dailymail.co.uk/news/article-3301234/Victoria-Albert-Museum-spurns-offer-Maggie-s-frocks-saying-lack-technical-quality-social-value.html.

22 Coleman and Ringrose, 5.

23 Coleman and Ringrose, 5.

24 Brewer and Hunter, 54.

25 Marie Lathers, *Space Oddities: Women and Outer Space in Popular Film and Culture, 1960–2000*, London: A&C Black, 2012, 145–181.

26 Lathers, 170–171.

Part 1

1 For more detailed information on developing a research plan, see pages 331–353 (for the first edition) of *The Norton Field Guide to Writing*.

Chapter 2

1 Christy Gavins, *Teaching Information Literacy*, Lanham, Maryland: Scarecrow Press, 2007, 37.

2 Gavins, 39–44.

3 MacDonald and MacDonald, *Successful Keyword Searching: Initiating Research on Popular Topics Using Electronic Databases*, Westport, CT: Greenwood Press, 2001, 8.

4 Joyce Duncan Falk, "Humanities," in Steven D. Atkinson and Judith Hudson, eds., *Women Online: Research in Women's Studies Using Online Databases*, New York: Haworth Press, 1990, 31.

5 Falk, 33.

6 Brooke Erin Duffy, *Remake, Remodel: Women's Magazines in the Digital Age*, Urbana, IL: University of Illinois Press, 2013, 81.

7 Zachary Kaiser, "Citation Bombing: Tactical and Symbolic Subversion of Academic Metrification," *Art Journal Open*, April 12, 2018, http://artjournal.collegeart.org/?p=9844.

8 Kaiser.

9 Jane Devine and Francine Egger-Sider, *Going beyond Google … Again*, Chicago: Neal-Schuman, an imprint of the American Library Association, 2014, 7.

10 Francesca Granata, "Fitting Sources—Tailoring Methods: A Case Study of Martin Margiela and the Temporalities of Fashion," in Heike Jenss, ed., *Fashion Studies: Research Methods, Sites and Practices*, London: Bloomsbury, 2016, 143.

11 Australian Dress Register, Last accessed May 21, 2018, http://www.australiandressregister.org/about/.

12 Liz Williamson, "Interlaced: Textiles for Fashion," in Bonnie English and Liliana Pomazan, eds., *Australian Fashion Unstitched*. Cambridge: Cambridge University Press, 2010, 105.

13 Christine Schmidt, "Against the Grain: Australia and the Swimsuit," in Bonnie English and Liliana Pomazan., eds., *Australian Fashion Unstitched*. Cambridge: Cambridge University Press, 2010, 172.

14 Kate Strasdin, Instagram post, July 10, 2017.

15 Europeana, Last accessed May 21, 2018, Europeanafashion.eu.

16 Agiatis Bernardou and Alastair Dunning, "From Europeana Cloud to Europeana Research," in Agiatis Bernardou, Erik Champion, Costis Dallas and Lorna M. Hughes, eds., *Cultural Heritage Infrastructures in Digital Humanities*, London: Routledge, 2018, 149–151.

17 Joy Spanabel Emery, *A History of the Paper Pattern Industry: The Home Dressmaking Fashion Revolution*, London: Bloomsbury, 2014, 2.

18 Emery, 2.

19 Additionally, to know the precise pressing of the record, such as whether it is the first UK pressing or a subsequent pressing, one has to check the numbers etched in the runout of the vinyl itself.

20 Emery, 2.

21 Google Cultural Institute, Last accessed May 21, 2018, https://www.google.com/culturalinstitute/beta/time?project=fashion&date=1835.

22 Justine de Young, "How to Research Fashion," February 1, 2018, Last accessed June 25, 2018, https://fashionhistory.fitnyc.edu/how-to-research-fashion/.

23 This figure is current as of June 23, 2018.

24 Susan Sontag, "The Avedon Eye," *Vogue*, December 1978, 104.

25 Elliott Smedley, "Escaping to Reality: Fashion Photography in the 1990s," in Stella Bruzzi and Pamela Church Gibson, eds., *Fashion Cultures: Theories, Explorations and Analysis*, Routledge: London, 2000, 155.

26 Sophia Kingshill, *Mermaids*, Toller Fratrum, Dorset: Little Toller Books, 2015, 26.

27 Kingshill, 26.

28 Kingshill, 131.

29 This hypothetical research problem was inspired by Maureen Callahan's 2014 book, *Champagne Supernovas: Kate Moss, Marc Jacobs, Alexander McQueen, and the '90s Renegades Who Remade Fashion*.

30 Gavins, 43.

31 Joanne Entwistle and Don Slater, "Models as Brands: Critical Thinking about Bodies and Images," in Joanne Entwistle and Elizabeth Wissinger, eds., *Fashioning Models: Image, Text, and Industry*, Berg: London, 2012, 16.

32 Kira Jolliffe and Bay Garnett, *The Cheap Date Guide to Style*, London: Universe Publishing, 2008, 16.

33 Kate Moss, qtd. In Lynn Hirschberg, "Kate Moss Loves the Camera as Much as It Loves Her," *W Magazine*, March 2017, 274.

Chapter 3

1 Naomi Rosenblum, *A World History of Photography*, 3rd ed., New York: Abbeville, 1997, 497.

2 Rosenblum, 498.

3 Rosenblum, 499.

4 Reproduced in Susan Sontag's *On Photography* (1977), 194–195.

5 Simone Santini, *Exploratory Image Databases: Content-based Retrieval*, San Diego: Academic Press, 2001, 3.

6 Santini, 3.

7 Santini, 5.

8 Santini, 5.

9 Santini, 6–7.

10 Santini, 6.

11 Santini, 6.

12 Santini, 10.

13 Santini, 18.

14 Santini, 17.

15 Loic Tallon, "Introducing Open Access at the MET," Metropolitan Museum of Art, Last accessed April 21, 2018, https://www.metmuseum.org/blogs/digital-underground/2017/open-access-at-the-met.

16 Hilda Davis, "The History of Seminole Clothing and Its Multi-Colored Designs," *American Anthropologist*, No. 974–980, 1955, 976.

17 Davis, 976.

18 See Appendix.

19 Design Pass Notes, "Millennial Pink Is the Colour of Now—but What Exactly Is It?," *The Guardian*, March 22, 2017, https://www.theguardian.com/artanddesign/shortcuts/2017/mar/22/millennial-pink-is-the-colour-of-now-but-what-exactly-is-it.

20 Marianne Vedeler, *Silk for the Vikings*, Ancient Textiles Series, Vol. 15, Oxford: Oxbow Books, 2014, 50–51.

21 Tin Eye, Last accessed May 21, 2018, https://tineye.com/.

22 Google Reverse Image Search, Last accessed May 21, 2018, https://reverse.photos/.

23 Hunter Davies, *The John Lennon Letters*, New York: Little, Brown and Co., 2012, 380.

24 Davies, 306.

25 Ray Coleman, *John Ono Lennon, Volume 2, 1967–1980*, London: Sidgwick & Jackson, 1984, 174.

26 Richard White, *Come Together: Lennon & McCartney in the Seventies*, London: Omnibus Press, 2016, 214.

27 White, 188.

28 John Lennon, qtd. In White, 188.

29 White, 180.

30 Many thanks to Christina Mitchell who responded to my query on the Facebook group Fashion Historians Unite! with the name of the pattern. Fashion Historians Unite! and crowdsourced scholarship in fashion and textile studies will be discussed in Chapter 3.

Part 2

1 Andy Hobsbawm, qtd. in Steve Hilton, "The Social Value of Brands," in Rita Clifton, ed., *Brands and Branding*, Vol. 43. New York: John Wiley & Sons, 2009, 47.

2 Hilton, 47.

3 Sava Saheli Singh, "Hashtagging #HigherEd," in *Hashtag Publics: The Power and Politics of Discursive Networks*, Bern, Switzerland: Peter Lang, 2016, 272.

Chapter 4

1 Such as in the Costume Society of America listserve debacle of January 2018, in which numerous subscribe and unsubscribe messages went out to the roughly 700–800 people on the list.

2 Tal G. Amit, response to a query on the Facebook group Fashion Historians Unite!, February 5, 2017.

3 Various, responses to a query on the Facebook group Fashion Historians Unite!, February 5, 2017.

4 Singh, 274.

5 Andrea Melvin, post to the Facebook group Fashion Historians Unite!, October 16, 2017.

6 @SarahLikesClothes, Instagram post, January 23, 2018.

7 Daren C. Brabham, "The Myth of Amateur Crowds: A Critical Discourse Analysis of Crowdsourcing Coverage," *Information, Communication & Society*, Vol. 15, 2012, 394–410.

8 The Purdue Owl, *Chicago Manual of Style*, 17th edition, Last accessed April 21, 2018, https://owl.english.purdue.edu/owl/resource/717/05/.

9 The Purdue Owl, *MLA Formatting and Style Guide*, Last accessed April 21, 2018, https://owl.english.purdue.edu/owl/resource/747/08/.

10 The Purdue Owl, *APA Formatting and Style Guide*, Last accessed April 21, 2018, https://owl.english.purdue.edu/owl/resource/560/10/.

11 Easybib.com, Last accessed May 21, 2018, http://www.easybib.com/guides/how-to-cite-an-instagram-post/.

12 Easybib.com.

13 Internet Archive, *Wayback Machine*, Last accessed September 4, 2018, https://archive.org/web/.

14 Caroline Rennolds Milbank, Instagram post.

15 Eleanor Houghton, Instagram post.

16 Thank you to Holly Kent for helping me come up with the term "research burst."

17 Singh, 268.

18 Singh, 268.

19 Amanda Sikarskie, Tweet, "Come to the #teachingfashionstudies panel this a.m. @ 10:30 to hear approaches to teaching fashion in the history classroom! #aha17," January 6, 2017.

20 Singh, 268.

21 Vanessa Rosales, Instagram post, 2016.

22 Singh, 269.

23 Amanda Sikarskie, Tweet, "A necklace chain makes a chic alternative to that boring conference lanyard [elephant emoji] #academicfashion #stylishacademic #styletip #aha17," January 6, 2017.

24 Singh, 274.

25 See for example Elias Aboujaoude's *Virtually You: The Dangerous Power of the e-Personality*, New York, W. W. Norton, 2011.

26 Roland Barthes, "Blue Is in Fashion This Year: A Note on Research into Signifying Units in Fashion Clothing," 37.

27 Barthes, 38.

28 Barthes, 40.

29 Barthes, 39.

30 Sherman Dorn, "Is (Digital) History More than an Argument about the Past?" in Jack Dougherty and Kristen Nawrotzki, eds., *Writing History in the Digital Age*. Ann Arbor: University of Michigan Press, 2013, 31.

31 Jenss, 13.

32 Dara Prant, "Polyvore Acquired by Global Fashion Platform Ssense, Fans Are Not Pleased," *Fashionista*, April 5, 2018, Last accessed May 21, 2018, https://fashionista.com/2018/04/ssense-acquires-polyvore-ends-operations.

33 Peter McNeil and Sanda Miller, *Fashion Writing and Criticism: History, Theory, and Practice*, London: Bloomsbury, 2014, 131.

34 McNeil and Miller, 132.

35 Alex Sayf Cummings and Jonathan Jarrett, "Only Typing? Informal Writing, Blogging, and the Academy," in Jack Dougherty and Kristen Nawrotzki, eds., *Writing History in the Digital Age*. Ann Arbor: University of Michigan Press, 2013, 253.

36 Singh, 272.

37 Singh, 272.

38 Cummings and Jarrett, 253–254.

39 Brent Luvaas, *Street Style*, London: Bloomsbury, 2016, 44.

40 Luvaas, 23.

41 Luvaas, 25.

42 M.A. Bazin, *L'Epoque sans nom*, 1833, qtd. In Robert Herbert, *Impressionism: Art, Leisure, and Culture in Parisian Society*, New Haven: Yale, 36.

43 Antonin Proust, qtd. In Herbert, 36.

44 Luvaas, 22.

45 *Shoes of New York*, Instagram, Last accessed May 21, 2018, https://www.instagram.com/shoesofnyc/.

46 Brent Luvaas, "Urban Fieldnotes: An Auto-Ethnography of Street Style Blogging," in Heike Jenss, ed., *Fashion Studies: Research Methods, Sites and Practices*, London: Bloomsbury, 2016, 83.

47 Luvaas, "Urban Fieldnotes," 98.

48 Minh-Ha T. Pham, *Asians Wear Clothes on the Internet: Race, Gender, and the Work of Personal Style Blogging*, Durham, NC: Duke University Press, 2015, 3.

49 *The Sartorialist*, Last accessed May 21, 2018, http://www.thesartorialist.com/.

50 *Business of Fashion*, Last accessed May 21, 2018, https://www.businessoffashion.com/.

51 *The Cut*, Last accessed May 21, 2018, https://www.thecut.com/.

52 Chiara Ferragni, *The Blonde Salad*, Last accessed May 21, 2018, https://www.theblondesalad.com/.

53 Henry Schermer and David Jary, *Form and Dialectic in Georg Simmels' Sociology*, London: Palgrave Macmillan, 2013, 89.

54 Schermer and Jary, 89.

55 Schermer and Jary, 90.

56 Schermer and Jary, 90.

57 Nik Cohn, qtd. in Christopher Breward, "The Dandy Laid Bare," in Stella Bruzzi and Pamela Church Gibson, eds., *Fashion Cultures: Theories, Explorations and Analysis*. Routledge: London, 2000, 236.

58 Breward, 235.

59 Schermer and Jary, 91.

60 Suzy Menkes, "The Circus of Fashion," *New York Times* Magazine blog, February 10, 2013, Last accessed May 21, 2018, https://www.nytimes.com/2013/02/10/t-magazine/the-circus-of-fashion.html.

61 Pham, 77.

62 Pham, 55.

63 Franca Sozzani qtd. In Duffy, 102.

64 Pham, 78.

65 Pham, 128.

66 Pham, 128.

67 Pham, 139–141.

68 Pham, 186.

69 Pham, 187.

70 Noel McLaughlin, "Rock, Fashion, and Performativity," in Stella Bruzzi and Pamela Church Gibson, eds., *Fashion Cultures: Theories, Explorations and Analysis*, London: Routledge, 2000, 266.

71 Fred David, qtd. In McLaughlin, 266.

72 Menkes.

73 McNeil and Miller, 137.

74 McNeil and Miller, 137.

Chapter 5

1 Granata, 142.

2 Scott Curtis, "Still/Moving: Digital Imaging and Medical Hermeneutics," in Lauren Rabinovitz and Abraham Geil, eds., *Memory Bytes: History, Technology and Digital Culture*. Durham, NC: Duke University Press, 222.

3 Curtis, 223.

4 Bron Meyer, *Skating with Bron Meyer*, 1921, 126.

5 Kathleen Baird-Murray, "Desperately Seeking Cleavage," *Vogue* (UK), December 2016.

6 Lara Rutherford-Morison, "Is Cleavage 'Over'? 'Vogue' Asks Women to Vote to Decide & the Internet Is Not Having It Today," *Bustle*, November 3, 2016, Last accessed May 21, 2018. https://www.bustle.com/articles/193077-is-cleavage-over-vogue-asks-women-to-vote-to-decide-the-internet-is-not-having.

7 Katherine Hill Winters, Museum Programs & Collections Associate at the Society of the Cincinnati, and Moderator, Fashion Historians Unite!, November 7, 2016.

8 Fiona Anderson, "Museums as Fashion Media," in Stella Bruzzi and Pamela Church Gibson, eds., *Fashion Cultures: Theories, Explorations and Analysis*, London: Routledge, 2000, 379.

9 Anderson, 376.

10 Anderson, 377.

11 Margaret Thatcher, qtd. In Robb Young, *Power Dressing: First Ladies, Women Politicians & Fashion*, London: Merrell, 2011, 35.

12 Young, 34.

13 Young, 35.

14 Young, 34.

15 Young, 34.

16 Jolliffe and Garnett, 94.

17 Young, 35.

18 Young, 35.

19 Cynthia Crawford, qtd. In Young, 35.

20 Young, 35.

21 Louisa Hadley, *Responding to Margaret Thatcher's Death*, London: Palgrave Macmillan, 2014, 51.

22 Young, 71.

23 Laurie Penny, "A Tory Wet Dream Comes True in May," *Morning Star*, May 13, 2010.

24 Laura Roberts, "Kitten-heeled Theresa May Opts for Flats on First Day as Home Secretary," *The Daily Mail*, May 14, 2010.

25 Young, 71.

26 Elizabeth Sanderson, "Theresa May Looks FAB in Her 'Thunderbirds' Jacket," *The Daily Mail*, May 29, 2010.

27 Cristina Odone, "Theresa May, What Did You Think You Looked Like in That Strapless Dress? Please Stop!," *The Telegraph*, November 12, 2013.

28 Edward Barsamian, "First Lady Melania Trump's Best Style Moments," *Vogue*, July 31, 2017, Last accessed October 30, 2018, https://www.vogue.com/article/first-lady-melania-trump-best-looks-celebrity-style.

29 Singh, 267.

30 The Business of Fashion, "Capsule Collections," Fashion A–Z, Last accessed October 30, 2018, https://www.businessoffashion.com/education/fashion-az/capsule-collections.

31 @DavidArmstrong, Tweet, "An early contender for the most moronic, insensitive and plain stupid marketing campaign of the year," October 13, 2016.

32 @deNutrients (Jennifer Depew), Tweet, "#justsayno to deadly Rx painkillers and say yes to fashion #justsaymoschino," October 26, 2016.

33 Anne D'Alleva, *Look! Again: Art History and Critical Theory*, Upper Saddle River, NJ: Prentice Hall, 2005, 128.

34 Barry Spunt, *Heroin and Music in New York City*, New York: Palgrave Macmillan, 2014, 2–3.

35 Spunt, 3.

36 Smedley, 155.

37 Spunt, 15.

38 Spunt, 15.

39 Spunt, 29.

40 Spunt, 29.

41 Spunt, 23.

42 Spunt, 16.

43 Marybeth Stalp, *Quilting: The Fabric of Everyday Life*, Dress, Body, and Culture ser., London: Berg, 2007.

44 Spunt, 123.

45 Georg Simmel, "Fashion," *The American Journal of Sociology*, Vol. LXII, No. 6, May 1957, 556.

46 Simmel, 543.

47 Simmel, 543.

48 Schermer and Jary, 103.

49 Schermer and Jary, 83–84, 86–88.

50 Simmel, 556.

51 Schermer and Jary, 83.

52 Callahan, 98.

Part 3

1 Giorgia Lupi and Stefanie Posavec, *Dear Data*, New York: Princeton Architectural Press, 2016, 52.

2 Lupi and Posavec, 88.

3 Lupi and Posavec, 88.

4 Lupi and Posavec, 90.

5 Lupi and Posavec, 92.

6 Lupi and Posavec, 91.

7 Lupi and Posavec, 91.

Chapter 6

1 Lupi and Posavec, x.

2 Jeffrey Roessner, "Revolution 2.0: Beatles Fan Scholarship in the Digital Age," in Kenneth Womach and Katie Kapurch, eds., *New Critical Perspectives on the Beatles: Things We Said Today*. New York: Palgrave Macmillan, 2016, 223.

3 Roessner, 230.

4 Roessner, 230.

5 John Theibault, "Visualizations and Historical Arguments," in Jack Dougherty and Kristen Nawrotzki, eds., *Writing History in the Digital Age*. Ann Arbor: The University of Michigan Press, 2013, 173.

6 Theibault, 177.

7 Edward Tufte, *Beautiful Evidence*, Cheshire, CT: Graphics Press, 2006, 13.

8 Tufte, 43.

9 Theibault, 173.

10 Theibault, 173.

11 Alberto Cairo, *The Functional Art: An Introduction to Information Graphics and Visualizations*, San Francisco: New Riders, 2013, 61.

12 Cairo, *The Functional Art*, 63.

13 Cairo, *The Functional Art*, 76.

14 Louis Sullivan, "The Tall Office Building Artistically Considered," *Lippincott's Magazine*, March 1896.

15 Cairo, *The Functional Art*, 32.

16 Lupi and Posavec, xi.

17 Lupi and Posavec, xi.

18 See Alberto Cairo's *The Truthful Art: Data, Charts, and Maps for Communication*, San Francisco: New Riders, 2016.

19 Cairo, *The Functional Art,* 51.

20 Theibault, 174.

21 Malcolm Bradbury, ed., *The Atlas of Literature*, London: De Agostini, 1996, 178.

22 Theibault, 178.

23 Roxanne O'Connell, *Visualizing Culture: Analyzing the Cultural Aesthetics of the Web*, New York: Peter Lang, 2014, 45.

24 O'Connell, 52.

25 As of April 2018, Polyvore is now defunct. The site was acquired by Ssense and subsequently shut down. For more on this development, see Chapter 3.

26 Stephanie D.H. Evergreen, *Effective Data Visualization, Effective Data Visualization: The Right Chart for the Right Data*, Los Angeles, CA: Sage Publications, 2017, 5.

27 E.B. White, qtd. In Cairo, *The Functional Art,* 61.

28 B. Schneiderman, "The Eyes Have It: A Task by Data Type Taxonomy for Information Visualizations," *Proceedings of IEEE Symposium on Visual Languages—Boulder, CO*, 1996, 336–343.

29 Angela Zoss, "Visualization Types—Data Visualization," *LibGuides at Duke University*, Last accessed May 21, 2018, http://guides.library.duke.edu/datavis/vis_types.

30 Cairo, *The Functional Art,* 154.

31 Moritz Stefaner, qtd in Cairo, *The Functional Art,* 318.

32 See Chapter 1 for more information about the Quilt Index.

33 Evergreen, 12.

34 Evergreen, 13.

35 Evergreen, 13.

36 Cairo, *The Functional Art,* 114.

37 Cairo, *The Functional Art,* 115.

38 Cairo, *The Functional Art,* 116.

39 Evergreen, 11.

40 Evergreen, 15.

41 Wordle—Beautiful Word Clouds, Last accessed May 21, 2018, http://www.wordle.net/.

42 "Easy Open Ended Verbatim Analysis with Word Clouds," *WordyUp*, Last accessed May 21, 2018, https://www.wordyup.com/.

43 Evergreen, 177.

44 Evergreen, 177.

45 Evergreen, 179.

46 "A Definitive Ranking of Macaron Flavors," *Huffington Post*, April 4, 2014, Last accessed May 23, 2018, https://www.huffingtonpost.com/2014/04/04/macaron-flavors_n_5084278.html.

47 Wordle—Advanced, Last accessed May 21, 2018, http://www.wordle.net/advanced.

48 Cairo, *The Functional Art,* 36.

Chapter 7

1 Judith A. Tyner, *The World of Maps: Map Reading and Interpretation for the 21st Century*, New York: The Guilford Press, 2015, 179.

2 Tyner, 179.

3 Jeremy Black, *Maps and History: Constructing Images of the Past*, New Haven, CT: Yale University Press, 1997, 234.

4 Thiebault, 175.

5 Black, 236.

6 Black, 213.

7 Black, 213.

8 "Lost Spitalfields," *Spitalfieldslife*, Last accessed May 21, 2018, http://spitalfieldslife.com/2013/07/06/lost-spitalfields/.

9 Adam Geczy, *Fashion and Orientalism: Dress, Textiles and Culture from the 17th to the 21st Century*, London: Bloomsbury, 2013, 46.

10 Tyner, 24.

11 Tyner, 124.

12 Tyner, 124.

13 Tyner, 59.

14 Tyner, 78.

15 Tyner, 78.

16 Ian Gregory and Paul Ell, *Historical GIS: Technologies, Methodologies and Scholarship*, Cambridge: Cambridge University Press, 2007, 21.

17 Gregory and Ell, 89.

18 Stephen Robertson, "Putting Harlem on the Map," in Jack Dougherty and Kristen Nawrotzki, eds., *Writing History in the Digital Age*. Ann Arbor: The University of Michigan Press, 2013, 186–187.

19 Gregory and Ell, 18.

20 Cairo, *The Functional Art*, 51.

21 Theibault, 178–179.

22 Black, 216.

23 Pupul Jayakar, "Indian Fabrics in Indian Life," *Textiles and Ornaments of India, New York: Museum of Modern Art* (1955): 15–23, 16.

24 Monroe Wheeler, ed., *Textiles and Ornaments of India, New York: Museum of Modern Art*, 1955, 11.

25 Wheeler, 11.

26 Jayakar, 20.

27 Jean-Christophe Plantin, *Participatory Mapping: New Data, New Cartography*, 2014, 28.

28 Plantin, 31–32.

29 Plantin, 30.

30 Plantin, 33–34.

31 Plantin, 33–34.

32 Tyner, 127.

33 Vedeler, 111.

34 Vedeler, 111.

35 Vedeler, 58.

36 Vedeler, 58.

37 Vedeler, 67.

38 Mario Novak, "Health, Diet, and Lifestyles of Early Medieval Populations in the Eastern Adriatic Region (Sixth–Twelfth Centuries)," Paper given at International Medieval Congress, May 11, 2017.

39 Vedeler, 71.

40 Vedeler, 74.

41 Vedeler, 72.

42 Vedeler, 72–73.

43 Vedeler, 70.

44 Vedeler, 70.

45 Black, 207.

46 Black, 207.

47 Vedeler, 71–92.

48 Black, 236.

49 Vedeler, 111.

50 Richard Kurin, *Hope Diamond: The Legendary History of a Cursed Gem*, New York: Smithsonian Books, in association with HarperCollins, 2007, 27.

51 Kurin, 20–21.

52 Kurin, 30.

53 Kurin, 31.

54 This feature of the terrain of the Deccan Plateau may be named after the ancient Greek gorgon Medusa, a relic of the Greek's brief foray into India during the Hellenistic period.

55 "Welcome," OpenStreetMap, Last accessed May 22, 2018, https://www.openstreetmap.org/welcome.

56 From: *Reports of the Missionary and Benevolent Boards and Committees to the General Assembly of the Presbyterian Church in the United States of America*, 1891, 299.

57 Evergreen, 103–132.

58 Vikram Chandra, *Geek Sublime: The Code of Beauty, the Beauty of Code*, Minneapolis, MN: Graywolf Press, 2014, 31.

59 Lupi and Posavec, xi.

60 October 19, 2017 saw the #fashioniskale symposium at the Museum of Modern Art, New York, on sustainability and instant gratification in fashion. When I proposed this book to

Bloomsbury in 2016, I had titled this case study, "Fashion Is Kale" to reflect the bringing of Elizabeth Hawes into the present through data visualization. Clearly, the time for updating spinach has come. I have now changed the title of the case study to "Coding *Fashion Is Spinach*," both to differentiate from this other use of the phrase and to reflect the importance of code and coding in this case study.

61 Lupi and Posavec, xi.

62 Cairo, *The Functional Art*, 347.

63 My apologies for the black and white reproduction of the images.

64 Elizabeth Hawes, *Fashion Is Spinach*, New York: Random House, 1938, 3.

65 Hawes, 4.

66 Hawes, 7.

67 Hawes, 6.

68 Hawes, 8.

69 Shulman, Alexandra. "Vogue Editor Alexandra Shulman's Fashion Rules," *The Guardian*, October 28, 2016, Last accessed May 21, 2018, https://www.theguardian.com/media/2016/oct/28/alexandra-shulman-vogue-editor-fashion-rules?CMP=fb_gu.

70 Hawes, 8.

71 Jolliffe and Garnett, 76–83.

72 Jolliffe and Garnett, 76.

73 Jolliffe and Garnett, 85.

74 Mrs. Spinach, "Where It All Began: A Tribute to 'Fashion Is Spinach' (the Book)," FashionisSpinach.com, June 14, 2014, Last accessed May 21, 2018, http://www.fashionisspinach.com.

75 Hawes, 5.

Conclusions

1 Harriet Walker, *Less Is More: Minimalism in Fashion*, London: Merrell, 2011, 9.

2 Donald Judd, qtd. In Walker, 9.

3 Walker, 9.

4 Walker, 10.

5 Walker, 14.

6 Walker, 14.

7 Walker, 10.

8 Jil Sander qtd. In Walker, 10.

9 Lisa Armstrong, "Fashion Talk: Catwalk Report '98," *Vogue* (UK), January 1998, 102, 105.

10 Walker, 11.

11 Walker, 11.

12 Walker, 10.

13 Walker, 163.

14 Suzy Menkes, "The Circus of Fashion," *New York Times Magazine* blog, February 10, 2013, Last accessed May 21, 2018, https://www.nytimes.com/2013/02/10/t-magazine/the-circus-of-fashion.html.

15 J.J. Martin, "Countess Marta Marzotto in Her Moroccan Home," *The Wall Street Journal*, August 21, 2013, Last accessed May 21, 2018, https://www.wsj.com/articles/countess-marta-marzotto-in-her-moroccan-home-1377106502.

Post-script

1 Kristen Bateman, "Anna Magnani, the Most Important Italian Film Star You've Never Heard Of, Finally Gets Her Due," *Vogue*, May 24, 2016, Last accessed May 22, 2018, https://www.vogue.com/article/anna-magnani-lincoln-center-film-retrospective-fashion-influence.

2 Donatella Versace qtd. In Stella Bruzzi and Pamela Church Gibson, eds., *Fashion Cultures: Theories, Explorations and Analysis*, London: Routledge, 2000.

Bibliography

Aboujaoude, Elias. *Virtually You: The Dangerous Power of the E-Personality*. New York: W. W. Norton, 2011.

Adams, Hazard. *Critical Theory since Plato*. 2nd ed. Boston: Cengage, 1992.

American Council on the Teaching of Foreign Languages, *ACTFL Standards for Foreign Language Learning: Preparing for the 21st Century*, 2012. http://www.actfl.org/sites/default/files/pdfs/public/StandardsforFLLexecsumm_rev.pdf.

Anderson, Fiona. "Museums as Fashion Media." In Bruzzi, Stella and Pamela Church Gibson, eds. *Fashion Cultures: Theories, Explorations and Analysis*. London: Routledge, 2000.

Andrews, Richard. *Research Questions*. London: Continuum, 2003.

Armstrong, Lisa. "Fashion Talk: Catwalk Report '98." *Vogue* (UK), January 1998.

Atkinson, Steven D. and Judith Hudson, eds. *Women Online: Research in Women's Studies Using Online Databases*. New York: Haworth Press, 1990.

Austin, Michael, dir. *Princess Caraboo*. TriStar Pictures, 1994.

Baird-Murray, Kathleen. "Desperately Seeking Cleavage." *Vogue* (UK), December 2016.

Baker, Chris. "The London Regiment in 1914–1918." *The Long, Long Trail: The British Army in the Great War of 1914–1918*. http://www.1914-1918.net/58div.htm.

Ball, Helen K. "Quilts." In Knowles, J. Gary and Adra L. Cole, eds. *Handbook of the Arts in Qualitative Research*. Los Angeles, CA: Sage Publications, 2008.

Banks, M. *Visual Methods in Social Research*. London: Sage Publications, 2001.

Barndt, Deborah. "Touching Minds and Hearts: Community Arts as Collaborative Research." In Knowles, J. Gary and Adra L. Cole, eds. *Handbook of the Arts in Qualitative Research*. Los Angeles, CA: Sage Publications, 2008.

Barone, Tom. "Going Public with Arts-Inspired Social Research: Issues of Audience." In Knowles, J. Gary and Adra L. Cole, eds. *Handbook of the Arts in Qualitative Research*. Los Angeles, CA: Sage Publications, 2008.

Barone, Tom. "How Arts-based Research Can Change Minds." In Cahnmann-Taylor, Melisa and Richard Siegesmund, eds. *Arts-based Research in Education*. New York: Routledge, 2008.

Barone, Tom. "Making Educational History: Qualitative Inquiry, Artistry and the Public Interest." In Ladsen-Billings, G. and W.F. Tate, eds. *Education Research in the Public Interest*. New York: Teachers College Press, 2006.

Barsamian, Edward. "First Lady Melania Trump's Best Style Moments." *Vogue*. July 31, 2017. Last accessed October 30, 2018. https://www.vogue.com/article/first-lady-melania-trump-best-looks-celebrity-style.

Barthes, Roland. "Blue Is in Fashion This Year: A Note on Research into Signifying Units in Fashion Clothing." In Roland Barthes. *The Language of Fashion*. Trans. Andy Stafford. Eds. Andy Stafford and Michael Carter. Oxford: Berg, 2006.

Barthes, Roland. *Camera Lucida*. New York: Hill and Wang, 1981.

Barthes, Roland. "Fashion and the Social Sciences." In Roland Barthes. *The Language of Fashion*. Trans. Andy Stafford. Eds. Andy Stafford and Michael Carter. Oxford: Berg, 2006.

Barthes, Roland. "From Gemstones to Jewellery." In Roland Barthes. *The Language of Fashion*. Trans. Andy Stafford. Eds. Andy Stafford and Michael Carter. Oxford: Berg, 2006.

Barthes, Roland. *The Language of Fashion*. Trans. Andy Stafford. Eds. Andy Stafford and Michael Carter. Oxford: Berg, 2006.

Bateman, Kristen. "Anna Magnani, the Most Important Italian Film Star You've Never Heard Of, Finally Gets Her Due." *Vogue*. May 24, 2016. Last accessed May 22, 2018. https://www.vogue.com/article/anna-magnani-lincoln-center-film-retrospective-fashion-influence.

Baudrillard, Jean. *The Mirror of Production*, trans. Mark Poster. New York: Telos Press, 1975.

Bayley, Stephen. "Forward." In *Commerce and Culture: From Pre-Industrial Art to Post-Industrial Value*. Tunbridge Wells: Penhurst Press Ltd., 1989.

Bayley, Stephen. "Watteau, Art and Trade." In *Commerce and Culture: From Pre-Industrial Art to Post-Industrial Value*. Tunbridge Wells: Penhurst Press Ltd., 1989.

Behar, Ruth. "Between Poetry and Anthropology: Searching for Languages of Home." In Cahnmann-Taylor, Melisa and Richard Siegesmund, eds. *Arts-based Research in Education*. New York: Routledge, 2008.

Behar, Ruth. "Ethnography and the Book that Was Lost." In Knowles, J. Gary and Adra L. Cole, eds. *Handbook of the Arts in Qualitative Research*. Los Angeles, CA: Sage Publications, 2008.

Bender, Marilyn. *The Beautiful People*. New York: Coward-McCann, 1967.

Benjamin, Walter. "The Work of Art in the Age of Mechanical Reproduction." In Bayley Stephen, ed. *Commerce and Culture: From Pre-Industrial Art to Post-Industrial Value*. Tunbridge Wells: Penshurst Press Ltd., 1989.

Berlo, Janet C. and Ruth B. Phillips. *Native North American Art*. Oxford: Oxford University Press, 1998.

Bernardou, Agiatis, Erik Champion, Costis Dallas and Lorna M. Hughes, eds. *Cultural Heritage Infrastructures in Digital Humanities*. London: Routledge, 2018.

Bernardou, Agiatis and Alastair Dunning. "From Europeana Cloud to Europeana Research." In Bernardou, Agiatis, Erik Champion, Costis Dallas and Lorna M. Hughes, eds. *Cultural Heritage Infrastructures in Digital Humanities*. London: Routledge, 2018.

Bernstein, Bruce. "The Booth Sitters of Santa Fe's Indian Market: Making and Maintaining Authenticity." *American Indian Culture and Research Journal*. Vol. 31, No. 3 (2007): 49–79.

Bhattacharya, Kakali. "Voices Lost and Found: Using Found Poetry in Qualitative Research." In Cahnmann-Taylor, Melisa and Richard Siegesmund, eds. *Arts-based Research in Education*. New York: Routledge, 2008.

Black, Jeremy. *Maps and History: Constructing Images of the Past*. New Haven, CT: Yale University Press, 1997.

Blumenfeld-Jones, Donald. "Dance, Choreography and Social Science Research." In Knowles, J. Gary and Adra L. Cole, eds. *Handbook of the Arts in Qualitative Research*. Los Angeles, CA: Sage Publications, 2008.

Boelstorff, Tom. *Coming of Age in Second Life*. Princeton, NJ: Princeton University Press, 2008.

Bolmar, Lydia and Kathleen McNutt. *Art in Dress*. Peoria, IL: The Manual Arts Press, 1916.

Bornhak, Akim, dir. *8 Miles High*. Warner Brothers, 2007.

Bowman, Nancy H. et al. *Successful Fashion Shows*. New York: Journal of Retailing, 1938.

Boyle, Sian and Josh White. "Victoria and Albert Museum Spurns Offer of Maggie's Frocks Saying They Lack 'Technical Quality' and Only Have 'Social Value.'" *The Daily Mail*. November 2, 2015. Last accessed May 21, 2018. http://www.dailymail.co.uk/news/article-3301234/Victoria-Albert-Museum-spurns-offer-Maggie-s-frocks-saying-lack-technical-quality-social-value.html.

Brabham, Darren C. "The Myth of Amateur Crowds: A Critical Discourse Analysis of Crowdsourcing Coverage." *Information, Communication & Society*. Vol. 15 (2012): 394–410.

Brackman, Barbara. *Encyclopedia of Appliqué*. Lafayette, CA: C&T Publishing, 2009.

Brackman, Barbara. *Encyclopedia of Pieced Quilt Patterns*. Paducah, KY: American Quilter's Society, 1993.

Brackman, Barbara. *Patterns of Progress: Quilts in the Machine Age*. Los Angeles, CA: Autry Museum of Western Heritage, 1997.

Bradbury, Malcolm. ed. *The Atlas of Literature*. London: De Agostini, 1996.

Brecht, Bertolt. "Radio as a Means of Communication: A Talk on the Function of Radio." http://www.nyklewicz.com/brecht.html.

Breward, Christopher. "The Dandy Laid Bare." In Bruzzi, Stella and Pamela Church Gibson, eds. *Fashion Cultures: Theories, Explorations and Analysis*. London: Routledge, 2000.

Brewer, John and Albert Hunter. *Foundations of Multimethod Research: Synthesizing Styles*. Thousand Oaks, CA: Sage Publications, 2006.

Bruzzi, Stella and Pamela Church Gibson, eds. *Fashion Cultures: Theories, Explorations and Analysis*. London: Routledge, 2000.

Buckley, Reka and Stephen Gundle. "Flash Trash." In Bruzzi, Stella and Pamela Church Gibson, eds. *Fashion Cultures: Theories, Explorations and Analysis*. London: Routledge, 2000.

Bullock, Richard. *The Norton Field Guide to Writing*. New York: Norton & Co., 2006.

Burris-Meyer, Elizabeth. *This Is Fashion*. New York and London: Harper & Brothers, 1943.

Butchart, Amber Jane. *Nautical Chic*. New York: Abrams, 2015.

Byrde, Penelope. *Jane Austen Fashion: Fashion and Needlework in the Works of Jane Austen*. Ludlow: Excellent Press, 1999.

Cahnmann-Taylor, Melisa and Richard Siegesmund, eds. *Arts-based Research in Education*. New York: Routledge, 2008.

Cairo, Alberto. *The Functional Art: An Introduction to Information Graphics and Visualization*. San Francisco: New Riders, 2013.

Cairo, Alberto. *The Truthful Art: Data, Charts, and Maps for Communication*. San Francisco: New Riders, 2016.

Caldwell, James T. "Unicode: A Standard International Character Code for Multilingual Information Processing." In Mair, Victor H. and Yongquan Liu, eds. *Characters and Computers*. Amsterdam: IOS Press, 1991.

Callahan, Maureen. *Champagne Supernovas: Kate Moss, Marc Jacobs, Alexander McQueen, and the '90s Renegades Who Remade Fashion*. New York: Touchstone, 2014.

Cammell, Donald and Nicolas Roeg, dirs. *Performance*. Warner Brothers, 1970.

Catlin, George. *Illustrations of the Manners and Customs of North American Indians*. London: Henry G. Bohn, 1866.

Champion, Erik. "The Role of 3D Models in Virtual Heritage Infrastructures." In Bernardou, Agiatis, Erik Champion, Costis Dallas and Lorna M. Hughes, eds. *Cultural Heritage Infrastructures in Digital Humanities*. London: Routledge, 2018.

Chandra, Vikram. *Geek Sublime: The Beauty of Code, the Code of Beauty*. Minneapolis, MN: Graywolf Press, 2014.

Clifton, Rita. *Brands and Branding*. Vol. 43. New York: John Wiley & Sons, 2009.

Clough, Peter, ed. *Narratives and Fictions in Educational Research*. Maidenhead: Open University Press, 2002.

Cohen, Stanley. *Folk Devils and Moral Panics*. 3rd ed. London: Routledge, 2002.

Cole, David R. "Lost in Data Space." In Coleman, Rebecca and Jessica Ringrose, eds. *Deleuze and Research Methodologies*. Edinburgh: Edinburgh University Press, 2013.

Coleman, Ray. *John Ono Lennon, Volume 2, 1967–1980*. London: Sidgwick & Jackson, 1984.

Coleman, Rebecca and Jessica Ringrose, eds. *Deleuze and Research Methodologies*. Edinburgh: Edinburgh University Press, 2013.

Cortada, James W. "Genealogy as a Hobby." In Aspray, William and Barbara M. Hayes, eds. *Everyday Information*. Cambridge, MA: The MIT Press, 2011.

Cox, Margaret. *Life and Death in Spitalfields, 1700 to 1850*. New York: Council for British Archaeology, 1996.

Crabtree, Caroline and Christine Shaw. *Quilting, Patchwork, and Appliqué: A World Guide*. London: Thames & Hudson, 2007.

Cummings, Alex Sayf and Jonathan Jarrett. "Only Typing? Informal Writing, Blogging, and the Academy." In Dougherty, Jack and Kristen Nawrotzki, eds. *Writing History in the Digital Age*. Ann Arbor: The University of Michigan Press, 2013.

Curtis, Scott. "Still/Moving: Digital Imaging and Medical Hermeneutics." In Lauren Rabinovitz and Abraham Geil, eds. *Memory Bytes: History, Technology and Digital Culture*. Durham, NC: Duke University Press, 2004.

d'Alleva, Anne. *Look! Again: Art History and Critical Theory*. Upper Saddle River, NJ: Prentice Hall, 2005.

Davies, Hunter, ed. *The John Lennon Letters*. New York: Little, Brown and Company, 2012.

Davis, Hilda. "The History of Seminole Clothing and Its Multi-Colored Designs." *American Anthropologist* 57, No. 5 (1955): 974–980.

"A Definitive Ranking of Macaron Flavors." *Huffington Post*. April 4, 2014. Last accessed May 23, 2018. https://www.huffingtonpost.com/2014/04/04/macaron-flavors_n_5084278.html.

de Groot, Jerome. *Consuming History: Historians and Heritage in Contemporary Popular Culture*. London: Routledge, 2009.

Deleuze, Gilles and Felix Guattari. *A Thousand Plateaus*. Minneapolis: University of Minnesota Press, 1987.

Depew, David and Laura Rigal, eds. *Memory Bytes: History, Technology, and Digital Culture*. Durham, NC: Duke University Press, 2004.

Design Pass Notes. "Millennial Pink Is the Colour of Now—but What Exactly Is It?" *The Guardian*. March 27, 2017. Last accessed May 21, 2018. https://www.theguardian.com/artanddesign/shortcuts/2017/mar/22/millennial-pink-is-the-colour-of-now-but-what-exactly-is-it.

Devine, Jane and Francine Egger-Sider. *Going beyond Google … Again*. Chicago: Neal-Schuman, an imprint of the American Library Association, 2014.

Diamond, C.T. Patrick and Christine Van Halen-Faber. "Apples of Change: Arts-based Methodology as a Poetic and Visual Sixth Sense." In Mitchell, Claudia, Sandra Weber and Kathleen O'Reilly-Scanlon, eds. *Just Who Do We Think We Are? Methodologies for Autobiography and Self-Study in Teaching*. New York: Routledge Falmer, 2005.

Donmoyer, Robert and June Yennie Donmoyer. "Readers' Theatre as a Data Display Strategy." In Knowles, J. Gary and Adra L. Cole, eds. *Handbook of the Arts in Qualitative Research*. Los Angeles, CA: Sage Publications, 2008.

Dorn, Sherman. "Is (Digital) History More than an Argument about the Past?" In Dougherty, Jack and Kristen Nawrotzki, eds. *Writing History in the Digital Age*. Ann Arbor: The University of Michigan Press, 2013.

Dougherty, Jack and Kristen Nawrotzki, eds. *Writing History in the Digital Age*. Ann Arbor: The University of Michigan Press, 2013.

Drucker, Johanna. "At the Intersection of Computational Methods and the Traditional Humanities." In Simonowski, Roberto, ed. *Digital Humanities and Digital Media: Conversations on Politics, Culture, Aesthetics, and Literacy*. Urbana, IL: Open Humanities Press, 2016.

Duffy, Brooke Erin. *Remake, Remodel: Women's Magazines in the Digital Age*. Urbana: University of Illinois Press, 2013.

Dunlevy, Mairead. *Pomp and Poverty: A History of Silk in Ireland*. New Haven, CT: Yale University Press, 2011.

Eicher, Joanne B. "Editing Fashion Studies: Reflections on Methodology and Interdisciplinarity in The Encyclopedia of World Dress and Fashion." In Jenss, Heike, ed. *Fashion Studies: Research Methods, Sites and Practices*. London: Bloomsbury, 2016.

Eichler, Margaret. *Nonsexist Research Methods*. London: Routledge, 1987.

Eisner, Elliot. "Art and Knowledge." In Knowles, J. Gary and Adra L. Cole, eds. *Handbook of the Arts in Qualitative Research*. Los Angeles, CA: Sage Publications, 2008.

Eisner, Elliot. "Persistent Tensions in Arts-based Research." In Cahnmann-Taylor, Melisa and Richard Siegesmund, eds. *Arts-based Research in Education*. New York: Routledge, 2008.

Eisner, Elliot. "The Promise and Perils of Alternative Forms of Data Representation." *Educational Researcher*. Vol. 26, No. 6 (1997): 4–10.

Elliott, Jane. *Using Narrative in Social Research: Qualitative and Quantitative Approaches*. Thousand Oaks, CA: Sage Publications, 2005.

English, Bonnie and Liliana Pomazan, eds. *Australian Fashion Unstitched*. Cambridge: Cambridge University Press, 2010.

Entwistle, Joanne and Elizabeth Wissinger, eds. *Fashioning Models: Image, Text, and Industry*. London: Berg, 2012.

Evergreen, Stephanie D.H. *Effective Data Visualization: The Right Chart for the Right Data*. Los Angeles, CA: Sage Publications, 2017.

Faiers, Jonathan. "Dress Thinking: Disciplines and Interdisciplinarity." In Nicklas, Charlotte and Annebella Pollens, eds. *Dress History: New Directions in Theory and Practice*. London: Bloomsbury, 2015.

Falk, Joyce Duncan. "Humanities." In Atkinson, Steven D. and Judith Hudson, eds. *Women Online: Research in Women's Studies Using Online Databases.*. New York: Haworth Press, 1990.

Fallaci, Oriana. *The Egotists: Sixteen Surprising Interviews*. Chicago: Henry Regnery Company, 1963.

Fanning, Robbie and Tony Fanning. *Here and Now Stitchery from Other Times and Places*. New York: Butterick Publications, 1978.

"Fashion: Beach Plums: Native American Fashions." *Vogue*. Vol. 127, No. 2 (Febuary 1, 1956): 190–191.

Finley, Susan. "Arts-based Inquiry in *QI*: Seven Years from Crisis to Guerilla Warfare." *Qualitative Inquiry*. Vol. 9, No. 2 (2003): 281–296.

Finley, Susan. "Arts-based Research." In Knowles, J. Gary and Adra L. Cole, eds. *Handbook of the Arts in Qualitative Research*. Los Angeles, CA: Sage Publications, 2008.

Flanagan, J.F. *Spitalfields Silks of the 18th and 19th Centuries*. Leigh-on-Sea: F. Lewis, 1954.

Fletcher, Mandie, dir. *Absolutely Fabulous: The Movie*. BBC Films, Fox Searchlight Pictures, 2016.

Gavins, Christy. *Teaching Information Literacy*. Lanham, Maryland: Scarecrow Press, 2007.

Geczy, Adam. *Fashion and Orientalism: Dress, Textiles and Culture from the 17th to the 21st Century*. London: Bloomsbury, 2013.

Gerdts, William. *American Impressionism*. New York: Abbeville Press, 2001.

Gillow, John and Bryan Sentance. *World Textiles: A Visual Guide to Traditional Techniques*. London: Thames & Hudson, 1999.

Glazier, Richard. *A Manual of Historic Ornament*. Mineola, New York: Courier Corporation, 1948.

Gosse, Douglas. "Queering Identity(ies) and Fiction Writing in Qualitative Research." In Cahnmann-Taylor, Melisa and Richard Siegesmund, eds. *Arts-based Research in Education*. New York: Routledge, 2008.

Granata, Francesca. "Fitting Sources—Tailoring Methods: A Case Study of Martin Margiela and the Temporalities of Fashion." In Jenss, Heike, ed. *Fashion Studies: Research Methods, Sites and Practices*. London: Bloomsbury, 2016.

Gray, David E. *Doing Research in the Real World*. 2nd ed. Los Angeles, CA: Sage Publications, 2009.

Gregory, Ian and Paul Ell. *Historical GIS: Technologies, Methodologies, and Scholarship*. Cambridge: Cambridge University Press, 2007.

Gurung, Regan A.R., Nancy L. Chick and Aeron Haynie, eds. *Exploring Signature Pedagogies*. Sterling, VA: Stylus, 2009.

Gwynn, Robin D. *The Huguenots of London*. Brighton: Alpha Press, 1998.

Hadley, Louisa. *Responding to Margaret Thatcher's Death*, ed. Ser. Palgrave Pivot. London: Palgrave Macmillan, 2014.

Hamilton, Mary Lynn. "Using Pictures at an Exhibition to Explore My Teaching Practices." In Mitchell, Claudia, Sandra Weber and Kathleen O'Reilly-Scanlon, eds. *Just Who Do We Think We Are? Methodologies for Autobiography and Self-Study in Teaching*. New York: Routledge Falmer, 2005.

Hawes, Elizabeth. *Fashion Is Spinach*. New York: Random House, 1938.

Hawes, Elizabeth. *Why Is a Dress?* New York: Viking Press, 1942.

Hawes, Elizabeth and James Thurber. *Men Can Take It*. New York: Random house, 1939.

Hayward, Philip. *Making a Splash: Mermaids (and Mer-Men) in 20th and 21st Century Audiovisual Media*. Bloomington: Indiana University Press, 2017.

Herbert, Robert. *Impressionism: Art, Leisure & Parisian Society*. New Haven, CT: Yale University Press, 1988.

Hill, Colleen. *Fairy Tale Fashion*. New Haven, CT: Yale University Press, 2016.

Hilton, Steve. "The Social Value of Brands." In Rita Clifton., ed. *Brands and Branding*. Vol. 43. New York: John Wiley & Sons, 2009.

Hirschberg, Lynn. "Kate Moss Loves the Camera as Much as It Loves Her." *W Magazine*, March 2017.

Horwell, Veronica. "Erica Wilson Obituary." *The Guardian*. January 2, 2012. Last accessed May 21, 2018. https://www.theguardian.com/lifeandstyle/2012/jan/02/erica-wilson

Huges, Christina, ed. *Disseminating Qualitative Research in Educational Settings: A Critical Introduction*. Maidenhead: Open University Press, 2003.
Huston, John, dir. *The African Queen*. Horizon Pictures, Romulus Films, Ltd., United Artists, 1951.
Inciardi, James A. *The War on Drugs*. 4th ed.. Boston, MA: Pearson, 2008.
Jenss, Heike, ed. *Fashion Studies: Research Methods, Sites and Practices*. London: Bloomsbury, 2016.
Jolliffe, Kira and Bay Garnett. *The Cheap Date Guide to Style*. London: Universe Publishing, 2008.
Jones, Liz and Ian Barron. *Research and Gender*. London: Continuum, 2007.
Kaiser, Susan B. and Denise Nicole Green. "Mixing Qualitative and Quantitative Methods in Fashion Studies: Philosophical Underpinnings and Multiple Masculinities." In Jenss, Heike, ed. *Fashion Studies: Research Methods, Sites, and Practices*. London: Bloomsbury, 2016.
Kaiser, Zachary. "Citation Bombing: Tactical and Symbolic Subversion of Academic Metrification." *Art Journal Open*. April 12, 2018. http://artjournal.collegeart.org/?p=9844.
Kamposiori, Christina, Claire Warwick and Simon Mahony. "Building Personal Research Collections in Art History." In Bernardou, Agiatis, Erik Champion, Costis Dallas and Lorna M. Hughes, eds. *Cultural Heritage Infrastructures in Digital Humanities*. London: Routledge, 2018.
Kerouac, Jack. *On the Road*. New York: Viking Press, 1957.
Kingshill, Sophia. *Mermaids*. Toller Fratrum: Little Toller Books, 2015.
Knowles, J. Gary and Adra L. Cole, eds. *Handbook of the Arts in Qualitative Research*. Los Angeles, CA: Sage Publications, 2008.
Kurin, Richard. *Hope Diamond: The Legendary History of a Cursed Gem*. New York: Smithsonian Books, in association with HarperCollins, 2007.
Larocca, Amy and Rebecca Ramsey. "How Maximalism Is Changing the Shape of Fashion." *The Cut*. February 12, 2016. Last accessed May 21, 2018. https://www.thecut.com/2016/02/trends-maximalist-toolbox.html
Lathers, Marie. *Space Oddities: Women and Outer Space in Popular Film and Culture, 1960–2000*. A&C Black, 2012.
Laver, James. *Taste and Fashion, from the French Revolution to the Present Day*. London, Toronto etc.: G.G. Harrap and Company Ltd., 1945.
Lawner, Lynne. *Harlequin on the Moon: Commedia dell' Arte and the Visual Arts*. New York: Harry N. Abrams, 1998.
Leonard, Robert Z., dir. *Ziegfeld Girl*. Metro-Goldwyn-Mayer, 1941.
Lewis, Frank. *James Leman: Spitalfields Designer*. Leigh-on-Sea: F. Lewis, 1954.
Lomas, Clare. "'I Know Nothing about Fashion'. There's No Point in Interviewing Me: The Use and Value of Oral History to the Fashion Historian." In Bruzzi, Stella and Pamela Church Gibson, eds. *Fashion Cultures: Theories, Explorations and Analysis*. London: Routledge, 2000.

Lupi, Giorgia and Stefanie Posavec. *Dear Data*. New York: Princeton Architectural Press, 2016.
Luvaas, Brent. *Street Style: An Ethnography of Fashion Blogging*. London: Bloomsbury, 2016.
Luvaas, Brent. "Urban Fieldnotes: An Auto-Ethnography of Street Style Blogging." In Jenss, Heike. ed. *Fashion Studies: Research Methods, Sites and Practices*. London: Bloomsbury, 2016.
MacCauley, Clay. *Seminole Indians of Florida*. Washington, DC: Bureau of American Ethnology, 1887.
MacDonald, Randall M. and Susan Priest MacDonald. *Successful Keyword Searching*. Westport, CT: Greenwood Press, 2001.
MacLure, Maggie. "Classification or Wonder? Coding as an Analytic Research Practice in Qualitative Research." In Coleman, Rebecca and Jessica Ringrose, eds. *Deleuze and Research Methodologies*. Edinburgh: Edinburgh University Press, 2013.
Maira, Sunaina. "Temporary Tattoos: Indo-Chic Fantasies and Late Capitalist Orientalism." *Meridians: Feminism, Race, Transnationalism*. Vol. 3, No. 1 (2002): 134–160.
Malin, Peta. "An Ethico-Aesthetics of Heroin Chic: Art, Cliché and Capitalism." In Guillaume, Laura and Joe Hughes, eds. *Deleuze and the Body*. Edinburgh: Edinburgh University Press, 2011.
Martin, J.J. "Countess Marta Marzotto in Her Moroccan Home." *The Wall Street Journal*. August 21, 2013. Last accessed May 21, 2018. https://www.wsj.com/articles/countess-marta-marzotto-in-her-moroccan-home-1377106502.
Marx, Leo. *The Machine in the Garden: Technology and the Pastoral Ideal in America*. New York: Oxford University Press, 1964.
Mason, Darielle. *Kantha: The Embroidered Quilts of Bengal from the Jill and Sheldon Bonovitz Collection and the Stella Kramrisch Collection of the Philadelphia Museum of Art*. Philadelphia: Philadelphia Museum of Art; New Haven, CT: Yale University Press, 2009.
McCall's. *McCall's Needlework Treasury: A Learn & Make Book*. New York: Random House, 1964.
McGann, Jerome. "Marking Texts of Many Dimensions." Schreibman, Susan, Ray Siemens and John Unsworth, eds. *A Companion to Digital Humanities*. New York: John Wiley & Sons, 2004. 198–217.
McLaughlin, Noel. "Rock, Fashion and Performativity." In Bruzzi, Stella and Pamela Church Gibson, eds. *Fashion Cultures: Theories, Explorations and Analysis*. London: Routledge, 2000.
McNeil, Peter and Sanda Miller. *Fashion Writing and Criticism*. London: Bloomsbury, 2014.
McNiff, Shaun. "Art-based Research." In Knowles, J. Gary and Adra L. Cole, eds. *Handbook of the Arts in Qualitative Research*. Los Angeles, CA: Sage Publications, 2008.

Menkes, Suzy. "The Circus of Fashion." *New York Times Magazine* blog. February 10, 2013. Last accessed May 21, 2018. https://www.nytimes.com/2013/02/10/t-magazine/the-circus-of-fashion.html.

Meyer, Bron. *Skating with Bron Meyer*. New York: Doubleday, Page, and Company, 1921.

Miller, Lesley Ellis. *Selling Silks: A Merchant's Sample Book*. London: V&A Publishing, 2014.

Mitchell, Claudia, Sandra Weber and Kathleen O'Reilly-Scanlon, eds. In *Just Who Do We Think We Are? Methodologies for Autobiography and Self-Study in Teaching*. New York: Routledge Falmer, 2005.

Mola, Luca. *Silk Industry of Renaissance Venice*. Baltimore, MD: Johns Hopkins University Press, 2000.

Mrs. Spinach, "Where It All Began: A Tribute to 'Fashion Is Spinach' (the Book)." FashionisSpinach.com. June 14, 2014, Last accessed May 21, 2018. http://www.fashionisspinach.com.

Mulvaney, Jay. Jackie: *The Clothes of Camelot*. New York: St. Martin's Press, 2001.

Nahshon, Edna, ed. *Jews and Shoes*. New York: Berg, 2008.

Novak, Mario. "Health, Diet, and Lifestyles of Early Medieval Populations in the Eastern Adriatic Region (Sixth-Twelfth Centuries)." Paper given at International Medieval Congress. Kalamazoo, MI. May 11, 2017.

Nowviske, Bethany. "How to Play with Maps." In Panofsky, Ruth and Kathleen Kellett, eds. *Cultural Mapping and the Digital Sphere: Place and Space*. Calgary: University of Alberta Press, 2015.

Nye, David. *American Technological Sublime*. Cambridge, MA: The MIT Press, 1994.

O'Connell, Roxanne M. *Visualizing Culture: Analyzing the Cultural Aesthetics of the Web*. New York: Peter Lang, 2014.

Odone, Cristina. "Theresa May, What Did You Think You Looked Like in That Strapless Dress? Please Stop!" *The Telegraph*. November 12, 2013.

Osborn, Don. *African Languages in a Digital Age*. Cape Town: HSRC Press, 2010.

Paine, Sheila. *Embroidered Textiles: Traditional Patterns from Five Continents with a Worldwide Guide to Identification*. London: Thames and Hudson, 1990.

Panofsky, Ruth and Kathleen Kellett, eds. *Cultural Mapping and the Digital Sphere: Place and Space*. Calgary: University of Alberta Press, 2015.

Penney, David W. *North American Indian Art*. London: Thames & Hudson, 2004.

Penney, David W. and George C. Longfish. *Native American Art*. New York: Hugh Lauter Levin, 1994.

Penny, Laurie. "A Tory Wet Dream Comes True in May." *Morning Star*. May 13, 2010.

Pham, Minh-Ha T. *Asians Wear Clothes on the Internet: Race, Gender, and the Work of Personal Style Blogging*. Durham, NC: Duke University Press, 2015.

Phelan, Raymond and Dorothy Wishman, dirs. *Nude on the Moon*, Moon Productions. 1961.

Plantin, Jean-Christophe. *Participatory Mapping: New Data, New Cartography*. New York: John Wiley & Sons, 2014.

Prant, Dara. "Polyvore Acquired by Global Fashion Platform Ssense, Fans Are Not Pleased." *Fashionista*. April 5, 2018. Last accessed May 21, 2018. https://fashionista.com/2018/04/ssense-acquires-polyvore-ends-operations.

Prown, Jules David and Kenneth Haltman, eds. *American Artifacts: Essays in Material Culture*. East Lansing: Michigan State University Press, 2000.

Prosser, Jon and Catherine Burke. "Image-based Educational Research: Childlike Perspectives." In Knowles, J. Gary and Adra L. Cole, eds. *Handbook of the Arts in Qualitative Research*. Los Angeles, CA: Sage Publications, 2008.

The Purdue Owl. *APA Formatting and Style Guide*. Last accessed April 21, 2018. https://owl.english.purdue.edu/owl/resource/560/10/.

The Purdue Owl. *Chicago Manual of Style*. 17th ed. Last accessed April 21, 2018. https://owl.english.purdue.edu/owl/resource/717/05/.

The Purdue Owl. *MLA Formatting and Style Guide*. Last accessed April 21, 2018. https://owl.english.purdue.edu/owl/resource/747/08/.

Rafele, Antonio. *Representations of Fashion: The Metropolis and Mediological Reflection between the Nineteenth and Twentieth Centuries*. San Diego, CA: Hyperbole Books, 2013.

Rambukkana, Nathan, ed. *#Hashtag Publics: The Power and Politics of Discursive Networks*. New York: Peter Lang, 2015.

Renoir, Jean, dir. *The Golden Coach*. Delphinus, Hoche Productions, Panaria Film, 1952.

Richards, Keith and James Fox. *Life*. New York: Little, Brown, and Co., 2010.

Ridenour, Carolyn S. and Isador Newman. *Mixed Methods Research: Exploring the Interactive Continuum*. Carbondale: Southern Illinois University Press, 2008.

Roberts, Laura. "Kitten-heeled Theresa May Opts for Flats on First Day as Home Secretary." *The Daily Mail*. May 14, 2010.

Robertson, Stephen. "Putting Harlem on the Map." In Dougherty, Jack and Kristen Nawrotzki, eds. *Writing History in the Digital Age*. Ann Arbor: The University of Michigan Press, 2013.

Roessner, Jeffrey. "Revolution 2.0: Beatles Fan Scholarship in the Digital Age." In Womach, Kenneth and Katie Kapurch, eds. *New Critical Perspectives on the Beatles: Things We Said Today*. New York: Palgrave Macmillan, 2016.

The Rolling Stones. *Beggars Banquet*. 1973. Decca Records. Vinyl.

The Rolling Stones. *Goatshead Soup*. 1973. Rolling Stones Records. Vinyl.

The Rolling Stones. *Some Girls*. 1978. Rolling Stones Records. Vinyl.

Rosales, Vanessa. *The Digital Fashion Gaze*. MA thesis. Parsons, The New School, 2014.

Rose, Gillian. *Visual Methodologies: An Introduction to Researching with Visual Methods*. 4th ed. Los Angeles, CA: Sage Publications, 2016.

Rosenblum, Naomi. *A World History of Photography*. 3rd ed. New York: Abbeville, 1997.

Rossman, G.B. and B.L. Wilson. "Numbers and Words: Combining Qualitative and Quantitative Methods in a Single Large Scale Evaluation." *Evaluation Review*. Vol. 9, No. 5 (1985): 627–643.

Rothstein, Natalie. *Spitalfields Silks*. London: H.M. Stationery Office, 1975.

Roulston, Kathryn, Roy Legette, Monica Deloach and Celeste Buckhalter. "Troubling Certainty: Readers' Theatre in Music Education Research." In Cahnmann-Taylor, Melisa and Richard Siegesmund, eds. *Arts-based Research in Education*. New York: Routledge, 2008.

Rutherford-Morison, Lara. "Is Cleavage 'Over'? 'Vogue' Asks Women to Vote to Decide & the Internet Is Not Having It Today." *Bustle*. November 3, 2016. Last accessed May 21, 2018. https://www.bustle.com/articles/193077-is-cleavage-over-vogue-asks-women-to-vote-to-decide-the-internet-is-not-having.

Said, Edward W. *Orientalism*. Harmondsworth: Penguin, 1995.

Saldaña, Johnny. "The Drama and Poetry of Qualitative Method." In Cahnmann-Taylor, Melisa and Richard Siegesmund, eds. *Arts-based Research in Education*. New York: Routledge, 2008.

Sanderson, Elizabeth. "Theresa May Looks FAB in Her 'Thunderbirds' Jacket." *The Daily Mail*. May 29, 2010.

Sandino, Linda and Matthew Partington. *Oral History in the Visual Arts*. London: Bloomsbury, 2013.

Santini, Simone. *Exploratory Image Databases: Content-based Retrieval*. San Diego, CA: Academic Press, 2001.

Schermer, Henry and David Jary. *Form and Dialectic in Georg Simmels' Sociology*. London: Palgrave Macmillan, 2013.

Schmidt, Christine. "Against the Grain: Australia and the Swimsuit." In English, Bonnie and Liliana Pomazan, eds. *Australian Fashion Unstitched*. Cambridge: Cambridge University Press, 2010.

Schmuck, Christine and Virginia Jewel. *Fashion Illustration*. New York and London: Whittlesey House McGraw-Hill Book Co., 1937.

Schneiderman, B. "The Eyes Have It: A Task by Data Type Taxonomy for Information Visualizations." In *The Craft of Information Visualization*, pp. 364–371. Morgan Kaufmann, 2003.

Schreibman, Susan, Ray Siemens and John Unsworth, eds. *A Companion to Digital Humanities*. New York: John Wiley & Sons, 2004.

Schwartzburg, Lauren. "Why Millennial Pink Refuses to Go Away." *New York Magazine*. March 19, 2017. http://nymag.com/thecut/2017/03/why-millennial-pink-refuses-to-go-away.html.

Scott, Philippa. *The Book of Silk*. London: Thames & Hudson, 1993.

Shakespeare, William. *Othello*. Oxford: Clarendon Press, 1975.

Shulman, Alexandra. "Vogue Editor Alexandra Shulman's Fashion Rules." *The Guardian*. October 28, 2016. Last accessed May 21, 2018. https://www.theguardian.com/media/2016/oct/28/alexandra-shulman-vogue-editor-fashion-rules?CMP=fb_gu.

Sikarskie, Amanda Grace. *The Duprees of Spitalfields*. Amazon CreateSpace, 2015.

Sikarskie, Amanda Grace. "Erica Wilson: The Julia Child of Needlework." *WGBH Open Vault*. Last accessed May 21, 2018. http://openvault.wgbh.org/exhibits/needlework/article.

Sikarskie, Amanada Grace. *Fiberspace*. Doctoral dissertation. Michigan State University, 2011.

Sikarskie, Amanda Grace. *Textile Collections: Preservation, Access, Curation, and Interpretation in a Digital Age*. Lanham, MD: Rowman & Littlefield, 2016.

Simmel, Georg. "Fashion." *The American Journal of Sociology*. Vol. LXII, No. 6 (May 1957) (reprint): 541–558.

Simonowski, Roberto, ed. *Digital Humanities and Digital Media: Conversations on Politics, Culture, Aesthetics, and Literacy*. London: Open Humanities Press, 2016.

Singh, Sava Saheli. "Hashtagging #HigherEd." In Rambukkana, Nathan, ed. *#Hashtag Publics: The Power and Politics of Discursive Networks*. New York: Peter Lang, 2015.

Slippers, Bibi. "Emoji in die skriptorium." In *Fotostaatmasjien*. Cape Town, South Africa: Tafelberg, 2016.

Smedley, Elliott. "Escaping to Reality: Fashion Photography in the 1990s." In Bruzzi, Stella and Pamela Church Gibson, eds. *Fashion Cultures: Theories, Explorations and Analysis*. London: Routledge, 2000.

Sontag, Susan. "The Avedon Eye." *Vogue*, December 1978.

Sontag, Susan. *On Photography*. New York: Farrar, Straus and Giroux, 1977.

Spanabel Emery, Joy. *A History of the Paper Pattern Industry: The Home Dressmaking Fashion Revolution*. London: Bloomsbury, 2014.

Spunt, Barry. *Heroin and Music in New York City*. New York: Palgrave Macmillan, 2014.

Stalp, Marybeth. *Quilting: The Fabric of Everyday Life*. Dress, Body, and Culture ser. London: Berg, 2007.

Stanley, John Mix. *Portraits of North American Indians*. Washington, DC: Smithsonian Institution, 1852.

Steinberg, Marc William. *Fighting Words: Working-Class Formation, Collective Action, and Discourse in Early Nineteenth-Century England*. Ithaca, NY: Cornell University Press, 1999.

Stevenson, Margaretta and Fashion Group Inc. *How the Fashion World Works; Fit Yourself for a Fashion Future*. New York and London: Harper, 1938.

Stobart, Jon and Bruno Blondé, eds. *Selling Textiles in the Long Eighteenth Century: Comparative Perspectives from Western Europe*. Basingstoke: Palgrave Macmillan, 2014.

Stoddard, Patricia. *Ralli Quilts: Traditional Textiles from Pakistan and India*. Atglen, PA: Schiffer Publications, 2003.

Striphas, Ted. *The Late Age of Print: Everyday Book Culture from Consumerism to Control*. New York: Columbia University Press, 2009.

Strong-Wilson, Teresa. "White Female Teacher Arrives in Native Community with Trunk and Cat': Using Self-Study to Investigate Tales of Traveling White Teachers." In Mitchell, Claudia, Sandra Weber and Kathleen O'Reilly-Scanlon, eds. *Just Who Do We Think We Are? Methodologies for Autobiography and Self-Study in Teaching*. New York: Routledge Falmer, 2005.

Sullivan, Louis. "The Tall Office Building Artistically Considered," *Lippincott's Magazine*, March 1896.

Susann, Jacqueline. *Valley of the Dolls*. 5th ed. New York: Random House, 1969.
Tallon, Loic. "Introducing Open Access at the MET." Metropolitan Museum of Art. Last accessed April 21, 2018. https://www.metmuseum.org/blogs/digital-underground/2017/open-access-at-the-met.
Thiebault, John. "Visualizations and Historical Arguments." In Dougherty, Jack and Kristen Nawrotzki, eds. *Writing History in the Digital Age*. Ann Arbor: The University of Michigan Press, 2013.
Thomas, Mary. *Mary Thomas's Embroidery Book*. Mineola, New York: Courier Dover Publications, 1936.
Thomas, Christopher. *Life and Death in London's East End: 2000 Years at Spitalfields*. London: Museum of London Archaeology Service, 2004.
Thunder, Moira. *Spitalfields Silks*. V&A Pattern. Vol. 4. London: V&A Publishing, 2011.
Tortora, Phyllis G and Keith Eubank. *Survey of Historic Costume: A History of Western Dress*. 6th ed. New York: Fairchild Books, 2015.
Tufte, Edward. *Beautiful Evidence*. Cheshire, CT: Graphics Press, 2006.
Tyner, Judith A. *The World of Maps: Map Reading and Interpretation for the 21st Century*. New York: The Guilford Press, 2015.
Ulrich, Laurel Thatcher. "Pens and Needles: Documents and Artifacts in Women's History." *Uncoverings*. Vol. 14 (1993): 221–228.
Uhrmacher, P. Bruce and Jonathan Matthews, eds. *Intricate Palette: Working the Ideas of Elliot Eisner*. Upper Saddle River, NJ: Pearson Education, Inc., 2005.
Uzanne, Octave, Mary Sophia Hely-Hutchinson Lody and François Courboin. *Fashion in Paris; the Various Phases of Feminine Taste and Aesthetics from the Revolution to the End of the XIXth Century*. London: W. Heinemann, 1901.
Vadim, Roger, dir. *Barbarella: Queen of the Galaxy*. Marianne Productions, Dino de Laurentiis Cinematografica, Paramount Pictures, 1968.
van Halen-Faber, Christine and C.T. Patrick Diamond. "A History of the Arts in Educational Research: A Postmodern Guide for Readers-Flâneurs." In Knowles, J. Gary and Adra L. Cole, eds. *Handbook of the Arts in Qualitative Research*. Los Angeles, CA: Sage Publications, 2008.
van Ruymbeke, Bertrand and Randy Sparks, eds. *Memory and Identity: The Huguenots in France and the Atlantic Diaspora*. Columbia: University of South Carolina Press, 2003.
Vaughn, K. "Pieced Together: Collage as an Artists' Method for Interdisciplining Research." *International Journal of Qualitative Methods*. Vol. 4, No. 1. Article 3 (2005): 27–52.
Vedeler, Marianne. *Silk for the Vikings*. Ancient Textiles Series, Vol. 15. Oxford: Oxbow Books, 2014.
Vice. *The Vice Guide to Sex Drugs and Rock and Roll*. New York: Warner Books, 2003.
Walker, Harriet. *Less Is More: Minimalism in Fashion*. London: Merrell, 2011.
Weber, Sandra. "The Pedagogy of Shoes: Clothing and the Body in Self-Study." In Mitchell, Claudia, Sandra Weber and Kathleen O'Reilly-Scanlon, eds. *Just Who Do*

We Think We Are? Methodologies for Autobiography and Self-Study in Teaching. New York: Routledge Falmer, 2005.

Weber, Sandra. "Visual Images in Research." In Knowles, J. Gary and Adra L. Cole, eds. *Handbook of the Arts in Qualitative Research*. Los Angeles, CA: Sage Publications, 2008.

Wheeler, Monroe, ed. *Textiles and Ornaments of India*. New York: Museum of Modern Art, 1955.

White, Richard. *Come Together: Lennon & McCartney in the Seventies*. London: Omnibus Press, 2016.

Whitley, Lauren D. *Hippie Chic*. Boston, MA: MFA Publications, 2013.

Williamson, Liz. "Interlaced: Textiles for Fashion." In English, Bonnie and Liliana Pomazan, eds. *Australian Fashion Unstitched*. Cambridge: Cambridge University Press, 2010.

Wilson, Erica. *Erica*. Television Series. Boston, MA: WGBH, 1971–2 and 1975–6.

Wilson, Erica. *Erica Wilson's embroidery book*. New York: Scribner, 1973.

Wilson, Erica. *Erica Wilson's Quilts of America*. New York: Oxmoor House, 1979.

Wilson, Erica. *More Needleplay*. New York: Charles Scribner's Sons, 1979.

Wilson, Erica. *Needleplay*. New York: Charles Scribner's Sons, 1975.

Wilson, Henry. *Pattern and Ornament in the Arts of India*. London: Thames & Hudson, 2011.

Womach, Kenneth and Katie Kapurch, eds. *New Critical Perspectives on the Beatles: Things We Said Today*. New York: Palgrave Macmillan, 2016.

Women's Wear Daily. *Fifty Years of Fashion. The Evolution of Women's Styles in America from 1900 to 1950 Documented Sketches and Text from the Costume Library of Women's Wear Daily*. New York: Fairchild Publications, 1950.

Wood, Margaret. *Native American Fashion: Modern Adaptations of Traditional Designs*. New York: Van Nostrand Reinhold Company, 1981.

Young, Agnes Brooks. *Recurring Cycles of Fashion, 1760–1937*. New York and London: Harper & brothers, 1937.

Young, Robb. *Power Dressing: First Ladies, Women Politicians & Fashion*. London: Merrell, 2011.

Zoss, Angela. "Visualization Types—Data Visualization." *LibGuides at Duke University*. Last accessed May 21, 2018. http://guides.library.duke.edu/datavis/vis_types.

Join the Conversation on Instagram!

If you enjoyed this book, please tag us on Instagram @sikarska and @bloomsburyfashion #digifashionresearchbook.

Index

Absolutely Fabulous 38
academic communication 78–82
academic conferences 76–7
academic fashion 78, 88–9
The African Queen 76
Altamont Speedway 84
Alt, Emmanuelle 90
American Historical Association 77–8
American Memory 55
angel numbers 134
annotation. *See* document annotation
applied theory 95
areal symbols 149, 174
Armstrong, Louis 107
Armstrong, Violet 30
artificial intelligence 11, 174–5
Australian Dress Register 29
Australian fashion industry. *See* Fashion industry, Australia
AutoCAD. *See* computer-aided design
auto-ethnography 88
Avedon, Richard 48
Avon 27, 33
azimuthal projection 142–3

Barbarella (1968) 15–17
Babbage, Charles 157
Bailey, David 48, 76
Balenciaga 76
bar graph 127, 129
Barthes, Roland 81–2, 109
The Beatles 34, 62, 113
Beaton, Cecil 47, 100
bebop 107
bee swarm plot 121
Benjamin, Walter 109
Berg Fashion Library 10, 28, 36
big data 13, 88
binaries 8, 157
The Black Queen 15–17
black and white photography 145
blogging 87–9, 91–4, 108
blogosphere 85, 90–1
The Blonde Salad 88, 168
Blumenfeld, Erwin 48
bomber jackets 78
Boolean queries 21, 32, 39, 41, 47, 174
boots. *See* shoes
breasts. *See* cleavage
bricolage 82–3
British fashion industry. *See* Fashion industry, Britain
bubble chart 118, 121, 129, 174
Burton, Sarah 166
Busteed, Kimberly 30
bustle 80
Byzantine
  dress 150–1
  purple 61

CAD. *See* computer-aided design
Cairo, Alberto 68, 116–19, 122, 129, 137, 158, 160
Calloway, Cab 107
Capsule Collection 96, 103–9. *See also* Moschino
cartes-de-visite 47
Cartier 153
cartograms 150, 174
Cassini, Oleg 103
Castiglione, Countess of 45–6
Central Saint Martins 93
Cheap Date (magazine) 44
Chicago Manual of Style 73–4
choropleth maps 149
Christie, Agatha 49–51
citation bomb 26
citations, research 73–5
cleavage 12, 95, 97–8
Cleveland-McGill Scale 127, 129, 174

Clinton, Hillary 103, 106
Coachella 141–3, 149
coding and code 14, 157–8, 160, 174
color, importance of 60–1, 119–21, 144–5
Commercial Pattern Archive 10, 28, 33–4
communication, academic. *See* academic communication
computer-aided design 136
computer intelligence. *See* artificial intelligence
computer vision 52–3, 56, 58
conferences, academic. *See* academic conferences
conic projection 142–3
content-based image retrieval 54, 58, 61, 63
copyright 55, 154, 176
costume design. *See* period films
Costume Institute 28, 32, 93, 121
costume, use as a term 2–3
Creative Commons 31, 55, 174
crowdsourcing 35, 63, 70, 85, 136, 147, 174–5
cultural appropriation 162
Cunningham, Bill 85–6
cylindrical projection 142–3, 174

Daguerre, Louis 47
daguerreotype 86
Dahl-Wolfe, Louise 48
dandy 88–9
databases 9–11, 21, 24–30, 32–5, 37–40, 47, 51–4, 56, 58–9, 63, 65, 95, 127, 130–1, 135–6, 143, 146, 149, 154, 156, 174–6
data visualization 14, 17, 48, 68, 96, 110–40, 144–6, 156, 158–61, 174–7. *See also* literary visualization
Day, Corinne 44
deconstruction 96
deformation. *See* zones of least deformation
deja vu 51
Deleuze, Gilles 6
democracy 89–90
density. *See* information density
dialectic 13, 89, 96, 98, 109. *See also* Hegel; Simmel, Georg
Dietrich, Marlene 47
Dior, Christian 70, 167
discursive communities 72, 78, 103, 174
document annotation 159–60, 174
Dolce & Gabbana 1, 76, 162, 173
donut chart 130–1, 175
Dora the Explorer 139
Dress Discover 10, 28
dress, use as a term 2–3
drugs. *See* heroin chic;
Dublin Core 27, 33, 175
Dupree family 26
dyes and dyestuffs 7, 61, 70
Dynasty 101

echo chambers 91, 99, 103, 108, 175
Edwardiana 89
Elizabeth II 30
embroidery 33, 165
emojis 12, 17, 78–82, 104, 111, 113–14, 158, 175
emoticons 78, 82, 175
Equal Rights Amendment 55–6, 167
ethics 11, 13, 82, 93, 119
ethnography. *See* auto-ethnography
Europeana 10, 12, 28, 30–3, 35, 55
European Economic Community 101
Excel (application) 156

Facebook 11–13, 66–8, 70–1, 73–5, 85, 95, 100
family history 51
family trees 121
fashion, academic. *See* academic fashion
fashion blogger poses 90–1. *See also* blogging
fashion, definition of 2
fashion diary. *See* blogging
Fashion Historians Unite! 11, 67–8, 70–1, 99
Fashion industry, Australia 29–30, 33
Fashion industry, Britain 101–2
Fashion Institute of Technology 34–6

Fashion Is Spinach 9, 14, 83, 157–8, 160, 162–3, 191
fashion journalism 110, 115, 119
Fashion Law Institute 84
Fashion Photography Archive 10, 28, 36–9, 41–3
Fashion Studies Journal 93
fashion, use as a term 2–3
Fashion Week 74, 86, 88, 168
  Stockholm 94
Faux, Susie 103
femininity 88, 92, 166. *See also* high femininity
feminism 96, 167
Ferragamo, Salvatore 101
Ferragni, Chiara 88, 168
fetish commodity 109. *See also* Benjamin, Walter
FIDM 10–11, 27–8, 32–3, 68
First Ladies 13, 55–6, 97, 103
flâneur 87
folksonomy 149, 175
Fonda, Jane 15, 17
Fonteray, Jacques 17
Ford, Betty 55–6
Fox Historic Costume Collection 68–9
Fox Talbot, William Henry 47
fragrance 33, 108
Frissell, Toni 48
futurism 15–17

Galanos, James 68–9
Garthwaite, Anna Maria 72
Geographic Information Systems 14, 143–4, 146–7, 150, 152, 175
#GeorgianJanuary 72
geospatial turn 144, 149, 175
Gerber Accumark. *See* computer-aided design
Gestalt theory 129
GIS. *See* Geographic Information Systems
globalism 3, 167
global village. *See* McLuhan, Marshall
Goat's Head Soup 76
The Gold Coach 59–60, 172
Google Earth 143–4
Google Reverse Image Search. *See* reverse image search
grandparents 51
Grand Rapids Public Museum 70–1
Granny Takes a Trip 62
Gucci 1, 13, 55, 97, 103, 149, 171

Hadid, Gigi 168
Hall, Jerry 40–1, 53–4, 167
handbags 101, 108, 113
  charms 1, 110, 167
Harlem 144
harlequin pattern 58–60, 172
Harper's Bazaar 48, 93, 162
Harry Potter 139
hashtags 11–12, 25, 67–8, 70, 72, 76–8, 103–5, 174–5
Haussmann, Baron 86–7
"have a nice day" 62
Hawes, Elizabeth 9, 14, 83, 158, 162–3
Hearst, Gabriela 76
Heavenly Bodies 68
Hebdige, Dick 4
Hegel 89
heliography 47
Hepburn, Audrey 76
Hepburn, Katherine 76
hermeneutics 3, 12–13, 96–9, 103–4, 108–10, 118
  hermeneutic circle 97, 158
Hermès 96
heroin chic 38, 106. *See also* opiates
hex codes 60–1, 175
high femininity 167
hijab 98
Hippie Trail 121, 152
histogram 121
historicism 166
Ho, Lisa 30
Holmes, Nigel 115, 118
Hope Diamond 153, 171
Hope, Henry Philip 153
Huguenots 26, 140
hustling 107

iAnnotate 159
ichimatsu 48, 58–9
icon array 127, 175
Iman 167
India 145–6, 153–5
influencers 90, 93
information density 118, 121, 142, 144, 149, 175
information literacy 21
information transparency 118, 144, 175
Instagram 10–12, 17, 30, 66–79, 81–93, 95, 105, 107–8, 157, 162, 176
intellectual property 79
intelligentsia 90
internationalization. *See* globalism
International Quilt Study Center & Museum 7
Inuyasha 48, 50

Jagger, Mick 25–6, 44, 76
James, Charles 121
Japanese dress. *See* kimono
Jenkins, Henry 113
Jents, Beril 29
Johnston, Steve 85
Jones, Terry 85
Judd, Donald 165

kagome 48, 58
Karan, Donna 104
Kennedy, Jackie 103
Kent, Holly 176
Kerouac, Jack 158
keywords 21, 24–5, 27, 32, 39–41, 45–6, 136, 154, 174
kimono 48–9, 57–8, 113, 166
kirmiz 61
kitsch 16, 166
Kollur 153–4, 156

labor, unpaid 92
Lacroix, Christian 167
Lagerfeld, Karl 120
Lange, Dorothea 86
Lanvin, Jeanne 25–6, 70
Lauren, Ralph 103
Lectra Modaris. *See* computer-aided design
leg-of-mutton sleeves 35, 56
Lennon, John 61–3, 65
leopard print 13, 102, 168
Lévi-Strauss, Claude 5
Leyster, Judith 31, 88
Libre Office 129
lichen purple. *See* Byzantine, purple
linear symbols 149
linear visualization 149, 175
linked open data 30–1, 175
listservs 11, 67
literary visualization 160
lollipop plot 156, 175
The Lord of the Rings 139
Los Angeles County Museum of Art 55
Louis XIV 153
Lovelace, Ada 157
Lupi, Giorgia 111–13, 116, 158

macarons 133
machine learning 149, 174–5
Magnani, Anna 51, 59–60, 171–3
Map Communication Model 146, 175
mapping 6, 9, 14, 118, 139–41, 143–55, 157, 159, 161, 163, 174
  qualitative and quantitative 149
Marco Polo 153
Margiela, Martin 28, 32, 35, 95
Marxism 96
Marzotto, Marta 168
maximalism 6, 8, 17, 24, 96, 99, 165–7
May, Theresa 13, 102
McCartney, Stella 168
McLuhan, Marshall 84
McQueen, Alexander 38, 44, 166
memory 29, 46, 49, 51–2, 55, 58, 107, 140
Mendeley 159
Menkes, Suzy 90, 167
Mercator projection 142–3. *See also* cylindrical projection
mermaids 38–41, 43, 53
metadata 10, 12, 26–8, 30, 32–4, 36, 39, 41, 56, 61, 174–5
  scheme 27–8, 39, 174–5

meta (prefix) 27
Met Gala 15, 68
methods books 9
Metropolitan Museum of Art 31, 48–9, 55, 68, 93, 121. *See also* Costume Institute
Milan 144, 148–9, 156
millennial pink 60. *See also* color
minimalism 3, 14, 16, 23–4, 105, 165–8
  pretty 166
Minnesota Dressmakers 10, 28, 33
mixed methods research 1, 3–8, 14–15, 88, 116, 152, 171, 176. *See also* maximalism
mobile 12, 33, 54, 79, 137, 152, 159, 162
models (fashion) 24, 36, 39–41, 44, 81, 86, 91–2, 95, 102, 173–5
Modemuze 10, 28, 33
modernity 2, 109, 165–6
Modern Language Association 73
modesty 89, 109
Mods and Rockers 89–90
mood board 76, 83, 119, 176
Moschino 9, 13, 96, 103–6
Moss, Kate 9–10, 38–9, 41–2, 44, 63, 65, 145
Mother's Little Helper 106
Motupalli 153
Mouzat, Virginie 90
muckrakers 86
Mugler, Thierry 134, 167
  and Mugler Circle 134
multidimensional visualization 117, 119, 121, 144, 176
Museum at FIT. *See* Fashion Institute of Technology
Museum of Modern Art (MoMA) 83–4

Napoleon III 86
neogeography 147, 176
nested area graph 156, 176
Net-a-Porter 162
network visualization 121, 176
'the new black' 121
New Look 70
The New School 93
New York Fashion Week. *See* Fashion Week
Niépce, Joseph Nicéphore 47
Norse. *See* Vikings
Noughties.
  2000s fashion 167
Nude on the Moon 16
nudie suit 108
Nylon magazine 93

On the Road 158
open access 30, 55, 87, 149, 176
OpenStreetMap 14, 140–1, 144, 147–9, 154, 156
opiates 104, 106–7
Opium (fragrance) 108

paisley 102
Pallenberg, Anita 15–17, 44, 110
panniers 35–6, 70
Parsons, Gram 108
Parsons School. *See* The New School
participant observation 85–6, 176
participatory turn (in mapping) 146. *See also* crowdsourcing
PDF documents. *See* document annotation
peach emoji 80. *See also* emojis
peacocks 7, 168
Penn, Irving 48
perception (visual) 61, 131, 145, 152
perfume. *See* fragrance
period films 59–60
photography
  documentary 37, 86
  history of 47–8
  runway 36–7, 39, 41, 48, 86. *See also* street style
pie chart 102, 121, 127, 129–32, 135, 140, 156, 158, 160, 175–6
Pierson, Louis 45–6
pink. *See* millennial pink
Pinterest 10–11, 68, 119
planar visualization. *See* Mapping
plus-size fashion 161–2
Pockets of History 10, 29, 33
podcast 74, 93
Poiblanc, Ludivine 90

point symbols 149
polka dot map. *See* simple dot distribution map
Polyvore 82–3, 119
Porter (magazine). *See* Net-a-Porter
Posavec, Stefanie 111–13, 116, 158
poses. *See* fashion blogger poses
positivism 4–5
post-colonialism 95–6
postmodernism 1, 4, 6, 96
post-structuralism 5, 96
power dressing 101
prescription drugs, in fashion. *See* Moschino
Prince (the artist) 130, 132
Princess Caraboo 53–4
prints. *See* maximalism
projections. *See* azimuthal projection; conic projection; cylindrical projection
provenance 29, 61, 63, 70, 80, 175
Prynne, Hester. *See The Scarlet Letter*
psychoanalysis 95–6, 99, 108
public domain 11, 31, 55, 92, 156, 176
publishing, scholarly 11, 26, 34, 54, 72, 76
punk style 19, 44, 85
purses. *See* handbags
pussy bow blouse 13, 97–8, 103

qualitative methods 4–8, 17, 143, 149–50, 152, 156–8, 174, 176
quantitative methods 5–8, 13, 17, 110, 143, 149, 156, 158, 174, 176
Queen Elizabeth II. *See* Elizabeth II
query by example 56, 60, 176
Quilt Index 10, 27, 29, 33, 123, 126–8, 130–1, 135–6
quilts 7, 11, 121, 123, 127, 130, 135, 145–6. *See also* ralli

Rabanne, Paco 17
Rajasthan. *See* India
ralli 121, 145–6
Rawlings, John 48
Reddit 68
remote sensing 143, 176
research bursts 17, 76, 176
Reutlinger Studio 47
reverse image search 11, 46, 61–3, 176
Ricci, Nina 41, 43
Richards, Keith 110
robe de style 70–2
Rockers. *See* Mods and Rockers
Rolling Stones 62, 76, 106

Saint Laurent, Yves 31, 108
Sander, Jil 166
The Sartorialist 88
Savannah College of Art & Design 93
The Scarlet Letter 106
Schön magazine 93
Schuman, Scott 86
Scott, Jeremy. *See* Moschino
search engine optimization (SEO) 25–6, 176
Seeberger Frères 47
selfies 77, 88, 90
self-styling. *See* style, personal
Seminole patchwork 58
semiotics 44
sewing patterns 33–4
shame 13, 106, 109–10
shippo 48, 57–8
shoes 12, 17, 79, 102, 113, 142, 161, 168
Shoes of New York 87
shopping 14, 83, 86, 101, 160–2
signs. *See* semiotics
silk 14, 17, 26, 61, 76, 140–2, 150–3, 166, 171
similarity mismatch 52–3
Simmel, Georg 78, 88–9, 106, 108–10
simple dot distribution map 149
Simplicity (patterns) 34
single number visualization 123, 126–8, 130, 156, 160, 176
Sitbon, Martine 41–2
sketching 122
Slippers, Bibi 80
Smithsonian 153
Snow, John 139–40, 146
source code. *See* code
Sozzani, Franca 90
spiders 26, 176
Spitalfields 26, 140–1, 147, 153, 166

stacked proportional area chart. *See* nested area graph
Steele, Valerie 94
Stefaner, Moritz 122
Steichen, Edward 47
STEM disciplines 92
street style 36, 85–8, 101–2, 176
structural equation modeling (SEM) 5
structuralism 5, 96
style, personal 78, 86, 88, 92–3
Stylish Academic 73, 75, 77–8, 88–9, 93
subaltern groups 89
swimwear 30

Tableau (software) 68, 122
tag. *See* hashtags
tag clouds. *See* word clouds
Takahashi, Rumiko 48. *See also Inuyasha*
Tapestry 10, 29, 33
Tavernier, Jean-Baptiste 153–4
Teddy Boys 89–90
temporal visualization 121, 144, 177
Terry, Kate 166
Thatcher, Margaret 12–13, 100–2
thematic maps 141, 145–6, 149, 157, 174
Thingverse 136
3D modeling 121, 136–7, 177
thrifting 162
Tiffany blue 60–1. *See also* color; hex code
Tin Eye 11, 61, 63
topographic maps 142, 146
Topshop 98, 101
Trainspotting 110
transparency. *See* information transparency
Trump, Melania 13, 97, 99, 103
Tufte, Edward 115–16, 118
Tumblr 68
turkey red 61. *See also* color; hex code
Twitter 12, 66–8, 72–5, 77–8, 84–5, 95, 98–100, 102, 104–5

unicode 79
Unravel 74, 93
Urban Fieldnotes 87

Valley of the Dolls 106
van der Rohe, Ludwig Mies 1
Vanity Fair 90
veiling 76
Venturi, Robert 1, 16
Venus de Milo 137
Vernacular
    language 107, 157
    style 91
Versace 29, 101, 173
    Donatella 172
    Menswear Archive 33
Victoria and Albert Museum 12, 30, 93, 100
Vikings 14, 150, 152
violin plot 121
Vionnet, Madeleine 31, 168
visualization. *See* data visualization
visual rhetoric 119
Vogue 12, 34, 47–8, 90, 93, 97–8, 105, 107, 161, 166–7, 171
volumetric visualizations 121, 177
volunteered geographic information 147, 176

Warhol, Andy 84
Waterhouse, Dawn 30–1
Wayback Machine 75
weaving. *See* silk
web crawlers. *See* spiders
wedding dress 30, 47
Where's Wally? 58
White, E.B. 119
whitework 126
Wikipedia 12, 72
Williams, Betty 33
Winnie the Pooh 139
Woolf, Virginia 118
word clouds 13, 121, 131–4, 140, 156, 160
Wordle 131, 134–5
WordyUp 131, 134
Worthing, Helen Lee 47
writing assignments 19, 59, 99
Wylie, Mina 30

zones of least deformation 142–3
Zotero 35